Bureaucracy and Rural Development in Malaysia

GAYL D. NESS

Bureaucracy
and
Rural Development
in Malaysia

A Study of Complex Organizations
in Stimulating Economic Development
in New States

UNIVERSITY OF CALIFORNIA PRESS
Berkeley and Los Angeles 1967

UNIVERSITY OF CALIFORNIA PRESS
BERKELEY AND LOS ANGELES, CALIFORNIA

CAMBRIDGE UNIVERSITY PRESS
LONDON, ENGLAND

FOR JEANNINE

Preface

In Southeast Asia the Federation of Malaysia is unique in its modern development. All countries of the region, as indeed all new states of the world, have created national development plans and often new organizations to implement those plans. Of these countries, only the Federation of Malaysia and Singapore have achieved any success in their development programs. Malaysia and Singapore alone appear to have made serious and sustained attempts to translate their development programs into action.

For anyone concerned with the process of economic development, one of the most depressing experiences in this region is to make the rounds of government offices, to hear of plans and reorganization, and to come away with the certain knowledge that little or nothing that was said in the air-conditioned offices bears any resemblance to what will actually be done on the ground. It is easy to draft plans and projects; it appears almost impossible to move any project out of the office and onto the ground.

In this depressing scene Malaysia appears freakishly unique. In land development, irrigation, road-building, schools, adult education, and in many other specific projects one can trace the development of an idea, the mobilization of administrative and financial resources to give life to the idea; finally one finds it actually coming to life in the work that is being done.

This study is an attempt to understand Malaysia's experience. Reduced to its most fundamental element, we would argue that the delicate demographic balance of the country—the 50 percent Malays and 40 percent Chinese—is the basic moving force behind this success in public investment. This delicate balance made the public investment program an urgent necessity to the new leaders. This balance, too, provided an outlet for revolutionary energies in the direction of public investment, rather than in the direction of a take-over of the private economy—a pattern that has already all but destroyed the economies of Burma and Indonesia.

It is important to analyze the manner in which the body of flesh and blood has been built on the skeleton. With every new move, with every reorganization, with every formulation of organizational goals and every decision to embark upon a new program, the pattern of development activities is built. At every turn there are many alternatives, some of which will lead to chaos, many of which will simply lead in different directions, perhaps to greater or lesser successes. Thus to understand Malaysia's unique experience in development planning and execution, we shall be concerned with the development of its total pattern, with the formation and operation of the organizations that have been responsible for the public investment program.

Malaysia's dramatic successes have been largely in public investment. Other indicators of growth, including per capita real income or product, are less encouraging. When measured in constant prices, they show a slight gain. However, since such a large part of the value of the product derives from the foreign sale of rubber, it makes more sense to measure product in current prices: here Malaysia has shown a decline in per capita product because of falling rubber prices. Nonetheless, the economy seems healthy and buoyant.

From this observation emerges the question of the relation between economic development—the continued rise in real product per capita—and public investment. What does Malaysia's success in road-building mean for the economy? The gestation period of such infrastructure construction is long; the full returns in any event are not obtained for years. In addition, it is not known what other changes such developments bring in their wake. To what extent do they extend the market, effect the commercialization of hitherto subsistence areas, and change the values, attitudes, and social organization of the country? There is some reason to believe that road-building, the construction of items of physical infrastructure, achieves these ends, but it is not known how long this takes and to what extent it is done. Within the next half century, it should be possible to use the growing body of data on the economies of Southeast Asia to discover, in comparative studies, the impact of public investment on economic development. As yet it is too early.

Individual biases and values will not be exorcised, no matter how powerful is the norm of objectivity in the social sciences. It is useful, therefore to state beforehand those biases of which an author is aware. In the first place, I agree with Colin Clarke that economic growth is economic progress—I think economic growth is a good thing. It pleases me to see it achieved, it distresses me to witness its failure, especially when the failure is due to misdirected policies. I can see little sense in the romantic argument that happy people in poor countries ought to be left alone. Whether they are happy is irrelevant, for the drive for economic development that causes such turmoil in the poor country is led for the most part by the elites of those countries themselves. The drive for modernization is a fact; there seems to be no turning back.

The romantic argument seems unreal to me also in another sense. I cannot see that it is better to be hungry than to be well fed. I cannot see that high infant mortality, high morbidity rates, and the physical and intellectual isolation of the traditional village are features to be valued. Economic development means doing away with hunger, sickness, and intellectual stupor. To the argument that it also means stomach ulcers, mental diseases, and unhappiness, two answers are available. First, there is no unequivocal evidence that economic development or modernization does increase these social and psychological ills. Second, I would not accept the argument that economic growth ought to bring "happiness"; this is too elusive and unoperationalized a term to propose as the end of any action. I am with the later nineteenth century utilitarians who made the move from happiness to liberty as the ends of government. Economic growth provides more liberty, more effective alternatives to a population. It provides them with more ways to develop the talents they have—for good or for evil. This is an end I hold to be good.

Following from this bias for economic development, I have a bias for Malaysia because it has achieved success in public investment and in its accommodation of ethnic interests. All of this has made me probably a less than fully objective observer of Malaysia—I am perhaps too sympathetic with the nation's problems and too impressed with the solutions it has achieved. I cannot be less. The reader will have to make the appropriate adjustments for himself if he is willing to wade through this mass of detail.

I spent approximately three years (1961–1964) in Malaysia. I used published documents to build up a picture of both public and operative goals, analyzing debates and statements in the legislature, budgets of the federal and state governments, and the organizations concerned with development. The most important data, however, came from interviews with the officers concerned with the programs, and with other observers in Malaysia, foreign and domestic. Interview materials were gathered slowly during the entire three-year period. I attempted to develop a survey instrument that could be applied systematically, but abandoned the efforts. In general I found it necessary to apply an evaluation of what was being said in an interview, and I could work out no suitable method of applying such an evaluation to a survey instrument. Especially in an interview that stretches over more than an hour, and then continues over a "stengah" at the rest house or over cocktails at a party, people contradict themselves directly and indirectly, often more than once on the same subject. It is not that they lie or deliberately attempt to deceive the questioner, though this does happen. It is merely a reflection of the great human capacity for holding conflicting ideas with little strain. The survey instrument normally achieves something like a snapshot of ideas, sentiments, and knowledge. I found it more useful to attempt to gain a more lifelike, moving version of the same phenomenon.

In such a field situation, one learns much from conflict. The public policy of an official, proclaimed in a dozen statements, acquires a different meaning in one intemperate moment when the official gives vent to his real feelings. Both sets of data are important: the public stance and the personal sentiments. The survey instruments tend to pick up only the more tempered, public stance.

To a large extent, therefore, through long and unsystematic discussions with a wide variety of people I have built a picture of how the organization of development works. Those who know the Malaysian situation can judge this work by the degree to which it agrees with their own experience in the country. Those who do not know the country are able to judge only the extent to which the argument seems to make sense. I have tried to include sufficient detailed description to allow those not familiar with Malaysia to make a more independent assessment of this argument for themselves. To the extent that readers are able to use my own data to present counter-interpretations to my own, I shall consider my description useful.

I have found the analysis of organizational goals perhaps the single most useful analytical key for this study. This has provided at least three advantages. First, it provides a comparative framework, which gives the Malaysian experience and the Malaysian study broader and more powerful intellectual implications than those defined by its own national boundaries. I should argue that there are both operational and analytical lessons to be learned from the Malaysian experience—

lessons that are applicable to other attempts to stimulate development and to other attempts to undersand how development is stimulated. Second, this approach focuses attention upon both the work
and the ideology or world view of the organization. Finally, and
following from the second, this approach offers the most systematic
entrée into the important problem of the articulation of society and
bureaucracy. That is, the dynamics of complex organizations in economic development in the twentieth century will be provided in
major part by the manner in which those organizations come to terms
with their environments. For major development organizations this

means that the goals must reflect the peculiar accommodation of
social forces that has been achieved in the political arena. Thus I
find the clearest understanding and the most powerful predictive
concepts provided by the analytical strategy taken in this study: from
broad social organization, through the articulation and balance of
interest in the political arena to the formulation of organizational

goals and the allied issue of the power and competence available to achieve, or work toward the achievement of, goals.

On 16 September 1963 the Federation of Malaya merged with Singapore and the British Borneo colonies of Sabah and Sarawak to become the Federation of *Malaysia*. In August 1965, Singapore separated from Malaysia and became an independent state. Throughout this analysis, I have used the term *Malaya*. This is not to suggest that I judge the larger Federation lacking in viability. It is merely that my analysis is confined to the eleven states of the original Federation of Malaya, and is also confined to the time when that name was official. I have not considered it appropriate to attempt to discuss here the implications of Malaysia for the use of complex organizations in development. On the whole, I think that influence is not significant in this case. It was in the eleven states of the original

Federation that the politics of accommodation were developed, and it was there that the fundamental pattern of development stimulation was created. To be sure, Malaysia has had some effect. There has been an increase in military expenditures, indicating some return to order goals, and there has been some consequent cutback in development activities. This, however, has been a result of Indonesia's *Konfrontasi* policy, rather than an effect of Malaysia itself. And even that military threat, I should argue, has not fundamentally altered the relationship between complex organizations and economic development that these pages seek to expose.

I have used the Chinese form, common in Malaya, in rendering Chinese names—surname followed by given names—except in the case of H. S. Lee, whose name appears in this form even in Malaya. In the tables, a dash (—) stands for "not applicable" or "nonexistent"; three short dashes (---) for "negligible"; and n. a. for "not available."

ACKNOWLEDGMENTS

This is my first major opportunity to acknowledge the myriad intellectual debts I have acquired. I am grateful to Professors Robert A. Nisbet and Kenneth E. Bock for first stimulating my interest in the sociological perspective. Professors Reinhard Bendix, Herbert Blumer, Wolfram Eberhard, and Philip Selznick in Sociology and Cho-ming Li in Economics provided sustained assistance and encouragement as well as excellent instruction through my graduate studies at the University of California in Berkeley.

I am also indebted to my colleagues and one-time fellow graduate students of the "subseminar." Dorothy Anderson Mariner, William H. Friedland, and Ernest Landauer contributed to the early formulation of my ideas on social change and economic development. Robert Alford also joined in those stimulating critical discussions.

The field work for the study was done under a fellowship from the Institute of Current World Affairs in New York. I am deeply grateful for the freedom allowed by the fellowship and for the encouragement and stimulation offered by its director, Richard H. Nolte. I do not believe that scientific orientations are a license for bad writing. I have tried to write clearly and concisely and with the aim of conveying something of the real human lives and experiences involved in the situation I was studying. If I have achieved any success in this endeavor, much of the credit must go to Richard Nolte, who encouraged me and assisted me in effective communication.

In Malaysia I met the full cooperation of government officers. The Ministry of Rural Development was exceptionally helpful and open. I was allowed to follow on inspection trips, to examine records, and to question officers at will. From the minister to district officers and below, people were always willing to take time from the great pressures of their work to answer my questions, to discuss openly their problems, and to share their hopes and fears with me. I owe a great deal to their assistance and friendliness, and to the additional honor they did me by being genuinely interested in what I was doing.

In Malaysia itself Drs. Thomas R. McHale and Clifton R. Wharton, Jr. offered encouragement, assistance, and friendship. They read, and made pertinent comments on, an earlier draft of the manuscript.

Professors J. Norman Parmer of Northern Illinois University and Robert O. Tilman of Yale University also read and commented upon the manuscript.

My wife, to whom this book is dedicated, bore with cheerful courage the great burden of living with a research project. I shall hope this book will be some small reward for her efforts and for the difficult time during which she carried on alone because of it.

Of course, I accept sole responsibility for whatever follies, mistakes, and bad judgments appear here.

G.D.N.

Ann Arbor
June 1966

Contents

I

NEW STATES, ECONOMIC DEVELOPMENT AND COMPLEX ORGANIZATIONS: A PARADIGM

The drive for modernization in the new Afro-Asian states is one of the major forces of the mid-twentieth century. All processes associated with this drive—the demise of colonialism, the rise of nationalism, and the creation of new sovereign states; the transformation of low-income, quasi-stable subsistence economies into highly productive commercial and industrial economies; the transformation of congeries of isolated agriculture-based communities into complex urbanized societies; and above all the waning of fatalism, bringing a demand for an end to the old order and an attempt to build a new society—all of these connote a revolution of major proportions from which no part of the world is isolated. Such a revolution could not fail to capture the minds of statesmen, journalists, and scholars. True to their reflective nature, mirroring the major social problems of the day, the social sciences have also made the new states a central object of study. The rapidly growing body of social science literature on the modernization of the new states shows both a fruitful application of new analytical tools and a pervasiveness of concern that extends analysis to almost every conceivable aspect of the problem.

One aspect of this modern development, however, has received rather little attention, despite its apparently great importance for the process: the relation between complex organizations and modernization. One of the most common features of the new states is the creation of new organizations specifically charged with planning and implementing programs of development. It has become fashionable, even somewhat compulsive, to have a planning organization, a national development plan, and specific implementing organizations. Even in states with apparently little concern in government for modernization, as in Brunei or Nepal, one still finds planners and beautifully bound national development plans. In addition to the specific task of planning, a wide range of subsidiary and implementing tasks have been adorned with the status symbols of their own organizations. The myriad agencies for community development, for cooperative development, for enticing foreign and local investors, for social and technological advance of the peasantry, and for the coordination of all government agencies have become a natural part of the social landscape of the new states. A significant feature of these planning and developing organizations is that they are new. For the most part they have emerged only since 1945, or since the independence of the state concerned.

The recent use of complex organizations to stimulate modern development in the new states is thus the central observation that has motivated this study.

There are both common and unique elements in this observation. The faith of the new states today is, for example, not unlike the belief in progress of the nineteenth-century West. The drive for modernization, the great faith placed in political independence, the faith in industrialization and its temples of steel mills and atomic plants, and the faith in the ability of the new state to gain standards of productivity and living comparable with the industrialized nations is not unlike the belief in progress that accompanied Western industrialization in the nineteenth century. The parallel extends even to the rejection of modernization in the new states. In the new state's search for identity, in the attempt to recreate the indigenous "village socialism" of the precolonial period, in the desire to be uncommitted, and in the verbal rejection of things Western—in all of these can be seen parallels with the romantic utopian rejections of early industrialization in the West.

The organizational pattern of modern development, on the other hand, is unique. The current widespread use of complex organizations to stimulate development represents something of an inversion of the process of bureaucratization and industrialization observed in the West. Though the modern bureaucratic organization emerged in some forms before the nineteenth century, its development is closely linked with the process of industrialization in that century. The modern organization was strengthened by, became pervasive in, and in turn furthered the development of, the modern industrial society.[1] In the Western experience bureaucratization was a function—in the pure mathematical sense—of industrialization or modernization. In the new states, on the other hand, bureaucratization preceded the major spurt to modernization. Bureaucratization came first in the colonial period, reflecting the transplantability of at least the formal structure across national and cultural boundaries and into a wide range of substantive fields. This occurred, to be sure, along with a period of economic development, but this was a development essentially of export economies, implying an unbalanced and incomplete kind of modernization. Today in the new states, previously established bureaucracies are being used to stimulate a more complete and balanced kind of modernization.

If the recent use of *complex organizations* to stimulate *modernization* in the *new states* is the motivating observation of the study contained in this book, its central argument is that these three phenomena are interdependent or interrelated parameters of analysis. The complex organization, modernization, and the new states go together naturally. This argument can be developed in greater detail in the form of a triangular paradigm, proposing a sociological affinity between the three phenomena,[2] considered in three pairs.

NEW STATES AND THE COMMITMENT TO MODERNIZATION

The category of *new states* derives its analytical power largely from the importance for those states of a recent colonial or dependent status.[3] This importance is especially compelling in the demand for modernization, itself a vague though useful concept. As generally used, modernization refers to the creation of a complex of institutions that resemble those of the industrialized nations. Politically, modernization

---

[1] See, for example, Max Weber's discussion of modern capitalism in *General Economic History*, London, n.d., pp. 275 ff.

[2] The sources of this paradigm are too numerous to be listed here. Useful summaries of the type of material from which it is drawn are given in the following: Max F. Millikan and Donald L. M. Blackmer, *The Emerging Nations*, Cambridge, 1961; Bert F. Hoselitz and Wilbert E. Moore (eds.), *Industrialization and Society*, New York, UNESCO, 1963; Edward Shils, "Political Development in the New States," *Comparative Studies in Society and History*, I and II, Vol. II, pp. 265–92 and 379–411; and J. H. Kautsky, *Political Change in Underdeveloped Areas*, New York, 1962.

[3] For this reason the Latin American states have been explicitly omitted from this discussion, though they share many of the characteristics of the non-industrialized societies with the new states.

implies an independent state or political community that has a government with some roots in the population, with at least an ideological
commitment to the welfare of the population, and with rather extensive control over the population. This sets political modernity apart
from absolutism in which the welfare of the ruler is the dominant consideration of government. It also sets political modernity apart from
colonialism, with its dependent polities. Economically, modernization
implies a mode of production and a set of economic institutions that
bring continued increases in human productivity, and a widespread—
though not necessarily equal—sharing of the increased product by all
members of the society. Socially, modernization implies the predomi-
nance of a wide range of heterogeneous, limited-purpose groupings, a
division of function and specialization of groups. Perhaps more fundamentally, it represents an extension of the base of concerted action.[4]

For the new states the economic aspects of modernization present a
more explicit and visible, and therefore a more powerful, set of goals
than do the political or social aspects. Independence implies the taking
of power by indigenous leaders. This in itself is a dramatic and visible,
if only partial, achievement of political modernization. The more intractable problems of the consolidation of power and the creation of a
political community often continue to plague the new leaders, but
these problems are not as visible and not as easily communicated as
other problems. The problems of building a new society, of creating
the base for new types of groupings, and of extending the base of concerted action are vague and difficult to define, and involve considerable
ambivalence.

In contrast with these problems, the problems of economic modernization are readily visible, as are at least some of the goals. The great
disparity between rich nations and poor nations, made painfully con-
spicuous by every automobile and transistor radio, and by the rapid
spread of the fruits of modern productive economies, forcefully focuses
attention on the problem of poverty and the rewards to be won through
economic modernization. The existence of modern economic organizations or enterprises in the new states only serves to sharpen this focus.
The persistent demand for steel mills or factories and for local ownership of the organizational means of production gives to the economic
aspects of modernization a force and explicitness that is lacking in the
political and social aspects.

The recent colonial past has wide ramifications for economic modernization or economic development throughout the new state. Three

---

[4] This is what Clifford Geertz calls the integrative revolution. See his *Agricultural
Involution*, Berkeley and Los Angeles, 1963.

considerations, however, are of major significance: the issue of opposition or struggle, the issue of democracy or a mass following, and the issue of the character of leadership.

First, the winning of independence involved a struggle against a metropolitan power. Regardless of how peaceful the struggle, and in many cases it was far from peaceful, it generated strong oppositional sentiments in the new leadership.[5] The emerging nationalist leaders became anticolonial leaders, often also anti-Western. Strength was gained for the nationalist cause by increasing the power of the anticolonial sentiments. As the nationalist leaders began to see the world around them and to contrast the low standards of living of their own countries with those of the metropolitan countries, there emerged a strong tendency to blame this disparity upon colonialism and the dominance of the metropolitan power. Even more, there was a tendency to identify poverty itself with political dependence, and to argue that only an independent nation could direct its development inward for the benefit of its own people and thus effectively achieve the economic modernization that separated the metropolitan from the colonial populations.[6]

Nor did the new leaders have to turn exclusively outward to see dramatic economic disparities between rulers and ruled, or between free and subject states. In their own states the old colonial rulers were separated from the native ruled by a wide gulf that equated race or skin color with wealth and power. The insults of the color bar, manifested in "Europeans Only" clubs and in "bridge parties," were pervasive and deeply wounding. Along with the sense of physical inferiority engendered by the color bar was the experience of economic deprivation. The Allied and Japanese slogans of World War II and the flood tide of the value of self-determination with the war's end only served to strengthen the sense of insult and deprivation, to make it more intolerable, and thus to increase the oppositional character of the nationalist struggle and the nationalist leaders.

Thus the new commitment to modernization, in large part a commitment to economic modernization, derived much of its power from the oppositional nature of nationalism, from the demand to acquire what the foreign rulers of the past had allegedly withheld.

Second, since the struggle for independence was a struggle against

---

[5] Shils, *op. cit.*

[6] One of the earliest references I have found to this argument comes from the Indian nationalists about 1900, who argued that Japan had achieved more industrial growth in one generation as a free state than had India in over a century of tutelage under the most industrial country in the world.

a physically superior metropolitan power in which the force of nationalist arms alone could not prevail, the colonial rulers' own political
philosophy shaped the arguments and attack of the new nationalists.
If they could not win by force alone, the nationalists could win by
appealing to the legitimacy of their aims, both in the world at large
and in the political centers of the metropolitan powers themselves.[7]
This meant that the political philosophy of liberal democracy, developed in the metropolitan countries in the preceding two centuries,
came to be used by the nationalists in their struggles for independence
in the mid-twentieth century. This was the point at which the metropolitan powers were most vulnerable, for they had themselves long
ago made the transition from the divine right of kings to the divine
right of the masses. Because of the physical superiority of the metropolitan powers the new nationalists could carry on a more effective
struggle in a foreign parliament or forum than on the battlefields of
their own countries.

There were variations to be sure, and in some cases both moral and
physical lines of attack were used. Great Britain and the United States
gave up their colonies more readily and more successfully than did the
Netherlands and France. Yet the legitimizing arguments of the nationalists were the same in all cases: the right of the ruled to choose their
rulers. The differences among the metropolitan powers meant that the
arguments of the nationalists would be presented in those centers of
power where the value of self-determination was strongest. For British
and American colonies, the nationalist arguments were presented in
London and Washington. For Dutch and French colonies, the nationalist arguments were presented in Lake Success (and later in New
York), and to a lesser extent in Amsterdam and Paris.

This form of struggle, determined by the values of the rulers, gave
to the new states an early commitment to liberal democratic institutions (which, to be sure, many have since lost). It not only made them
democratic in aspiration and ideology, it forced them to reinforce
their arguments for self-determination with a visible mass following,
a live indication that independence was indeed the wish of the
governed.

One of the most effective, or at least most common, ways to mobilize
a mass following was to play upon the sense of deprivation of the
independent peoples. Where no sense of deprivation existed, it had to
be created. Thus the new leaders expounded upon the great dis-

---

[7] The demise of gunboat diplomacy, we would argue here, has resulted as much
from the change of world values as from the change in the world balance of power,
though the two are difficult to separate.

crepancies between standards of living of the foreign rulers and the native ruled. Even more, the new leaders could promise that independence would eliminate this imbalance, would distribute the wealth more equally; or, more explicitly, that it would provide the population with the currently understood mechanisms of upward mobility.

This latter aspect of the promise brought education into the arena of aspirations for independence. More education, free universal education, has been a major aim of all new states and a major promise made by all nationalist leaders. It has also been a major force for mobilizing the masses behind the new leaders and the nationalist cause. To promise that all children regardless of skin color and wealth could receive an education was tantamount to promising all people that their children could have the good life. It was a promise that all could aspire to positions of honor and comfort, positions in the government service where one works with the mind rather than with the hands.

Thus, the commitment to economic modernization in the new states also derives its strength from the commitment to democracy or, more accurately, from the necessity to gain a mass following to legitimize both the nationalist struggle for independence and the continued rule of the new leaders in the post-independence period.

Finally, the character of leadership development has also strengthened the new states' commitment to economic modernization. Many leaders and parties that brought the country to independence are still in control of government.[8] For the most part the new leaders are of a new class and represent no established class themselves.[9] They are not of the class of traditional leaders with whom the colonial powers often made treaties and in whose name they indirectly ruled. Against the value of self-determination, which the new leaders have captured, the claim to traditional legitimacy of the old class of indigenous leaders is impotent.

Two factors strengthen the new leaders' commitment to economic modernization. First, they are generally educated parvenus. Not being of an established class of traditional leaders has meant that they have had little or no claim to wealth or status under the old system. Economic modernization means a destruction of the old economy— the old patterns of distribution as well as of production. In addition, a high premium is placed upon the skills of the educated elite. Thus

---

[8] This is partly because insufficient time has passed for the demise of the leaders for whom the achievement of independence was a great personal triumph, and partly a result of the widespread erosion of liberal democracy, or the advance of oligarchy, characteristic of the new states.

[9] Harry J. Benda, "Non-Western Intelligentsia as Political Elites," in J. H. Kautsky, *op. cit.*

the more indigenous people could take control of their own economy, and the more that economy were modernized, the greater would be the advantages of the new educated leaders.

Second is the less easily defined, but certainly no less powerful force of human enlightenment and the change of world values. As educated elites the new leaders were men of the world. Their horizons spread beyond the village or even the country of their birth. They were attuned to the large changes in world values since World War II. It is commonplace to note that there is nothing new in the poverty found in the new states today. There may be less poverty today than there was a century ago. Even if there were no change, however, the poverty and low productivity of the new states has been the common experience of man for centuries. What is new today is that this poverty has become unacceptable.[10] This is what is implied in the term "the revolution of rising expectations." This revolution was not, however, and in many cases is not yet, truly a mass revolution. It was originally a revolution of the educated elites who have become the new nationalist leaders. Far more than the physically and intellectually isolated peasants, the worldly and educated elites were caught up in, and helped to speed, the great change in world values. Because they were educated, the poverty of their lands first became intolerable for them.

Thus both the class position of the new leaders, and their initiation into the modern world, has strengthened their commitment to economic modernization.

ECONOMIC MODERNIZATION AND COMPLEX ORGANIZATIONS

The relation between economic development or modernization and the use of complex organizations for its stimulation is to be found partly in the nature of economic development and partly in the unique capacity of the complex organization to mobilize the resources required for development.

Economic development means essentially a long-term, sustained increase in per capita real product.[11] Historically such sustained increase has been associated with radical changes in the mode of production, in its technique, and in its organization. New tools and new techniques

---

[10] Even this phenomenon is not without its Western roots, for it can be argued to be essentially a result of the inexorable march of the West's two great revolutions: the industrial revolution with its seat in England and the political revolution with its seat in France. See, for example, Eric J. Hobsbawm, *The Age of Revolution*, London, 1962, *passim*.

[11] See Simon Kuznets, *Six Lectures on Economic Growth*, Glencoe, 1950, p. 14.

are required to produce sustained growth in productivity. Some increases can be achieved, of course, by more hours worked and by reducing underemployment of resources. However, the amount of time individuals work and the energy and industriousness with which they work depends on the larger organization of their lives. Time and energy are determined by the type and the extent of control exercised over individuals, the incentives they are given for work, and their relations with their fellows. Thus not only new tools, but new elements of social organization that are not always directly related to production, are required to produce a sustained increase in productivity.

One of the more visible and dramatic changes historically associated with economic development is a change in the industrial distribution of the labor force. The proportion, and often the absolute number, of workers in agriculture or in primary products declines. Unless land under cultivation can be expanded indefinitely, this decline in the agricultural work force is inevitable because of areal limitations. Secondary and tertiary industries are not as limited in this way, and can accommodate continued increases in human productivity along with increases in worker density. All industries tend to show an increasing mechanization along with increases in productivity. This is not always necessary in periods of three or four decades, as illustrated by agricultural increases in Meiji Japan, which were achieved without appreciable mechanization. In the long run, however, men with machines can produce more than men without machines, hence the association of mechanization with economic development. Along with mechanization, and probably more basic, is the application of science to the process of production. To some extent science can be substituted for mechanization, as again illustrated by Meiji agriculture, where the increases were achieved by better breeding and the increased use of commercial fertilizers. The more common experience with science and mechanization or technology, of course, is a multiplying and complementary relation between the two rather than a competitive relation. The experience of Japan and the possibility of substitution merely serves to indicate the great variety of forces that determine the speed and character of economic development.

Mechanization, science, and the changing industrial distribution of the labor force in turn imply urbanization and the growth of factories and offices as places of work—processes with ramifications in many directions. In one direction urbanization and industrialization mean an increase in the use of nonhuman sources of energy, the development of new power sources to run the machines and to accommodate

the high population densities of the modern society. In another direction the processes imply a depersonalization of human life. More
people work for others according to fixed schedules and in surround-
ings designed for productivity rather than for comfort. There is a
weakening of particularistic ties, especially kinship ties, allowing for
the use of more rational, standardized, and universalistic criteria for
allocating human resources. This in turn is associated with the creation of multiple centers of power and loyalty competing for the
allegiance and attention of the individual. In addition, the urban
industrial society both facilitates and demands a major change in the
institutions of socialization. Schools are more efficient than the family
in producing the specialized skills required in a highly productive
society, and they are more economical when situated in areas of high
population density, where transportation costs are low. At the same
time, schools contribute to the depersonalization of human relation-
ships that allows for a more rational allocation of human resources.

Another important correlate of economic development is an increase
in the scope of the market and in its complexity, a process commonly
subsumed under the rubric of commercialization, or the transition
from a subsistence economy to a market economy. An ever larger
proportion of goods produced and consumed passes through a market
or exchange system in which it acquires a monetary value. This
makes individuals both more productive and more dependent upon
one another. The growth of the market is strongly affected by the
development of instruments of communication. The construction of
roads, bridges, railways, ports, and the equally important extension
of the instruments of symbolic communication—radio, telephone, the
press, and television—add greatly to the speed with which producers
and consumers are functionally separated, yet integrated in the market.

Analytically, the fundamental process in economic development is
investment, though by this we mean something far broader than the
narrow national-income account definition. By considering investment
as a process, we refer to any increase in the productive capacity of any
part of the economic system, or of any factor of production. Thus
any addition to the physical items that produce wealth (communications facilities, power producers, and factories) and to the human
wealth-producing capacities (education, science, engineering, and
organization) is here considered an investment in the productive
capacity of the economy. In the long run the largest part of these
investments must come out of the wealth the economy itself produces.
In investment, especially in the broader sense used here, lies a critical
difference between the rich and the poor countries, the industrialized

and the underdeveloped countries. Here also lies one of the great problems of economic development in the poor countries of the modern world.

Because they are wealthy, because they enjoy high levels of human productivity, the industrialized economies find it relatively easy to engage in the wide range of investments in human and physical productive capacity required to sustain increases in human productivity. On the other hand, because they are poor and burdened with low levels of human productivity, the underdeveloped countries find it difficult to withhold sufficient wealth from consumption, or to mobilize sufficient unused wealth to increase their productive capacities. Thus in a very real sense, rich countries are rich because they are rich and poor countries are poor because they are poor. One need not, and indeed cannot, hold this proposition in its pure and static form, however. The rich nations of today were once poor nations, and not so very long ago, yet they did manage to change their modes of production and to reach conditions in which the maintenance of increases in human productivity is relatively easy. The rather dramatic nature in which the above proposition can be stated merely points to the magnitude of the problem of inducing or stimulating economic development in the poor new states.

The problem is exacerbated by the current impatience with poverty, the increasing inability to accept as inevitable the low levels of productivity that have for centuries been the common experience of man. Thus we have the great costs of stimulating economic development and the great demand for development. It is this that, in part, makes the complex organization a common feature not only of programs to stimulate economic development in the new states, but indeed a common feature of any highly productive industry or economy.

Modern social criticism has largely focused upon the unsavory aspects of the depersonalization characteristic of the complex organization. In the concern for this aspect of the organization, it is easy to overlook the great capacity of this form of social grouping—the fact that the great mobilization of human and material capital required to achieve sustained increases in human productivity could only be performed by the complex organization. To produce new sources of nonhuman power, to distribute this power, to build and maintain complex communications networks, to build schools and to produce technicians, administrators, and scientists, to mobilize wealth so that part can be saved and invested in further increases in productive capacity—all of this requires an ability to organize and mobilize human resources. Such mobilizing capacity with such permanence is to be found only in the modern complex organization, the organization that has limited goals and allocates its resources rationally. This allocation requires the creation of rules to be applied in standard fashion—files, and positions hierarchically arranged with clear definitions of responsibility and power.

The great and generalized capability of the complex organization lies behind the historical association of bureaucratization and economic development. There is, however, another set of forces that draws the complex organization more rapidly and more completely into the concern for economic development. The complex organization has become a repository of what competence now exists to increase directly the speed and to control the direction of the process of economic development. This is largely the result of the development of techniques of analysis in which modern organizations have played a major role. The techniques of national-income accounting, census, and other forms of survey analysis—techniques developed in the context and with the capacity of complex organizations—provide important tools for assessing the performance of an economy, for measuring human productivity and for discovering its probable correlates. The modern planning and developing organizations have the technical competence (potential if not always actual) to help assess and solve the problems of directing or stimulating economic growth. They can thus provide the basis for making decisions on programs and policies that enable new leaders to use the instruments of rule they inherited to make the changes they desire in their societies. Under certain conditions, the complex organization can also carry out the policies or programs required to stimulate economic development.

The close association between economic development and complex organizations thus reflects the great cost of economic development and the capacities of the complex organization to meet these costs speedily. The complex organization holds the promise of economic development.

NEW ORGANIZATIONS AND NEW STATES

The proclivity of the new states to create new development organizations derives in part from the dominant role of government in those states and in part from the central position of the administration in the nationalist struggle.

In the new states the central government often appears to hold a near-monopoly of organized powers, the powers of initiative. There is a great dearth of limited-purpose organization outside of government, and consequently an extreme concentration in government of the ability to initiate action.[12] The near-monopoly of organizational competence in the governments of the new states has three historical roots, all of which continue to affect developments in the post-independence period.

(1) One characteristic of a colonial experience is the creation of an organized state through powerful and extensive mechanisms of control. As a rule, colonialism brought effective central power to areas previously characterized by many small centers of weak control. Large areas that were characterized by chaos, anarchy, and chronic warfare were transformed into areas of peace, stability, and commerce. The colonial government created the structure of the modern state and the modern government. The business of establishing order in areas of disorder placed in the hands of the colonial governments the overwhelming majority of powers of initiative.

Though the colonial government created the structure of the modern state, it did not necessarily thereby create a political community, a state with major cohesive forces deriving from consensus or a generally shared set of politically relevant values. This is one of the tasks that has fallen to the governments of the new states. Like the colonial governments they, too, are concerned with the creation of order. To be sure, theirs is a different problem—that of creating a political community, consensus, or shared values on which the modern state can operate effectively. What the colonial governments originally accomplished through force, the governments of the new states must accomplish through the creation of a new culture. This task is largely defined by the government itself, and naturally places in the hands of government most powers of initiative. This is illustrated in the relation between formal structures of central and local governments in the new states. Where local government exists in the new states, it is primarily a structure created by the central government. It is almost never a real center of power against which the central government must struggle to obtain powers of initiative.[13]

(2) The central government has a near-monopoly of initiative powers not only because it was the original order-giving force, but also because indigenous private organization has been chronically weak in the

---

[12] Shils, *op. cit.*, has argued that this great, and probably increasing, gap between central initiative and lack of local initiative is one of the major obstacles to political modernization in the new states.

[13] There are differences between unitary and federal structures that should be analyzed here. The difference, with relevance to the problem of local initiative, may only be one of degree, but it may also be an important qualitative difference in the historical development of the new states.

colonies and in the new states. There have been two historical reasons
for this. First, private organization has been largely proscribed for non-
Western peoples, and has been allied with colonial rule for Westerners.
Private indigenous organization has always represented a threat to the
central government, because it has represented a threat to the maintenance of order. This was especially true when the forces of nationalism emerged, for indigenous organizations often aimed directly at
the termination of colonial government, sometimes regardless of how
nonpolitical their origins may have been.[14] Certainly in all colonial
areas, except in the American-Philippines relation, politics and political organizations were considered illegitimate, and the stereotype of
the fiercely antipolitical colonial officer is often more a reality than a
caricature.[15]

Long before politics, the requirements and rewards of the market
place provided a fertile field for the emergence of private organization.
The potential threat this offered to government monopoly initiative
powers was dampened either through proscription or cooptation and
alliance. Colonial areas have been almost universally plagued by the
emergence of what Furnivall called "the plural society." [16] The weakness and backwardness of indigenous peoples in economic affairs has
been opposed by the initiative, aggression, and success of immigrant
peoples. Colonial rule brought peace and stability, making conditions
favorable for trade. The ideology of laissez-faire that dominated the
colonial period opened the colonies to immigration. On the one hand
was the rapid immigration of traders taking advantage of the favorable conditions, and on the other hand was the rapid immigration of
labor—for the colonial areas were often underpopulated, or far enough
outside a money economy so that indigenous peoples would not re-
spond to the wage incentives (often very low) of the entrepreneurs
developing the territories. Against this rapid immigration, the colonial
government developed toward the indigenes a protective attitude—a
mixture of a divide-and-rule strategy;[17] a reflection of late nineteenth-
century anthropology that made colonial officers genuinely concerned

[14] See, for example, Harry J. Benda's discussion of the Sharikat Islam in Indonesia
in *The Crescent and the Rising Sun,* The Hague, 1958, *passim.*
[15] See below, p. 174, n. 2, for the author's direct experience of this phenomenon
in the British colony of North Borneo in 1962.
[16] J. S. Furnivall, *Netherlands India, a Study of Plural Economy,* Cambridge,
1944, *passim.*
[17] We shall argue below that the common "divide and rule" interpretation of
colonial policy assigns too much consistency, intelligence, and Machiavellianism to
colonial governments.

with native interests; an inability, especially where the Chinese immigrants were concerned, to understand and thus to control the immigrant elements; and in some cases a concern for making the territory self-sufficient in food, a policy that fit in well with the plantation economies characteristic of colonial areas. This protective attitude gave rise to a proscriptive orientation toward the organizations of the immigrants, thus obstructing their growth and development of initiative.

On the other hand, the foreign firms were a source of initiative. Their own organizational power, coupled with their political influence in the metropolitan countries and their club and school ties with colonial officers, produced an alliance between these two centers of initiative. In any event, these foreign firms would not be expected to maintain their extensive powers after independence, and in most cases they have not, though they have continued to be a source of initiative in the new states.

In the second place, the lack of development of the indigenous economies in the colonies has meant a lack of modern class development, on which organized initiative is often based. The colonies in most cases developed rapidly; the majority of new states will have difficulty in matching the rates of growth achieved during the best period of colonial rule. However, usually this was a development of what Levin has called an export economy.[18] Export economies are highly unbalanced, marked primarily by the dominance of primary product exports and luxury imports, and affecting only a small portion of the local population. The growth of an export economy is extremely limited, with little effect on the economy as a whole. Thus, though such indicators of growth as capital formation and total output may rise impressively, they are not followed by the changes in the society that would occur in a more balanced pattern of growth. This retarded indigenous economic development in the colonies has hindered the development of almost every form of modern organization, except the government bureaucracy. Cooperatives, trade unions, private schools and universities, associations of all types have been chronically underdeveloped in the colonial areas.

Not only government proscription of private organizations has retarded their development, especially in the case of cooperatives and trade unions. On the contrary, colonial governments often actively attempted to stimulate their development. More important was the

---

[18] Jonathan V. Levin, *The Export Economies,* Cambridge, 1960, *passim.*

characteristic of the society as a whole, which, largely unchanged by the development of an export economy, did not provide favorable conditions for the growth of modern organizations.[19]

Most factors that gave rise to the near-monopoly of government in modern organizational structures and thus in initiative powers have continued after the achievement of independence. In some cases these factors have become more pronounced in the new states. The shortage of trained administrators, the precariousness of new leaders in new governing institutions, and the weakness of the social base for organizational development produce pressures toward centralization of power. These remove the powers of initiative from local organizations, both public and private, thus further inhibiting their development. As the development of the capacity for effective and responsible action is retarded, the forces of centralization are strengthened, producing a vicious cycle that amplifies the basic weakness and further obstructs the development of local initiative.[20]

(3) The dominant role of government in the colonial territories and the new states has also been reinforced by the role the administration has played in the nationalist struggle. Both directly and indirectly the colonial administration was a prime mover in the nationalist struggle. Many of the new nationalist leaders obtained their early training in the colonial administration. The requirements and career possibilities originally brought local boys to the schools, provided the major focus for their career orientations, and initiated them to the modern world. The administration also provided the visible instrument of rule, the control of which became the major aim of the nationalists. Even in the very early stages of the nationalist movements, before they espoused independence, the new leaders emerged as a result of the demand for more local places in the administration. Before anyone thought of demanding independence, there were attempts to gain for local elites a larger share of the positions in the colonial administration.

As the nationalist movements gained force, especially in the postwar period when they were seeking self-rule, the administration became more and more an instrument with which, or around which, mass sentiments could be mobilized. Here the value of *new* organizations gained considerable strength. Pre-independence promises and post-independence activities performed the same functions of mobilizing

---

[19] We have discussed the general social conditions necessary for organizational development in "Cooperative Development and Industrial Capitalism in England and Denmark," *Berkeley Journal of Sociology*, Spring 1961, 1–15.

[20] Shils, *op. cit.*, has discussed this cyclical process of weakening local initiative in considerable detail.

mass sentiments. New organizations could give distinctiveness to the new governments; they could symbolize the difference between the old colonial leaders and the new nationalist leaders; they could be both symbolically free of the taint of the old regime, which was criticized in the nationalist struggle for its lack of concern for the governed, and organizationally free from the strictures placed upon initiative by the rules of the old administration. Thus new planning organizations and new development organizations have been both symbolically and structurally important in mobilizing mass support in the new states.

Finally, in the proclivity of the new states to create new organizations to stimulate development, one can see the force of countervailing powers. The new states are marked by export economies controlled by foreign firms whose technical capacities spread to every corner of the economies of the new states. Much of the modern drive for development in the new states aims, consciously or unconsciously, at transforming an export economy into an internally oriented and more balanced national economy. In the old export economy the foreign firms controlled a major share of the visible wealth. Here was an opportunity for indigenous leaders to acquire more wealth for the new state. In the first place government, the original organization, developed powers of taxation to share the wealth of the foreign firms. Next, indigenous organizations emerged, patterned on the foreign firms that had demonstrated wealth-producing capacities. Marketing boards and government enterprises in plantation and mineral extraction became common features of the new states.

In the bureaucracy, too, the countervailing forces are manifested. The original organizations demonstrated wealth-creating abilities; they were able to build roads and schools. New development organizations emerged to take up some of this power, to use it for other ends for other groups in the society.

Thus in the proclivity of the new states to use new complex organizations there is also a manifestation of a set of countervailing powers. New organizations were created to take up part of, and to share in, the powers and wealth of existing organizations created in the development of the colonial territory and its export economy.

The near-monopoly of organizational initiative in the new states calls attention to a distinction in types of organizations. In the industrial societies of the West we find a wide range of complex organizations. Some spring up almost *autochthonously* within the society. They are manifestations of perceptions by private individuals of problems or interests that can be served in sustained collective action, such as the community organizations, foundations, and private clubs. Other

organizations are *countervailing* organizations, emerging directly in reaction to existing organizations. Trade unions emerge to further
worker interests in the arena defined by the modern productive enterprise. Cooperatives emerge to further the interests of consumers and
producers in a market defined by existing commercial organizations.
Finally, other organizations are directly created as *subsidiaries* of a
parent organization. Government agencies, research organizations of
private firms, and even productive or distributive agencies of religious
organizations are common examples.

This set of distinctions is relevant to our original observation. In
the industrialization of the West in the nineteenth century, the organizational vanguard of development was the private, autochthonous,
market enterprise, though countervailing organizations such as trade
unions, and subsidiary organizations of government also played an
important role. In the new states economic development is being
stimulated predominantly by subsidiary organizations—specialized
agencies of the central government created to induce social and
economic change. One of the crucial distinctions is the difference in
organizational goals, and in the freedom to change goals.

For the analysis of goals, we shall use the typology proposed by
Amitai Etzioni: *order, output,* and *cultural.*[21] From our distinction of
organizational types, we can infer a continuum of freedom to choose
goals or of "goal stickiness," determined essentially by the constraints
upon goal choices exercised by external organizations. Goal choice or
goal change in the autochthonous organization is largely an internal
matter, effected by policy decisions wholly within the organization.
The constraints upon the autochthonous organization are only the
diffuse constraints of the entire society. Countervailing organizations
have limits set upon their choice of goals by the original organization
in the relationship. For example, trade-union goals are largely limited,
though not specifically determined, by the resources controlled by the
productive enterprise. Finally, subsidiary organizations have their goals
defined for them directly, and often specifically, by the parent organization. The goals of the subsidiary organization are essentially means
to other ends of the parent. In order to effect goal change, therefore,
the subsidiary organization must be able to demonstrate to the parent
that the means chosen are not appropriate, or not the most appropri-

---

[21] See his *Comparative Analysis of Complex Organizations*, New York, 1961,
passim. I have given the name *output* goal to Etzioni's *economic* goal. This is
primarily a stylistic change, recommended by our frequent use of the term economic
in the context of economic development. There is no change in definition; economic
or output goals indicate activity directed toward the production of goods or services.

ate, to achieve the ends of the parent. In the present context, this observation points to the necessity of distinguishing between the more general goals of government and the more specific goals of its subsidiary (development) organizations. We shall have cause to use this distinction in chapter IV.

Governments may be committed to economic development as a broad aim, but the creation of organizations to stimulate development requires a determination of their specific goals. Differences between development patterns in the nineteenth-century West and in the new states suggest a difference in the goals of the organizations in the two cases. The goals of the nineteenth-century autochthonous organizations were a function of some market mechanism. If the goals of a specific organization "did not pay," the entrepreneurs had freedom to change the goals and were indeed under pressure to do so. For the new subsidiary organizations of the new states the goals are stated by the parent organization and are a function of the perceptions of the new leaders, of their knowledge of the state of affairs, and of their ideas of the means appropriate to achieve their goals. From this two related problems arise. How is the performance of the new organization measured, and under what conditions will it be able to change its goals?

This distinction between organizational types and goals has carried us beyond the bounds of our paradigm and has changed its character somewhat. On the one hand the paradigm is now complete: (1) The colonial background of the new states and their consequent character of their struggle for independence and of their new leaders led to a commitment to economic development. (2) Both the problems of achieving development and the colonial bureaucratic heritage of the new states led to a use of modern complex organizations to stimulate economic development. (3) The struggle for independence plus the prior existence of wealth-creating organizations led to the proliferation of new development-stimulating organizations. In part, these new organizations furthered the nationalist cause by sustaining the distinctive image of the new governments; in part, they were reactions to the demonstration effect of the existing organizations.

On the other hand, the final observations of the paradigm raises a set of questions and defines a specific strategy of analysis. The paradigm is a closed analytical system. Three distinctly observable phenomena—the character and change of the polity, the economy, and the organizational complex—are argued to be functionally interrelated. Thus regardless of where we begin the analysis—with the new states, with the commitment to economic development, or with the organizations of development—the point of departure must be related to the other two phenomena. At the same time, the identification of subsidiary organizations, with their relative "goal stickiness" and their close connection with the parent organization, recommend the development organization as the most fruitful point at which to begin an analysis of the system.

The paradigm is not meant to be an exhaustive treatment of the unique relationship in our original observation. Such a treatment would have to take account of the variability of cultural background, colonial experience, and the processes of gaining independence in the new states. We have been content to disregard these important variables in order to focus upon more general processes, recognizing that this often does violence to specific historical experiences.

Nor do we imply that all relations we observe here are unique to the new states of the mid-twentieth century. At other times states have been committed to the process of stimulating economic development. Gerschenkron has made an excellent case for viewing this involvement itself as an important variable in the economic development of the West.[22]

Further, the proliferation of new government agencies may be seen as a characteristic of all modern governments. Some functions of this process may be the same as those proposed in our paradigm, such as the creation of distinctive images for new governing parties. Other functions may be reflections of similar changes in the base of power and subsequent attempts to alter the distribution of wealth. In this case, though the process and functions may be similar, the rate of change can vary. What appears as part of a long-term, secular change in the industrialized countries, appears as a radical change or discontinuous process in the new states.

Finally, the basic pattern of relationship in the new poor states may be currently duplicated in the old poor states of Central and South America. In the latter we can see similar stated commitments to economic development, and similar creations of new organizations to stimulate development. Our paradigm suggests, however, that the different class positions of the leaders in the old and new poor states will have a profound effect upon the processes of modernization in the two cases.

In drawing these three elements of our paradigm together in a

---

[22] Alexander Gerschenkron, *Economic Development in Historical Perspective,* Cambridge, 1962. See also S. M. Lipset's *The First New Nation,* New York, 1963, *passim,* where the role of local government in stimulating economic development in the post-revolutionary United States is analyzed.

single intellectual framework our paradigm is meant essentially to provide a set of *sentizing concepts*[23] that defines an issue, an aspect of human life of which we seek some understanding, and recommends a strategy of inquiry.

Following this recommendation, the object of this study is a new development organization in a new state. We shall focus attention upon the Ministry of Rural Development in Malaya. It will be useful to begin with a general discussion of the character of the society in which the Ministry emerged. This will be the subject of chapters II and III. Then we proceed to an analysis of the organizational experience that preceded the formation of the Ministry and helped to shape its goals and structure. We will then understand the relation between the Ministry and the larger society, the constraints upon the Ministry, and its impact on that society. The study is meant to provide some understanding of the historical relations observed more generally in our paradigm—an understanding of the relation between Malaya's commitment to economic development and the operation of its new development organizations.

---

[23] The term is Herbert Blumer's presented in seminar during the author's graduate study.

II

THE CHANGING MALAYAN SOCIAL SYSTEM – I: THE COLONIAL SYSTEM

The emergence and operation of an organization as important and forceful as Malaya's Ministry of Rural Development is a sociological phenomenon of major importance. It must be seen as a part of the pattern of larger movements or forces in the social system. The political, economic, and social forces from which the Ministry grew have a major determining influence on its orientation and actions, and in turn the actions of the Ministry itself affect the future development of the social system.

Modern Malaya can best be seen as two historically separate social systems. The system between 1874 and 1957 can be characterized as colonial, now being replaced by a national system. The important elements of the colonial social system are here described as a dependent paternalistic state, a colonial export economy, and an ethnic plural society. The emerging national social system is here seen to be composed of an independent parliamentary democratic state, an emerging modern industrial economy, and an emerging national plural society.

The dependent paternalistic state was characterized by control from outside the country, legitimized more by reference to what is good for the inhabitants than to their consent and desires. This state was replaced formally in 1957 by one based upon the consent of the governed, manifested in parliamentary elections. The colonial export economy was oriented outward for capital, management, and markets, with production and labor force concentrated in what are generally called primary or extractive industries. This economy is currently being replaced by one of predominantly nonagricultural forms of production and is tied to indigenous demands as well as to the demands of foreign markets. In the ethnic plural society the major groupings, the major specialization of functions were along ethnic lines. This type of society is now being replaced by one in which the basic point of reference and loyalty is the nation-state and in which major groupings come to have a widespread, national character. Designation of this type of society as a national *plural* society implies the acceptance of a wide range of group differences. That is, a national plural society refers to a society with a political community and with legitimate group differences. Implicit is the distinction between a plural society and a totalitarian society.

Although specific dates have been given for the beginning and end of the colonial social system, it is impossible to be precise about the timing of its total change. A social system does not change overnight. It is only possible to designate specific dates as indicators of a watershed in the continuous course of the history of a people. Generally it is possible to do this only some time after the fact, when a specific event can be said to have constituted a significant symbol of a major trend in the process. Such events, for instance, were the Pangkor Treaty of 1874, which brought the British government into direct intervention in the policies of the Malayan states, and the declaration of independence in 1957, which marked the end of direct British intervention. Both events were only individual happenings in gradual historical processes; they gain significance only because they clearly mark a major trend in those processes.

In this sense the designation of 1957 as the end of one system is rather tentative. As the course of Malayan history develops, it may seem more appropriate to shift the date backward, perhaps to the Japanese invasion, or forward to some major event yet to occur. For the present, however, the use of this date seems most appropriate, more so as it serves to indicate a major stimulus underlying the change of social system. We shall argue here that the colonial social system was a system in essential equilibrium. The elements of that system— the dependent state, the colonial export economy, and the ethnic plural society—fit together with a minimum of strain and a maximum of mutual support. The granting of independence, the emergence of an independent state, introduced new strains into the system. It made both the colonial export economy and the ethnic plural society untenable. Movements in the direction of a modern industrial economy and a national plural society thus bring the economy and the society into alignment with the new polity. We shall also argue that the emergence and operation of the Ministry of Rural Development is one of the most significant and comprehensive programs of action directly designed to relieve the strains of the emerging and as yet unbalanced system.

THE STATE

The traditional Malay[1] political system over which British colonial bureaucracy was laid at the end of the nineteenth century can best be described, using Leibenstein's phrase, as "the polity of a quasi-stable system at a low level of human and areal productivity." The largest units were states, headed by a sultan who, at least in the western states had more symbolic than real power. The states were organized around river valleys, as rivers afforded the only real means of trans-portation through the dense jungle of the peninsula. Below the level of the states were districts under the control of local chiefs; the districts were organized into villages controlled by local headmen and religious functionaries, the *imams*.

The social structure was marked by two major strata: rulers and subjects. The ruling stratum was an almost closed caste, with a value system that discouraged mobility or social achievement. The village was a geographic rather than a consanguineous unit, whose peasants engaged in rice-growing and fishing.

By current standards the land was adequate, and even underpopu-lated. Peasants could, and did, move to new areas to escape the harsh treatment of a chief or the consequences of the chronic warfare under which the area suffered. Sultans and district chiefs consolidated their power by retaining bands of personal followers. This required material resources, the major source of which were duties levied on the small traders entering the hinterland, and on the exporters of such products as tin. The capital of the state and district was thus generally situated at the mouth of a river or its tributaries, which placed the sultans and the district chiefs in a position to collect duties.[2] In the west coast states, especially during the nineteenth century, the exploitation of tin deposits in the interior provided sources of wealth for, and thus

[1] Following common usage, *Malay* refers to persons of the Malayo-Polynesian race living in Malaya. Malays are defined by the Constitution as those who adhere to the Islamic faith, habitually speak the Malay language, and follow Malay customs. *Malayan* refers to inhabitants or citizens of the Federation of Malaya, and includes members of all races or ethnic groups.

[2] Hence the common appearance of Kuala (river mouth) in Malayan town names: Kuala Lumpur, Kuala Selangor, Kuala Trengganu.

stimuli for the ambitions of, local chiefs, contributing to a decentralization of power and an increase in chronic warfare.

Wars between chiefs and between chiefs and sultans, rival interstate claims to succession, and court intrigues were characteristic of this traditional bloody and anarchic system. It can be described as a system in quasi-stable equilibrium, in part because the sultan provided a legitimizing symbol whose maintenance was in the interest of anyone in power or of any pretender to power. The peasants were concerned primarily with maintaining their village systems and families in a land that was relatively bountiful, and with keeping out of the way of the "fighting elephants," as the temporal powers were often called. There was little to be gained by the accumulation of capital. For the peasant this would only have invited confiscation, for as in most peasant systems, the rulers had a right to essentially all they could take. For the chiefs and sultans a constant distribution of wealth among followers was necessary to retain their services, which might at any time be needed in defense or attack. Thus the system was poor and life was cheap, but it did continue for some centuries, and it was brought to an end largely because of outside forces.[3]

Into this poor but quasi-stable system two sets of related outside forces were introduced: the Chinese and Western traders. Lying on the great trade route between India or the West and China, Malaya had long been in touch with travelers and traders from many lands. Chinese and Indian contacts date to before the Christian era. The Portuguese and the Dutch had conquered Malacca in the sixteenth century, after Islam had been brought to the entire archipelago. It was not until late in the eighteenth century and early in the nineteenth century, however, that the British inaugurated the modern period by founding first Penang and then Singapore. Also early in the nineteenth century, the Sultan of Johore helped push Malaya into the modern world by encouraging the immigration of Chinese to develop his land, largely through the production of pepper and gambier. By the middle of the century the Chinese were beginning to move into the tin fields of central Selangor and Perak. The Chinese involvement in tin mining greatly exacerbated the anarchic nature of the western Malay states, as clan wars were added to volatile Malay politics. From the point of view of Singapore and Penang traders, this called for British intervention to bring the peace and order needed to carry on trade. These traders applied pressure to induce the British government

---

[3] The above section draws largely on the work of J. M. Gullick, *Indigenous Political Systems of Western Malaya*, London, 1958, *passim*.

to intervene in Malaya, supported by the threat that Germany or France would intervene at the ostensible behest of some Malay rulers. The combination of trade-disrupting anarchy and the threat of intervention by other European powers induced the British government to enter into the Treaty of Pangkor with a Perak ruler in 1874. This was followed by a similar move in Selangor, and Malaya began to experience the peace and prosperity of "indirect" rule.

The original treaty arrangements were that the sultans would accept a British resident-adviser, whose advice would be followed in all things save religion and Malay customs. By 1895 this system had extended to Negri Sembilan and Pahang, which were in that year merged, together with Perak and Selangor, into the Federated Malay States, under a British resident-general. Early in the twentieth century the four northern states—Perlis, Kedah, Kelantan, and Trengganu—moved from Thai suzerainty to British protection, each obtaining the services of an adviser. Together with Johore, which had had a British consul since 1885 and had been under the influence of growing British interest in Singapore since early in the century, these states formed the Unfederated States of Malaya. Singapore, Malacca, and Penang (and for a short time a coastal area of Perak known as the Dindings) were bound together into the Straits Settlements, ruled from Singapore more directly as a colony of Great Britain. Thus by the end of the first decade of the twentieth century the pattern of British rule in Malaya was established. It was to remain, with a short break during the Japanese occupation of 1942–1945, until Malaya achieved independence in 1957.

The course of political development differed in the Federated and the Unfederated States. Even before their amalgamation in 1895, the Federated States tended toward centralization. Power was increasingly taken from the hands of the sultans and their local advisers and accumulated in the hands of the resident-general with his growing bureaucracy in Kuala Lumpur. Especially with the introduction of rubber and the European exploitation of tin, the demand for government services grew and resulted in the formation of technical bureaucratic departments for public health, public works, and education. The central government in Kuala Lumpur often found itself in conflict with both the colonial office, which tried to preserve the fiction of indirect rule, and the sultans themselves, who resisted, however meekly, the encroachments upon their power. Such conflict and resistance, however, were only rear-guard actions against the seemingly inexorable power of bureaucratization and rationalization. And favoring bureaucratization was another seemingly inexorable force—that of commercial or economic development.

Along with the consolidation of British power through the growth of a central bureaucracy, the state and district administrations were taken over by the small group of Britishers who formed the Malayan Civil Service. Assisted by Malays learning the art of administration, by Indians and, to a lesser extent, Chinese, this handful of officers[4] mobilized local resources to build roads, railroads, and public buildings, to control malaria, and in general to provide a favorable climate for foreign investment.

The Unfederated States developed at different rates: more rapidly in Johore and slower in the North. Johore has always been one of the more progressive Malay States. Its sultans have been more closely in tune with the growing commercial developments in Singapore. This allowed the state to advance economically while maintaining a great deal of indigenous control over the local administration. The growing central bureaucracy and the district administration were staffed largely by indigenous Malays, with some advice and assistance from British administrators who functioned largely in the state capital. In the north, the states of Perlis, Kedah, Kelantan, and Trengganu remained under the nominal suzerainty of Thailand until 1909.[5] As in Johore, the role of the British was limited to that of an adviser at the capital; state and district administration remained largely in the hands of the indigenous civil servants. Being farther from the centers of modern commerce and from the impact of both tin and rubber, these states were far less progressive economically than their sister Unfederated State, Johore.[6] They continued to be based upon Malay smallholding agriculture and to view the outside and the modern world more with suspicion than with open acceptance.

These differences between political developments in the states were, however, largely differences in the directness of British control and in the speed with which it was established. In all states British power was paramount. On all but a very few issues decisions rested with the British officials. The most important actions, often the only actions, were initiated by British officials, and the developments in England and policies of the British government were the most important

---

[4] Even at the end of the colonial system, in 1957, there were only 360 members in the Malayan Civil Service; see Robert O. Tilman, *Bureaucratic Transition in Malaya*, Durham, 1964, p. 73.

[5] Kelantan actually had had a British adviser since 1902; under Thai suzerainty this adviser was loaned to Thailand for posting to Kelantan.

[6] Actually some distinction can be made between all of the unfederated states on their degree of economic development. Of the northern states, Kedah was probably the most advanced, because of its proximity to Penang, and because of the early introduction of rubber into the state.

elements in Malayan politics. Decisions and policies carried out in Malaya were made far more often in England than in Malaya. Especially in the early years, until perhaps World War I, that center of power was activated by a commitment to development.[7] The development it stimulated and achieved in Malaya was truly remarkable, though paternalistic rather than democratic. In Malaya the foreign ruling power was carrying the white man's burden; it was not, nor was it even considering, preparing a land for eventual self-rule, even though it was often benevolent. In the latter part of the colonial period, in the 1920's and 1930's, the commitment to development could wane considerably, the entire policy could become more conservative and economically static, but this would not change the dependent and paternalistic nature of the state. In fact, as we shall argue later, the policy could become static and conservative precisely because the state was dependent rather than independent.

THE ECONOMY

The major economic effect of British rule in Malaya was the growth of a dual economy. This is meant not in the sense of Boeke, implying a precapitalist and a capitalist economy. It implies, rather, an economy with two different orientations and foci of activity. On the one hand was the modern colonial sector dominating the entire organization of production. The colonial economy was concentrated in modern trade, rubber production, and tin mining. It was an economy that was urban in culture, based upon urban markets, drawing managerial and organizational techniques from urban centers, and depending on urban resources and organizations for its capital mobilization. Its control was in the hands of British and other foreign firms and it drew into its orbit most Chinese and Indians in Malaya. It was concentrated in the Federated States and in Johore, as well as in the Straits Settlements.

On the other hand was the more traditional sector, most easily classified as a peasant sector. Its major products were rice and fish, its techniques of production were little affected by British intervention, and its markets, labor, and capital were largely indigenous and derived from a rural or peasant culture. It was dominated by Malays and was concentrated in the Unfederated States of the north and east. Rubber, however, provided a significant area of overlap between the modern

---

[7] James V. Allen, in a doctoral dissertation under preparation at the University of Malaya, argues persuasively that the early period of British rule was marked by a strong commitment to development, and the latter was marked by bureaucratic conservatism or even stagnation. He has labeled this the change from imperialism to colonialism. I am indebted to Mr. Allen for pointing this out.

and peasant sectors. Rubber cultivation could be easily articulated with peasant agriculture, and many Malays (including Indonesian immigrants) did in fact move into smallholder rubber planting, with holdings generally less than ten acres.

The dual character of the economy can best be seen, even as late as 1947, in the industrial distribution of the labor forces of Malaya's three main ethnic groups. About three-fourths of the peasant producers (fishermen and rice growers) were Malays, almost 90 percent of all rice growers were Malays, and about one-third of all economically active Malay males were in this peasant sector. Plantation agriculture was filled with an almost equal number of Malays, Indians, and Chinese, though each group was specialized within this broad industry. Approximately half the Malays in the industry were smallholders, and those working on estates (technically defined as planted areas over a hundred acres) were concentrated in weeding and casual maintenance work. Chinese were concentrated in both smallholding and the non-resident estate tapping labor. Indians were almost exclusively concentrated in the resident estate labor force. Mining, manufacturing, and utilities, comprising only slightly more than 10 percent of the total labor force, were dominated by Chinese. The tertiary industries, which accounted for about one-third of the labor force, were made up of about one-half Chinese and one-quarter each Malays and Indians. Within this sector, too, there was considerably more ethnic specialization than indicated by these figures. Half of the Malays in all tertiary industries were in government (including the police), where they made up more than half of all workers. The Chinese were heavily concentrated in private transportation, commerce, and finance; the Indians in public transportation (especially in the railways), in government, and to a lesser extent in urban commerce and finance. The ethnic composition of some industrial groups is shown in table II-1.

The Malay peasant economy, the dominant element in the traditional economy, was characterized by smallholdings, regardless of the crop: rice, rubber, or coconut.[8] Islamic law and rapid population growth appear to have resulted in highly fragmented smallholdings. Even at the end of the colonial period there was little modernization of peasant agriculture. Techniques of production were much the same as at the beginning of the century. Though commercial fertilizers had been introduced they were not in wide use,[9] and though some major irrigation schemes had been constructed, rice was mostly grown with

---

[8] See, for example T. Bryan Wilson, *The Economics of Padi Production in North Malaya*, Kuala Lumpur, 1958, *passim*.

[9] From interviews with field agricultural officers in Kedah and Penang.

TABLE II-1

ETHNIC CONCENTRATION IN MAJOR INDUSTRIES IN MALAYA 1947
(Showing economically active males only)

Industries	Total (thousands)	Malays (percent)	Chinese (percent)	Indians (percent)
Total	1,461.7	44	40	15
Agriculture	889.3	57	30	12
Peasant (including *Padi*)	508.3	70	27	1
Padi	333.2	88	10	---
Plantation	381.0	39	33	27
Mining	39.4	14	71	13
Manufacturing, construction, utilities	124.8	19	70	6
Tertiary	407.2	27	48	23
Government	104.9	54	11	30

SOURCE: Federation of Malaya, *Population Census*, 1957, Vol. 14, p. 31.

rainfall or traditional (though often very effective) small irrigation systems. Even in irrigated areas double-cropping was unusual, and was certainly not the norm for the entire sector. Still, per-acre yields of rice have been among the highest in Southeast Asia, though they are far below the yields of Japan.[10] Fishing was also characterized by the use of traditional techniques. Sail power predominated, and only the inshore surface fish were taken. While fish were widely distributed in the Malayan market, local rice appears to have been more confined to the traditional sector itself, to the extent that it was marketed at all. Through most of this century Malaya has been a net importer of rice. During the 1930's, for example, an average of slightly more than 300,000 tons was produced annually, but this amounted to only about 40 percent of total consumption.[11] The traditional sector has been nearly self-sufficient in rice, while imports have been largely for the urban areas and the modern sector.

Isolated physically and intellectually and dominated by old methods of production, it is little wonder that this traditional sector has been economically overshadowed by the modern. In the mid-1950's, it was

---

[10] The *FAO Yearbook of Food and Agricultural Statistics, 1957* gives Japanese yields as 208.7 bushels per hectare. Although Malaya has, according to this source, the highest yields in Southeast Asia, its yield is still only 98.5 bushels per hectare. Japanese yields in the first decade of the Meiji appear to have been about 70 bushels. See H. Rosovsky, *Capital Formation in Japan*, Glencoe, 1961, pp. 79 ff.

[11] D. H. Grist, *Malayan Agricultural Statistics, 1939*, Kuala Lumpur, Department of Agriculture, 1940, tables 28 and 31.

estimated that the traditional sector accounted for less than 25 percent of the gross national product.[12] In part this was certainly a result of a conscious government policy to protect the Malays. Malay Reservation Land Acts, the first of which was passed in 1913, designated large areas of land that could be allocated only to Malays. This policy has recently been criticized for precluding the use of land as loan security and thus depriving Malays of one important source of capital.[13] Government policy has also attempted to reserve smallholding rice production for the Malays, and also to keep Malays in this form of production. Non-Malays have been discouraged from growing rice, and requests for large tracts of land for mechanized rice growing have been explicitly refused.[14] There has also been a definite bias against allowing Malays to move into rubber production.[15] This has not been completely successful, as witnessed by the large number of Malays in smallholder rubber production, but it may have discouraged indigenous Malays, while not working so effectively for Indonesian immigrants.

The modern sector is dominated by three industries: trade, rubber, and tin, a brief analysis of which can illustrate the close functional articulation of the polity and the economy of the colonial system. Until the end of the nineteenth century Malaya's major value was its geographic position, dominating the trade routes between China and the West. Penang and Singapore were founded and grew to prominence as free ports, performing a valuable entrepôt function. In this Singapore has greatly outgrown the older Penang and has become one of the most important commercial centers in the entire Far East. Both Singapore and Penang provided important ports and some industrial functions for the states, which were the hinterland. The entrepôt functions, however, were localized and gave most economic stimulus to the immediate area of Singapore and less to Penang. There was a close articulation, through the agency house form of organization, of the trading and rubber and tin industries, but the trade function itself did not affect the Malay states to the same extent as Singapore. Thus for the purposes of this analysis the two major industries of Malaya were tin and rubber.

In the latter part of the nineteenth century tin was the most im-

---

[12] International Bank for Reconstruction and Development, *The Economic Development of Malaya*, Baltimore, 1955, p. 21.

[13] *Ibid.*, pp. 311–314.

[14] See Ding Eing Tan Soo Hai, *The Rice Industry in Malaya 1920–1940*, Singapore Studies in Borneo and Malaya, 1963.

[15] P. T. Bauer, *The Rubber Industry: A Study in Competition and Monopoly*, Cambridge, 1948, pp. 60–61.

portant source of wealth in Malaya. Around the end of the century
the approximately 40,000 tons exported annually provided more than
half of the revenues of the Federated Malay States.[16] Most of this tin
was mined by Chinese labor-intensive methods. There were a few
British mining operations, but on the whole European organizations
proved too costly for Malayan conditions, and until the end of World
War I mined only 25 percent of Malaya's exported tin. The introduction of tin dredges, which coincided with the exhaustion of some of
the rich and easily worked deposits that had been fertile fields for
Chinese organizations, gave a great advantage to European firms.
Dredges were too expensive for the clan capitalism of the Chinese, and
they were highly efficient in extracting tin from inaccessible swamp
lands and from low-grade ore deposits. Thus the dredges enabled the
European firms to overtake the Chinese, and by 1929 the European
organizations were producing about 60 percent of the exported tin.

It was, however, not only a technological and organizational advantage that gave the European firms the great lead over the Chinese.
The land policies, administered by the British administration, also
gave the British firms a legal advantage. This was especially evident in
the Perak land policies, but the same policy can be found in all important tin states. Large-scale, highly capitalized Western mining required extensive land and title surveys, to give investors the long-term
security of tenure they needed to make their operations profitable.
The more informal dealings between Chinese miners and Malay rulers
had reduced the land-title situation to a shambles. The necessity to
correct this led at the turn of the century to the closure of application
books for land in the Kinta valley, the richest tin-ore valley in the
world, and in the entire state of Negri Sembilan. As the land survey
was completed the districts of Negri Sembilan were open to application, but the rich Kinta valley remained closed. In 1907 the Kinta
lands were opened, but only on a limited scale and with stipulations
that favored the Western companies. While the books remained closed
the poor lands had to be worked and reworked, which provided an
advantage for Western technology in mining. Throughout the Federated States the government gave repeated consideration to taking
back all idle mining lands or lands on which the labor force was not
up to the required standard, in order to open these lands to investors
with labor-saving devices. "Thus, from 1906 onwards, the mining land
policy was in favour of large companies using machinery and labour-

---

[16] G. C. Allen and A. G. Donnithorne, *Western Enterprise in Indonesia and
Malaya*, London, 1957, pp. 156 and 297.

saving techniques of exploitation. In the nature of things, this policy favoured Western enterprise." [17]

In another way as well, land policy appears to have been directed to the stimulation of the modern sector, more or less exclusively. The attention to surveys and land policy was aimed at meeting the legal and administrative requirements of the modern sector, but was not of much benefit to the traditional sector. Soil surveys, needed to make diversified agriculture more efficient and productive, are still greatly lacking. Though the standardized land code applied to traditional agriculture as well as to the modern land-based industries, it appears to have been of little value to the peasants themselves. This is partly attested to by the chronic state of "arrears" in land registration. Though legally required to do so, many peasants do not record all transactions of land that take place, primarily because it is an expense in time and effort for which there are no apparent returns.[18]

The extraction of tin redounded to the advantage of more than the tin producers themselves. The revenues were used for public works— road- and railroad-building and other forms of overhead capital formation—that, though originally created primarily for the tin industry, provided external economies for other industries as well. One of the most important of these was rubber.

Rubber seedlings were first introduced into Singapore in 1877 at the initiative of Sir Clements Markham, head of the geographical section of the India Office, and Sir Joseph Hooker, head of Kew Gardens. Seeds were planted in the government's botanical gardens in Singapore and at the British residency in the royal town of Kuala Kangasr, Perak. The Singapore Gardens were established in 1857 and have provided a setting for research in tropical agriculture. Here, in its commitment to rationalization and to scientific research, Western organization made its first contribution to the development of Malaya's most important industry.

Little was done with rubber, however, until 1888 when H. N. Ridley became head of the Singapore Gardens. He experimented with and

---

[17] Lin Ken Wong, *The Malayan Tin Industry to 1914*, Tucson, 1965, p. 221. This is an excellent and well-documented account of the entire industry, especially important for its material on land policy. In effect land policy, as well as British administrators, tended to favor Chinese miners before the turn of the century. After that, however, the administrative sentiments changed along with increasing bureaucratization and gave preference to Western enterprise.

[18] G. Missen has reported a substantial discrepancy between land office records and actual holding and use of land in field research done in Kampong Jalan Sungai Lallang, near Seminyih, Selangor. Personal communication.

perfected the method of tapping rubber trees, thus solving one of the major problems of the industry. Ridley has been described as "a man of imagination and great firmness of purpose." [19] The latter soon earned him the names "mad Ridley" and "rubber Ridley," for his untiring efforts to interest government and planters in rubber cultivation. He met with more than the normal amount of opposition from unimaginative bureaucrats,[20] but he did find a few planters willing to try his seeds. At that time the government was willing to grant 1,000 acres of land to anyone who would establish a perennial crop, though many officials were not too happy about extending these provisions to rubber. Through Ridley's efforts at least a few small plantations of rubber were planted in Malaya by 1900; the largest was the Petaling estate, owned by a European tea planter in Selangor. In the person of Ridley, then, we find the West's second major contribution to the rubber industry, the imaginative innovator or entrepreneur, perhaps the single most important economic product of Western organization.

After planting, the rubber tree requires six to seven years before it can be tapped, and another approximately three years before it comes into full production. A maturing period of this length requires substantial amounts of capital for the development of an industry on a large scale. This requirement was met by the third major Western contribution to the industry: the private joint-stock company. Although there were Chinese and Indian planters, and after 1910 many Malay smallholders as well, by far the greatest contributors to the development of the industry as a whole were the Western merchant houses operating in Singapore, which could draw on the rich capital resources of the European markets. They were able to call upon various skills to increase efficiency. They found planters for the field work, accountants to provide reports for foreign shareholders, and agricultural scientists to increase productivity through research. By 1932 about half of the rubber acreage was in the form of estates (areas of more than a hundred acres), which had converted 1.9 million acres of dense Malayan jungle into highly productive land. About 1.2 million of those acres were owned by 793 European public-liability companies, and as many as one million estate acres were owned by the 479 companies whose estates were larger than 1,000 acres.[21]

---

[19] Allen and Donnithorne, *op. cit.*, p. 109.

[20] Ridley's account tells of one experience in which the Governor of Singapore, in an attempt to discredit Ridley's exotic experiments, sent natives to climb the trees in search of rubber. When they found none, the Governor had the trees destroyed and announced in the Government Gazette that the para rubber trees did not produce rubber. Cited in Allen and Donnithorne, *op. cit.*, p. 110.

[21] D. H. Grist, *Nationality of Ownership and Nature of Constitution of Rubber Estates in Malaya*, Kuala Lumpur, 1933, *passim*.

The final stimulus to the rubber industry came in the form of increased demands for the product, a result of the growth of the automobile industry and the perfection of the pneumatic tire. During the rubber boom of 1910 and 1911 Malaya exported only about 6,000 long tons. In only three years, in 1913, exports increased to 33,000 long tons. By 1919 the full effects of all major stimuli to the industry were felt, and Malaya reached an export tonnage of 200,000. By this time the structure of the industry was fairly well established, with substantial elements of growth built into it. Production in 1930 was about 400,000 tons[22] and went above 600,000 tons in the years just preceding independence.[23]

Though the agency houses were instrumental in developing the rubber industry, they were not in exclusive control of production. Malay, Chinese, and Indian farmers have moved into rubber planting with an alacrity and far-sighted economic rationality expected only of the ideal type *homo economicus*. Even when government policy favored his exclusive attention to rice or food production, the Malay peasant showed greater economic rationality in moving to rubber, for the comparative advantages of rubber- over rice-growing were often as high as 100 percent.[24] Thus by the time the structure of the rubber industry was established, Malay, Chinese, and Indian holdings of less than 100 acres made up about half of the total acreage, with Malays concentrated in the holdings under 10 acres, and the Chinese and Indians concentrated in the holdings between 10 and 100 acres.[25] Despite the importance of local producers, however, government policy on rubber actively favored the European sector and discriminated against the local sector; in the immediate pre-war years that policy actually acted to destroy part of the local sector. The major manifestations of this policy were restriction schemes.

After the World War I slump in the rubber market producers attempted to restrict output to force prices up. From 1922 to 1928 the Stevenson scheme restricted rubber planting in Malaya. Though it appears to have had some positive effect on prices, it had unfortunate effects on the Malayan industry and eventually was abandoned, in part

---

[22] G. C. Allen and A. G. Donnithorne, *op. cit.*, p. 295.

[23] Federation of Malaya, Department of Statistics, *Rubber Statistics Handbook, 1961*, Kuala Lumpur, 1962, p. 7.

[24] P. T. Bauer, *The Rubber Industry: A Study in Competition and Monopoly*, pp. 60–63.

[25] This description of the size of holdings differences among the different ethnic groups is actually a backward projection from a later period. The projection is generally accepted as reasonable, though reliable figures do not exist for the period before the 1930's. (D. H. Grist, *Nationality of Ownership, passim.*)

because the Netherlands Indies (Indonesia) did not join the scheme. The 1925–1926 famine prices for rubber stimulated a great increase in rubber smallholdings in Indonesia while Malayan smallholders were prevented from increasing (though it does not appear that the Malayan restrictions were fully enforced, or enforceable).

The International Rubber Regulation Scheme, introduced in 1934, in which the Netherlands Indies was a partner, attempted to restrict both production and planting, using the unrestricted period of 1929–1933 as a base for the calculation of quotas. Replanting was allowed up to 20 percent of the acreage in the base period; new planting was at first prohibited and later allowed up to 5 percent of the acreage in the base period. Production was restricted, through control of sales, to a proportion of the amount of the base period, with allowance made for acreage then in immature rubber. Estate production was controlled through control of sales at the point of export; smallholders were allotted coupons that allowed them to sell specified amounts, based on their production in the base period.

Even as early as 1935 "it was an open secret in Malaya that the European estates were treated preferentially, though the inequality was less than it had been under the Stevenson scheme." [26] Both the formal regulations and their application discriminated against the smallholders. On the two committees that drafted the regulations the smallholders were represented in the proportions 1 in 27 and 1 in 12. To gain information on the base period, questionnaires were sent to the estates, and government officers inspected smallholdings. Estates were seldom inspected when their completed questionnaires were returned. Smallholdings were inspected but generally underassessed because of their inaccessibility and because of official ignorance.

It does not appear that the smallholder felt he was suffering under the restrictions. The growing demand for rubber in the late 1930's and the fixed costs of estates resulted in strong demand for the smallholders' rubber coupons. Bauer reports that the smallholder could often sell his coupons for more than he would have received for tapping and selling his rubber without the restriction scheme. A U.S. Embassy official reported in 1939 that the smallholders regarded "their export coupons as a pension . . . and would almost certainly object to the discontinuance of control." [27] If the Malayan smallholder was going to his death, as Bauer argues, he was at least going happily.

The arrangements for replanting and new planting contained the most direct threat to the smallholders. On holdings of less than 100

---

[26] P. T. Bauer, *op. cit.*, p. 93.
[27] Cited in P. T. Bauer, *op. cit.*, p. 209.

acres, and certainly on those of less than 10 acres, replanting was generally impractical because according to the scheme, such a small portion of the stand could be replanted that the remaining stand would have greatly reduced new growth through shading and root competition. Furthermore, there was practically no technical advice open to the smallholders on the value of replanting and on the growing of high-yielding varieties of trees. The 5 percent new planting allowances were also of little value to the smallholders. The allowances were made in 1/20th acre grants. Often the grants to the smallholder were so small that it was not economic for him to go through the lengthy and costly process of applying for new land through the land office. If he did acquire new land, it was likely to be far from his original holding so that transportation costs would have made it uneconomic for him to tap rubber on that land. Finally, the regulation procedure was legal and complex and generally not understood by the smallholder, especially as there was almost no extension service to help him understand its provisions. Often the smallholder simply gave away or sold his new planting rights without any idea of their real value. While the estates were planting new trees on new and old land, thus reinvesting in their sector of the industry, the smallholder was consuming his capital without any reinvestment. It was obvious that this policy would eliminate the smallholder, but "the detailed record of the discussions preceding the 1934 agreement suggests that these provisions were drafted without consideration of this easily foreseeable long-term result." [28]

Both restriction schemes were predicated on a fantastic ignorance of the smallholder's operation. The Stevenson scheme was based on an estimate that the smallholders produced about half as much as the estates. When the restrictions were lifted in 1929, however, it was found that the smallholders produced as much as the estates. Government and agency officials explained this by "slaughter tapping." They thought the smallholders were cutting back bark faster than it could be replaced, and they predicted a drastic falling off of smallholder production in less than a year. They were confident of this in 1929 and in 1930, but a systematic investigation of smallholders showed that official explanations and predictions were completely wrong. There was far more smallholder acreage, and apparently the smallholders were also more efficient producers than had been believed. The planners were apparently wrong, but they were vindicated by their own restriction schemes, as table II-2 shows.

---

[28] *Op. cit.*, p. 173.

TABLE II-2

ANNUAL OUTPUT OF RUBBER PER MATURE ACRE ON
MALAYAN ESTATES AND SMALLHOLDINGS

Year	(pounds per acre) Estates	Smallholdings
1929	410	485
1930	380	460
1931	375	445
1932	365	385
1933	355	465
1934	regulations introduced	
1935	295½	240
1936	275	230
1937	375	330
1938	290	200
1939	290	200
1940	410	370

SOURCE: P. T. Bauer, *The Rubber Industry: A Study in Competition and Monopoly*, p. 97.

As might be expected, the share of the smallholder in total production fell as a result of the restriction scheme. In the years without restriction it averaged 45 percent, but by 1934, when the restrictions were introduced, it reached 50 percent. The average for the period 1935–1940 was 36 percent.[29] Bauer has estimated that the loss to the Malayan smallholder as a result of the entire underassessment of his production, acreage, and productivity amounted to about £10 million for the period of the regulation scheme. If current assessments of the ethnic specialization in size of holding and the backward projections of those assessments are correct, then the Malay smallholder must have lost proportionally far more than the Chinese or the Indian. It would be reasonable to assume this on grounds other than size of holding as well. Not only was the Malay smallholder least in a position to take advantage of replanting and new planting allowances, he was also generally physically and intellectually more isolated than the Chinese and Indian immigrants who had moved into the industry. Both as immigrants and as people from more economically or commercially advanced areas and occupations, the Indians and Chinese were in a better social and psychological position to understand the allowances of the regulation scheme. Thus the government's policy with respect to this major industry was not only to give preferential

[29] *Op. cit.*, p. 99.

treatment to Europeans, but to give lowest priority, and to burden with the greatest discrimination, those people whose interests and welfare they had undertaken to protect through the signing of formal treaties.

Bauer considers this process not so much a Machiavellian plot on the part of the estate holders to eliminate the smallholders as a result of ignorance. Other observers have seen in the process little more than the greed and venality of the estate holders. This analysis is not interested in fixing the blame but in understanding the actions that flow naturally from different systems or organizations. In Malaya's experience with rubber regulations, we can see clearly the close articulation of a dependent state and a colonial export economy. The ignorance that Bauer sees, or the venality that others see, played an important determining role in the development of the Malayan economy largely because it was unchecked by the interests of those against whom it worked. And it was unchecked because a large share of the producers affected by economic policies were unrepresented in the group that produced and administered those policies.

THE SOCIETY

The most striking characteristic of the colonial Malayan scene was, and remains today, its plural society. Everywhere in the country one can see evidence of major ethnic groups: Malays, Chinese, Indians, Eurasians, and Europeans.[30] They are brought together at the market place through common interests, and there they can be found in communication in the bazaar Malay that has become the lower *lingua franca* of Malaya. However, in their occupational specialization, in their widely different languages and styles of life, and in their religious differences, one can see the power of the forces that separate them.

Malaya's plural society is of relatively recent origin. A century ago there were less than a million people in the country, the overwhelming majority of whom were Malays (or Indonesians).[31] By the first decade of the twentieth century the population had reached almost 1.5 million, of whom 55 percent were Malays, 35 percent Chinese, and 10 percent Indians.[32]

---

[30] Common British colonial usage refers to ethnic groups as "communities." Except where necessary to retain the flavor of direct quotations, we shall use the term more common in the social sciences: ethnic group.

[31] M. V. Del Tufo, *A Report on the 1947 Census of Population*, Kuala Lumpur, 1948, p. 30.

[32] T. E. Smith, *Population Growth in Malaya*, Princeton, 1952, p. 8.

Most of the Chinese came from the south and southeast of China, originally as indentured laborers or at best as poor peasants.[33] The organizing units of the migration were clans, which in China had a geographic as well as a linguistic base. Since they came primarily to win wealth and then to return to China, the migrants generally came without their women. As late as 1931, of the 1.75 million Chinese in Malaya more than two thirds were born in China, and the sex ratio was one female to two males.[34] Though the Chinese brought some elements of their culture, most functionaries of the home society remained at home, at least during the early part of the migration. Priests, teachers, civil servants stayed behind; only the poor peasant came in search of wealth.

Something of the quantity and the quality of this migration can be seen in tables II-3 and II-4 which show the increase in numbers and

TABLE II-3

CHINESE IN MALAYA

Region	1850	1901	1911	1931
Straits Settlements	62,700	281,600	n.a.	659,200
Federated States and Johore	n.a.	268,900	n.a.	924,100
Unfederated States less Johore	n.a.	n.a.	49,400	115,900
Total	62,700	648,400		1,698,200

SOURCE: M. V. Del Tufo, *A Report on the 1947 Census of Population*, pp. 584–588.

the changing sex ratios. For purposes of this comparison Johore is grouped with the Federated Malay States with which it formed closer economic and demographic ties than with its sister Unfederated States of the North.

Linguistically the Chinese in Malaya are not homogeneous. In 1947 the five major dialect groups were as shown in table II-5.

In general the dialects are not mutually understandable. Among the less educated classes, Malay has often been a common tongue, but among the more literate, English serves this function. Since dialect also has kin implications, there has been some tendency toward occupational and areal specialization of the dialect groups, which often

---

[33] Victor Purcell, *The Chinese in Southeast Asia*, London, 1951. See also R. N. Jackson, *Immigrant Labour and the Development of Malaya 1786–1920*, Kuala Lumpur, 1961, chapters IV, VI, and XIV.

[34] T. E. Smith, *op. cit.*, p. 63.

form the basis of mutual-aid societies, chambers of commerce, schools, or other forms of voluntary organization.

Indians have been in contact with Malaya for many centuries and have left deep impressions on language, manner, and artifacts, espe-

TABLE II-4

CHANGING CHINESE SEX RATIOS IN MALAYA
(Females per 1,000 Males)

Region	1850	1901	1911	1931
Straits Settlements	178	286	n.a.	610
Federated States and Johore	n.a.	102	n.a.	465
Unfederated States less Johore	n.a.	n.a.	216	434
Total	178	195		510

SOURCE: See Table II-3.

cially of the aristocracy. The Indians did not migrate to Malaya in large numbers, however, until after the introduction of rubber. Early migration was under a system of indenture, but this was legally proscribed in 1910. Recruitment of labor for the rubber plantations con-

TABLE II-5

MAJOR DIALECT GROUPS OF
MALAYAN CHINESE 1947

(percent)	
Hokkien	32
Cantonese	25
Hakka	17
Tiechiou	14
Hailam	6

SOURCE: T. E. Smith, *The Population of Malaya*, p. 65.

tinued to be organized by *kanganis,* or Indian agents who recruited from their own villages or districts in India. Labor was much abused in the beginning, but conditions improved as both the Indian and

Malayan colonial governments extended protection to the workers.[35]

The main wave of Indian migration was directed at the estates. Indians came in relatively well-organized groups and have remained as isolated resident workers on the estates. Their ties with their homeland have been even stronger than those of the Chinese. There were regular remittances, often controlled by the *kangani*, frequent trips to India, and generally a permanent return home after a period of less than ten years in Malaya. The proportion of Indians born in Malaya was 12 percent in 1921; by 1931 this figure was only 31 percent.[36]

To the occupational specialization, a marked areal specialization of the ethnic groups has been added. In general Malays are confined to the rural villages or *kampongs*. Indians have been concentrated on estates, and Chinese in the towns. As late as 1947 the proportion of each ethnic group living in places of 1,000 or more was 11 percent for the Malays, 43 percent for the Chinese, and 34 percent for the Indians. The total urban population in that year consisted of 64 percent Chinese, 23 percent Malays, and 11 percent Indians.[37]

The support and maintenance of the ethnic plural society can best be seen in the schools, the most important institutions for the preservation of cultural identity. The colonial system contained four major school systems. The Malay vernacular schools catered primarily to rural Malays, providing primary education only. They had strong religious overtones and did relatively little to prepare boys and girls for life in the modern world. A variation of these were the Koranic schools that taught Malay children to read the Koran parrot-fashion. From these schools the children emerged illiterate, even in Arabic, the language of the Koran. They could pronounce, not understand, the written text. Chinese schools taught in Mandarin and were strongly oriented to the mainland, the source of teachers, textbooks, and curricula. After 1910 these schools became important institutions for the promotion of Chinese nationalism, and the Malayan government had to take steps to control them. Indian schools were provided on the estates by force of a government regulation of 1912. The regulations were not always enforced, and certainly not with the same vigor in all places. Most of these schools used Tamil as the medium of

---

[35] See, for example, Usha Mahajani, *The Role of Indian Minorities in Burma and Malaya*, New York, I.P.R., 1960, chapter IV; R. N. Jackson *op. cit.*, chapters V, IX, X, XII; and J. N. Parmer, *Colonial Labor Policy and Administration: A History of Labor in the Rubber Plantation Industry in Malaya, 1910–1941*, New York, 1960, *passim*.

[36] M. V. Del Tufo, *op. cit.*, p. 85.

[37] Federation of Malaya, Department of Statistics, *Population Census 1957*, Vol. 14, Kuala Lumpur, 1960, pp. 9 and 11.

instruction, but a few used Telegu or Punjabi. These schools, too, were oriented toward the homeland and to nascent Indian nationalism. Students from both Chinese and Indian schools emerged essentially ignorant of Malaya, and those from the Malay schools did not fare much better. The only really national schools were the English schools; even these were national only in that they instructed children of all ethnic groups, and gave them a common curriculum. These schools were heavily oriented toward England, however, or toward Christianity in the schools provided by Christian missions.

Thus the institution of education in colonial Malaya was essentially a divisive force in the society, tending to support its ethnic plural character. Some evaluation of the magnitude of this divisive force can be gained from the enrollment in the different types of schools (table II-6). For this we have used the 1949 figures. Earlier figures are low

TABLE II-6

SCHOOL ENROLLMENT IN MALAYA 1949

Type of School	Enrollment		Population Aged 5–15	Enrollment as percent of population
	Number	Percent		
Malay	238,592	44	674,994	35
Chinese	202,769	37	705,981	29
Indian	38,743	7	136,373	28
English	62,266	12	---	—
Total	547,370	100	1,536,878	36

SOURCE: Federation of Malaya, *Annual Report*, Kuala Lumpur, 1950, pp. 84 ff.
NOTES: The population figures are from the 1947 census. These figures are shown only to illustrate the magnitude of the problem and the extent to which it was being solved. The left-hand column shows the type of school, not the ethnic group of the students. From the literate population aged 20 and over shown in the 1959 census, it can be estimated that the English schools may have contained about 20 percent Malays, 20 percent Indians, and 60 percent Chinese.

either because of the disruption caused by the war, or because of the general underdeveloped character of the Unfederated States. During the immediate post-war period school enrollment increased rapidly and figures after 1949 begin to reflect this growth, which was partly a product of the emerging nationalist forces.

Table II-6 shows that in the latter stages of the colonial period, during which efforts were beginning to be made to build a national plural society in place of the ethnic plural society, about one-third of Malaya's children were in school. All but 12 percent of these were in schools that supported the ethnic plural society by increasing rather than by decreasing the ethnic identity of the groups.

It cannot be said that this was a deliberate policy. Some observers have argued that this is merely one more manifestation of the old *divide et impera* policy of the British.[38] Though there is certainly some evidence for this, the *divide et impera* theory attributes to the administration far more consistency, Machiavellianism, and perhaps even more intelligence than existed in fact. A pluralistic theory explains the situation far better than the more common conspiratorial theory. The pluralistic theory would argue that the major government motivation in the colonial education system was to provide clerks for the Malayan bureaucracy at minimum cost. However, the forces and demands the government encountered, both within and without its own ranks, was far from monolithic. There were lay individuals and groups interested in promoting education for their own cultural and economic reasons; there was much Christian mission activity that concentrated heavily on winning souls through treating the mind and the body; and there was the education department itself with its own standards, values, and professional codes. In addition, external groups were establishing their own schools. At times the institutions provided by these different centers of power engaged in activities that ran counter to the interests of government. When this happened, as when the Chinese schools became small Kuomintang headquarters, it became necessary for the government to extend greater control over them. In this sense government practice demonstrated not so much a consistent policy as a series of reactions to exigencies. Perhaps the only real elements of consistency in these reactions were the steady growth of all forms of education (including government support for private schools) and the continued argument from the treasury that government could afford no more. This was itself an inconsistent pattern of behavior, but it is the type of inconsistency to be expected in a pluralistic polity.

It still remains true, however, that the colonial government made no real attempt to build a unified national education system. Government permitted the establishment of mission schools, and even gave them some financial assistance. As the estate workers became protected, government gave some support to Tamil schools. Malay schools were

---

[38] See K. G. Treggoning, *"The Chinese and the Plural Society of Malaya,"* Symposium on Economic Problems of the Far East, University of Hong Kong, 1961, for a well-reasoned presentation of this argument.

established completely by government and gave instruction in the Malay language.[39] There is no more direct evidence than this of the functional compatibility of the plural society and the dependent state. A national consensus or a national consciousness was neither necessary nor desirable for the optimum functioning of the dependent state; on the contrary, a national consciousness might be disruptive. The colonial government has never looked with favor upon nationalist movements; the plural educational system that emerged under colonial rule was well suited to support that rule.

It remains only to note the religious specialization of the ethnic groups. Malays are almost exclusively Muslim. Chinese, as in China, practice a mixture of Confucian, Taoist, and Buddhist rites. Indians are primarily Hindus, with a few Muslims. Most of the Eurasians appear to be Christian, along with a small number of Chinese and Indians.

It is impossible either to omit or to include with any confidence a discussion of the value systems of Malaya's plural society. It cannot be omitted because much of the division in the society results from the differences in the value systems of the component parts. It is difficult to include because so little is known about it. A detailed discussion could be undertaken of the value systems of the Indians or the Chinese, and to a lesser extent of the Malays *in their own lands.* Here, however, only the Malays are in their own land. The other two communities are communities of migrants with special biases built into the migrant selection pattern. The value system of a migrant group always seems to differ from that of its parent society. It may be that the bias is to increase the concentration of achievement orientation among the migrants, but this is neither certain, nor does it say much about the specific content or symbols of the object of achievement.

A greater difficulty arises, however, from the peculiar effect the ethnic frontier can have upon value systems. We might accept as a general proposition that peoples with like value systems will merge and integrate with one another more easily than those with different value systems. However, this proposition becomes relatively weak when we recognize that a value system is not a stable and homogeneous thing appearing in the same way to all peoples at all times. A value

---

[39] K. G. Treggonning, *ibid.*, argues that "the educational policy in Malaya which supported Malay schools while tolerating Chinese language schools, may well have been influenced by the desire to establish two communities so that the balance would rest with the administration to divide and rule." He observes that in India, Burma, and Ceylon the British colonial government never established vernacular schools, adding that in none of these territories was the government faced with a Chinese problem similar to that in Malaya.

system can exert a relatively consistent set of constraining forces on a group of people, but that group still must interpret, primarily through actions, that value system to the group with whom they are in contact. Further, that value system must be interpreted by the group receiving the contact. Thus a new value system is likely to emerge in the process of culture contacts, defined in part by the character of that contact, and differing from the values of the parent groups not engaged in the contact. In Malaya, we would argue that the value systems of the plural society are emergents of that society. The way Malays conceive of the Indians and Chinese is also a part of Malay self-conceptions. The same can be said for the Chinese and Indians.

At the Malayan ethnic frontier, relatively few components of the value system appear to be of great importance. Even these must be presented tentatively, in part because there has been no systematic research of the values. What can be reported here is little more than what is generally believed to be the value system of the three major ethnic groups. Much of this is essentially what one group believes about the value system of the other. Nonetheless, this is important to the social process because it does affect the way in which one group acts toward another, even if both groups are wrong in their assessments of the other. There is also something of the self-fulfilling prophecy in this type of value contact.

It is widely believed that the Chinese are achievement-oriented, industrious, opportunistic, avaricious, and are sharp businessmen. Malays are held to lack achievement orientation, to be lazy, and to show a distaste of hard labor. At the same time they are believed to be loyal, polite, and proud. The Chinese are held to be self-possessed, the Malays headstrong and erratic. The Chinese are believed to be self-reliant, while the Malays rely upon government assistance and protection—a result of the spoon-feeding of colonial protection. The estate Indians are generally considered to be low in mental ability, lacking in self-reliance and achievement orientation. The urban commercial class of Indians, on the other hand, share many of the characteristics of the Chinese, especially in commercial and financial matters; they are not, however, thought to be as industrious or as work-oriented as the Chinese.

These are not presented as the real value systems of the respective ethnic groups, but as the picture of the values formed at the ethnic frontier, in which each group comes to see itself in part as the way it thinks other groups see it. Even to this extent the picture presented here is not accurate because it is not supported by systematic investigation. It is, however, the result of three years of observation and conversation with many groups in Malaya. Although it cannot be presented with any real confidence, neither can it be omitted because it forms an important background against which the picture of a plural society emerges in Malaya.

EQUILIBRIUM

The system we have been describing was one dominated by balancing or mutually sustaining forces. It was a system in essential equilibrium —not, by any means, in total equilibrium, a state unimaginable in any but abstract or ideal typical situations. However, barring the emergence of new exogenous forces,[40] it is possible to conceive of Malaya continuing as a colonial social system for some time into the future. The predominant forces in the major sectors of the system— the state, the economy, and the society—fit well together and gave the system a fair measure of stability.

The dependent and paternalistic nature of the government provided the proper setting for an outwardly oriented extractive economy. Government represented the external investors and to a certain extent the external consumers. The interests of these groups lay in low production costs, which in the labor-intensive export economy meant low wage levels. Whatever the motivation for government policies with respect to land, mining, rubber, and rice, those policies fit well with the colonial export economy. On the one hand, the economy did not need the stimulant of strong local demand for its products to maintain its dynamism; it did not matter how poor the Malayans were since they did not consume the products of the economy. On the other hand, since this was a labor-intensive economy in which labor was little more than a cost, it was economic to keep that cost as low as was commensurate with the maintenance of an efficient labor force. The discouragement of rubber smallholders, the encouragement of rice production, and even the attempt to increase food production with minimal investments in the application of science and technology, all contributed to the maintenance of low wage levels and thus to the viabil-

---

[40] Exogenous forces are not simply those physically external to the territory. They are outside in a functional sense, not deriving from the action in the system itself, though quite possibly with some effect on the system. For example, Japanese and Chinese nationalist movements only affected developments in the Malayan system, but were themselves not significantly affected by those developments. In our sense, these were exogenous forces. Other external forces were not, however, exogenous simply because they were external to Malaya. The actions of British stockholders, Members of Parliament, and retired Malayan civil servants were endogenous to the Malayan system, that is, a function (in the mathematical sense) of the system, even though they acted outside of Malaya itself.

ity of the economy. The education policy functioned, again whatever the
motivations, to provide a sufficient number of clerks for the bureaucracy
to keep costs of local administration low. At the same time, that policy
did not produce sufficient numbers of highly educated people to compete seriously with the foreign functionaries, nor sufficient numbers to
create a nationalist movement that would have threatened the very
existence of the government.

The ethnic plural society also flourished in the dependent state
when the indigenous peoples proved unwilling, and unsufficiently
driven or motivated, to work in the export economy. Under such conditions both the state and the economy stimulated the import of labor,
which eventually assumed such magnitude that it effectively divided
the society into two large ethnic categories. The education policy
sustained rather than weakened the plural character, thus precluding
the development of a national consensus. Significant sections of both
the Malay and Chinese population continued to feel that their respective interests would best be protected against the encroachments
of the other by continual benevolent and efficient British rule.

The colonial export economy also found most aspects of the ethnic
plural society useful and worked, often directly, to sustain the major
divisions. A foreign firm has always faced a major problem in controlling its staff, largely because it could not rely upon the general
expressive mechanisms of the society to control the behavior of its
personnel; and specific utilitarian mechanisms have probably never
been sufficient to provide the necessary control in any organization.
Control of the European staff was accomplished by emphasizing the
difference or uniqueness of the Europeans, creating a microcosmic
subculture that reflected the home culture. This subculture was maintained by a wide variety of specific mechanisms, such as the op-
probrium attached to "going native," the use of explicit sanctions
against marriage with local women,[41] and the exclusiveness of the
European club. For control of the local staff the *divide et impera*
policies often attributed to the government were directly in evidence.
Foreign businessmen in modern Malaya advocate the use of Chinese
as salesmen because of their local contacts and aggressiveness, to be
balanced by the use of Indians as accountants and bookkeepers. The
enmity between the Indians and the Chinese is said to prevent col-

---

[41] The role of marriage and European women in colonialism has received considerable literary attention, but little systematic sociological analysis. The coming
of the "mems" and the consequent domestication of the imperial adventurer can
be taken as a good indicator of the taming of the colonial frontier. It is unfortunate
that the significant role European women have played in the control of imperialism
and colonial institutions has not yet received systematic and imaginative treatment.

lusion between lower functionaries that could be detrimental to the firm.

The economy provided ample supports for the dependent state. The products of this economy were sufficiently valuable to give foreign investors, and the government in which they were represented (probably overrepresented), incentives for active participation in that economy. In England the Malayan economy provided ample rationale for the continuation of paternalistic rule. In Malaya, the economy was productive enough to provide revenues which the government invested in overhead capital in support of the colonial sector of the economy.

The picture of equilibrium is, to be sure, overdrawn. There were strains within the colonial social system, and given time these may have developed sufficient force to bring about the demise of that system. However, these strains were not responsible for the demise of the system in 1957. Colonialism in Malaya ended through the operation of outside forces rather than through the operation of forces developing in the system itself. The most powerful and immediate of the exogenous forces, of course, was the Japanese occupation. Even this, however, was more important for its impact on other outside forces than for its impact upon the forces at work in Malaya. While the Japanese occupation gave some support to the embryonic nationalist movements in Malaya, it was by no means responsible for bringing the colonial system to an end in the post-war years. Far more important was the ideological or value change precipitated by the Second World War. Out of that war came the fruition of the great political and philosophical movements of the eighteenth and nineteenth centuries. For the colonial areas one of the most important values in those movements was the value of self-determination. The Western world had made the great transition, in the words of Eric Stokes,[42] from the divine right of kings to the divine right of the masses, and World War II forced the Western world to extend its political formulas to the rest of the world.

For Malaya, then, independence came far more as a result of British political policies than as a result of strains within the Malayan colonial social system. Regardless of the larger exogenous forces at play, however, the actual changes involved in the demise of the colonial system and the emergence of a new system were hammered out in Malaya itself by individuals and groups working in that changing society. Thus we must turn to an analysis of these specific changes in order to see what kind of new system was emerging.

---

[42] Eric T. Stokes, *The English Utilitarians in India*, Oxford, 1959.

III

THE CHANGING MALAYAN SOCIAL SYSTEM—II: THE EMERGING INDEPENDENT SYSTEM

THE STATE

The first serious move of political reorganization in post-war Malaya was marked by the formation of the Malayan Union, inaugurated on 1 April 1947. It lasted less than a year, being superseded by the Federation of Malaya Agreement in February 1948. The Union abrogated the old treaties Great Britain had made with the Malay sultans. It welded together all the states into one union, in which the Malays had no special privileges and all races were given an equal position under the law. In addition, the sovereignty and prerogatives of the sultans were replaced by complete British jurisdiction in all matters. The British government forced the union agreement on the sultans, threatening to depose any who would not cooperate and to replace them with more pliant successors.[1]

Out of the extreme threat to Malay privileges posed by the Union agreement grew the first modern legitimate political organization of any significance in Malaya—the United Malay National Organization (UMNO). The UMNO was formed by Dato Onn bin Ja'afar, a leading Johore intellectual, together with a nucleus of Johore leaders. The party was established in March 1947, one month before the Malayan

---

[1] See T. H. Silcock and Ungku A. Aziz, "Nationalism in Malaya," in W. L. Holland (ed.), *Asian Nationalism and the West*, New York, 1953, pp. 267-347 for a good analysis of the forces that produced the Union plan.

Union was to be inaugurated. Under UMNO leadership the Malays, including the sultans, boycotted the opening ceremonies, and refused to accept seats in the Union's legislative council, which contained nominated unofficial as well as official members.

Malay opposition to the Union was well organized and disciplined, and it greatly impressed a British Parliamentary Commission sent to investigate political developments. Even Malay women were galvanized into action in resistance. At the same time, there was no support for government from the Indians and Chinese who stood to gain considerably from the Union's equal status provisions.[2] Finally, there was a forceful and significant opposition to the Union from the old British civil servants. They defended Malay cooperation with the Japanese by charging that the Malays had been deserted by the British, who failed to live up to their treaty responsibilities to protect the country.

In the final analysis, the Malayan Union proved abortive because of a combination of Malay and British parliamentary resistance and Chinese apathy. To Silcock and Aziz the apathy of the non-Malays was more important than Malay political organizational skill.

The Malays gained their advantage not by any specially brilliant political strategy, but by a very moderate degree of discipline and a limited capacity to stand firm or negotiate as the situation demanded. They could hardly have overcome effective opposition. . . . The government was forced to negotiate directly with the Malays to avoid a head-on clash in which they had no indication of even lukewarm political support from those who stood to gain from official policy.[3]

The experience demonstrated, however, at least to the Malays, that their interests could be protected and reform obtained by moderate constitutional means. This almost certainly would not have been the case had the Malays been faced with serious opposition from the other ethnic groups. Thus the successful Malay opposition to the Union was the first step in bringing Malaya along a path leading to a parliamentary democratic form of government.

Negotiations between the government and the Malays over the Malayan Union began as early as June 1947, only two months after the Union's beginning. In February 1948 the new Federation of

---

[2] Silcock and Aziz suggest this political apathy was due to the recognition of better opportunities in business, especially in the unsettled conditions of the immediate post-war years. It was also due to the recognition that success in politics was a dangerous kind of success, because it brought publicity and inevitably extortion from the Communists whose strength was gaining.

[3] T. H. Silcock and Ungku A. Aziz, *op. cit.*, pp. 303 and 306.

Malaya Agreement was signed. This returned to the sultans the prerogatives they had had before 1942, and even strengthened their
position in the Federated States, where the advance of the bureaucracy
had slowly eroded their powers. The agreement tightened citizenship
regulations for the non-Malays, but did grant them citizenship with
certain residency and language qualifications. Under the new agreement Malaya was governed by the British High Commissioner, advised
by his executive council and by a legislative council consisting of
appointed unofficial and official members. The states acquired legislative bodies parallel to those of the federal government and were led
by Chief Ministers or *Mentri Besar*.

The greater significance of the new agreement lies in its initiation
of a process that gradually took power from the bureaucracy and
placed it in the hands of local leaders, who were first appointed and
later elected. That is, a change was under way from a form of bureaucratic centralization to one of elective centralization. The administration of the states was standardized and made parallel with that of
the federal government. Functions of the states and the federal government were carefully differentiated. In the states power was increasingly taken from the British resident and placed in the hands of the
Mentri Besar. At the center the Federal Legislative Council brought
an increasingly representative character to the government. In 1951
local leaders were given quasi-ministerial responsibilities as members
for the specific departments concerned with internal development;
defense and foreign affairs remained in British hands. In addition to
their places in the legislative council, the members also occupied
positions on the executive council, a sort of pre-independence cabinet.
The federal secretariat was greatly pared down and the authority of
the Chief Secretary was progressively curtailed. In 1953 a further
advance was made as the British High Commissioner relinquished his
position as President of the Legislative Council, and the members of
the council elected their own speaker. Throughout the early years of
the 1950's, citizenship regulations were liberalized in both the federal
and state governments. By the time Malayans began to take part in
elections, 1952 for local and 1955 for federal elections, they had learned
that they could make rapid progress toward self-government by the
use of legitimate constitutional maneuvers.

The formation of political parties was as fluid and variegated as
could be expected under the conditions of emerging representative
government. The UMNO early took the lead in party politics and has
held it ever since. Dato Onn, its founder, attempted to transform the
party from an ethnic to an interethnic one, but in this he was singularly

unsuccessful. He resigned a number of times to force his views on the party and was called back by members who considered his leadership indispensable to the party's success. In 1951, however, Dato Onn was allowed to make his break complete, as the party refused to open its doors to full membership for non-Malays. At this time the UMNO elected as its new president Tungku Abdul Rahman, who has remained head of the party and Prime Minister since 1955. Dato Onn went on to form the Independence of Malaya Party (IMP), and later the Party Negara, both interethnic parties containing influential Chinese and Malay members.[4] For a short time UMNO members were allowed to hold positions in both UMNO and IMP. Then UMNO took a firm stand against Dato Onn and forced its members to choose between the two parties.

At the end of 1948 and early 1949, under the joint suggestion of Dato Onn, Malcolm MacDonald (then Governor-General of Malaya and Singapore) and other influential leaders of all ethnic groups, the Communities Liaison Committee was formed. The goal of the committee was to study the sources of interethnic conflict and to eliminate these so as to build a united Malayan nation. One of the first acts of the committee was to suggest, somewhat quietly, the formation of a Chinese political party parallel to UMNO. Out of this suggestion came the Malayan Chinese Association (MCA), formed in February 1949. The MCA made its initial impact on the Chinese by organizing a lottery, the proceeds of which were used for welfare services to assist the resettlement of Chinese squatters. Since only party members could take part in the lottery, the ranks of the party grew rapidly. In addition, the MCA provided an increasingly effective organizational alternative to the Communists, who were at this time operating as terrorists from Malay's dense jungles. During the Communist insurgency the MCA was instrumental in presenting a nationalist, non-Communist, pro-Malaya image of the Malayan Chinese.

In addition to the three major parties (UMNO, IMP, and MCA) a number of lesser parties came briefly into the arena. Most of these were of a left-wing or nationalist orientation. They were labor parties, democratic parties of minor intellectuals, lesser ethnic and interethnic parties. Many of these were of short duration or have remained, as in the case of the Labor Party, of very limited significance. One example

---

[4] The role of Dato Onn and the relations between the IMP and both Chinese and Malay leaders is the subject of the careful and very imaginative research now being undertaken by Raj Wasil at the University of Malaya's Department of History. I am deeply indebted to Dr. Wasil for sharing with me the results of his as yet unpublished work.

of these was a coalition to oppose the views of UMNO. In 1947 an All Malayan Council of Joint Action (AMCJA) welded together all ethnic and interethnic parties opposed to UMNO. Soon a Malay faction, Putera, split off from AMCJA, but continued to cooperate with it against UMNO. AMCJA became dominated by Chinese, and to a lesser extent Indian, interests, though it professed to be interethnic. With the outbreak of the Emergency in 1948 AMCJA collapsed as a legitimate party because it had been infiltrated by Communists. This collapse left the Chinese community with essentially no organized voice until the formation of MCA the following year.

The development of parties in Malaya's formative political years demonstrates the ethnic or "communal" base of group alignments. Only communal parties have been able to gain and hold a large following. Parties that were openly communal resisted attempts to make them intercommunal. Parties that were ideologically intercommunal soon became, if they were not from the beginning, the exclusive preserve of one community. At the same time, because of the generally even distribution of the ethnic groups, it soon became apparent that some form of ethnic accommodation or alliance would be necessary to win national elections.[5]

The first test move in the direction of communal party alliances came in 1952 with the Kuala Lumpur municipal elections. Rather quietly, in contrast with the fanfare that normally attended the formation of a new party in Malaya, the UMNO and the MCA formed an alliance against the IMP for the Kuala Lumpur municipal elections. Delivering Malay votes to Chinese candidates and Chinese votes to Malay candidates, the Alliance won nine of the twelve seats. Two went to the IMP and one went to an independent. The success of this local alliance led to the formation of a broader national Alliance between the MCA and the UMNO, to contest the local elections of 1953. Overwhelming Alliance success in these elections eclipsed the political leadership of Dato Onn and his IMP. The IMP passed out of activity and Dato Onn went into political retirement, emerging again in 1954 to form the Party Negara.

In the legislative council a political battle raged between the Alliance and Dato Onn, who continued as appointed Member for Home Affairs. Dato Onn clearly had the backing of the British, which gave

---

[5] See Margaret Clark, *The Malayan Alliance and Its Accommodation of Communal Pressures, 1952–1962*, unpublished M.A. thesis in history, University of Malaya, 1964 for a detailed analysis of these communal forces and their manifestation in the ruling Alliance Party.

him access to elements of the bureaucracy concerned with internal development. He formed the Rural and Industrial Development Authority, which was given much publicity as a dynamic and imaginative organization dedicated to the development of the rural areas. Alliance leaders carried on continued attacks against Dato Onn and consolidated their own ranks in the conflict. They pressed for, and won, British agreement for elections to the federal legislative council for 1955, with a majority of 52 elected seats over 46 appointed seats. In the elections issues Dato Onn was outmaneuvered and forced into the unenviable position of arguing for a delay in the movement to self-government.

In the elections of 1955 the two major contestants were the Alliance and Dato Onn's Party Negara. It was widely predicted, especially among the European community, that Party Negara would win a substantial majority. On the other hand, the Alliance had the backing of the Malay aristocracy and many Malayan intellectuals, as well as that of the wealthy and well-organized Chinese guilds and commercial community. Finally, the Alliance had expanded its base by drawing in the Malayan Indian Congress, the only really effective political leadership for the numerically insignificant Indian community. At the local level it was predicted that the Alliance would win the elections,[6] and when the votes were in, the Alliance had won 51 of the 52 elected seats. One lone seat went to the Pan Malayan Islamic Party from the Krian District, a densely populated rice district in Perak.

Dato Onn lost in his home constituency of Johore Bahru. His political star waned further when he contested a by-election in Batu Pahat a year later, losing by an overwhelming majority to the Alliance candidate. Up to this point Dato Onn's policy had been strongly interethnic. From early in the decade he argued that independence could only be won if the country could demonstrate to the British that the two major races could reach broad agreement on the accommodation of their diverse interests. Dato Onn mistook this requirement for that of complete interethnic political alignments. As it appears now, he was much ahead of his time, advocating alignments that were essentially unacceptable both to Malaya's masses and to her lower level elites. The mistake cost Dato Onn his political life. After his defeat he turned increasingly to what are called in Malaya "communal" appeals. Finally in 1959 he won a seat in the House of Parlia-

---

[6] L. A. P. Gosling, in a personal communication, tells of his own interviews in the states of Trengganu and Kedah just before these elections. He reports that the *penghulus* predicted the outcome of the elections in their *mukims* with unfailing accuracy.

ment from a constituency in the backward and Malay-dominated state of Trengganu. Until his death in 1962 he remained one of Malaya's most articulate and intelligent, but also one of its most lonely, opponents of government.

It is not surprising that Dato Onn misjudged the character of both the interethnic requirements of independence and the interethnic possibilities of the Malayan electorate. Silcock and Aziz, two astute observers of the Malayan scene, also completely misjudged the situation in 1952.[7] They saw the 1952 success of the Alliance largely as a matter of personalities rather than political issues. They pointed out that the IMP contained both Malay and Chinese candidates. Thus the conflict appeared to be between factions within each ethnic group. At the same time they found the Alliance dominated by the interests of short-term expediency. The 1952 Kuala Lumpur electorate was Malay-dominated, but the majority of the campaign funds came from the Chinese. From this they predicted that the future advantages of the Alliance would be doubtful, especially with the extension of the franchise. They argued that extremists in each ethnic wing would pull the Alliance apart and weaken its opposition to the IMP, which they considered the healthiest force in Malayan politics. "The developments of the past two years have merely ensured that when this [further local elections] does occur some at least of the parties will be intercommunal, and this must be recognized as a considerable gain." [8]

The 1955 and 1959 elections, with the continued success of the Alliance and the demise of openly intercommunal parties, have shown how wrong these observers were. They suffered from the same misperceptions that afflicted Dato Onn and many intellectuals viewing the Malayan scene. This misperception consisted of both an abhorrence of the perceived irrationalities of communal alignments in politics, and a failure to appreciate the cohesive power that success in elections can exercise on the strange bedfellows of modern party politics.

In the 1955 elections the Malays were heavily overrepresented. Though they constituted only 49 percent of the population, they made up 84 percent of the electorate.[9] This meant that at least 60 percent of the electorate was a rural Malay electorate (that is, from places less than 1,000). In the 1959 elections the proportion of Chinese in the electorate had increased to 37 percent and the total electorate grew

[7] T. H. Silcock and Ungku A. Aziz, *op. cit.*, pp. 331 ff.

[8] *Op. cit.*, p. 366.

[9] T. G. McGee, "The Malayan Elections of 1959: A Study in Political Geography," *The Journal of Tropical Geography*, October 1962, pp. 70–99.

from 1.2 million to 2.1 million. Even with this increase, however, a minimum of about half the electorate was rural Malay, and, as in most parliamentary democracies, the rural voter was considerably over-represented in the legislature. The major appeal of the Alliance in 1955 was its stand for independence for the country, and a great increase in education. Independence was achieved on 31 August 1957. In 1959 the Alliance campaigned on its past programs, promised greater benefits for the Malays in the rural areas, and an end to the Emergency.

Though it was largely successful in 1959, the Alliance suffered some defeats. It lost the two east coast states of Kelantan and Trengganu to the Pan Malayan Islamic Party,[10] and it lost a number of west coast urban seats to the Socialist Front and to the People's Progressive Party, a mildly left-wing party appealing primarily to Chinese and Indians in Ipoh, the capital city of Perak. The losses to the Pan Malayan Party came as a shocking surprise to the Alliance, though these certainly could have been foreseen had any surveys been carried out prior to the elections. It was a shock because it represented a loss of support in what had previously been a virtually impregnable stronghold of the UMNO, the rural Malays.

These large political developments since 1946 have demonstrated to the Malayan population and its leaders that interests could be advanced through legitimate parliamentary maneuvers and the type of manipulation of the electorate characteristic of successful politics in any open democratic system. They have also demonstrated that the diverse interests of ethnic groups could be protected in a viable national state by a combination of ethnic political alignments and organized interethnic accommodation. All of this has helped to strengthen Malayan commitment to modern parliamentary democratic government. In addition, another powerful force working negatively to strengthen this commitment was the Communist insurgency commonly known as the Emergency, which lasted officially from 1948 until 1960.

At the end of the war the Communist-led anti-Japanese guerilla forces in the jungles emerged and began to transform their program from a para-military to a modern political character. They began to form and to take over labor unions, voluntary organizations, political parties, and the Chinese schools. For two years they practiced what have become familiar tactics of front organization control, violence

---

[10] The Alliance recovered Trengganu in late 1961. This development is covered in some detail in chap. IX.

and agitation. Then in 1948 they embarked on a course of guerilla terrorism.[11] Their plan was to disrupt the economy, to paralyze the rubber and tin industries, to cut off the income of a large number of Malayans, and to cut off Great Britain's most important source of U.S. dollars. The insurgents began in Central Perak and Johore, engaging in a series of murders to intimidate both European planters and miners and Malayan workers.

The British-Malayan government was rather slow to react to that wave of violence. Not until June was a state of emergency declared, but only for restricted districts of Perak and Johore. This was followed by more violence, however, and in July the state of emergency was extended to the entire country. In the next few years the character of the Emergency, as it has come to be called, took shape. The Communists may have had between 5,000 and 7,000 guerilla troops living in the jungles. They styled themselves the Malayan Races Liberation Army, led by a Penang Chinese, Chin Peng. The vast majority of the guerillas, over 90 percent, were Chinese. They attacked estates and mines, laid road and rail ambushes, and engaged in single murders of special opponents, all of which were effective in terrorizing the population. Though the Communists took their toll of European planters and miners, their most common victims were Malayan Chinese. By the formal end of the Colonial period in 1957, 2,456 civilians had been killed, of which 1,700 were Chinese, as against 1,848 police and Home Guard, and 508 army were killed.[12]

By the end of 1948 it was clear that the Communists had not achieved their objective and it seemed doubtful that they could. Though the wave of killings was to increase greatly, during the early stages of the Emergency the economy was disrupted, but not paralyzed.

---

[11] There is some question whether the policy shift was a result of an internal decision in Malaya, or part of a world-wide Communist policy change, communicated to the Malayan party at the Calcutta Communist Conference in February 1948. The timing of the Malayan outbreak and that in other countries of Southeast Asia just after the conference appears more than coincidental. However, Ruth McVey, in *The Calcutta Conference and the Southeast Asian Uprisings*, Cornell Modern Indonesia Project, Interim Report Series, Ithaca, 1958, expresses doubt that the decision for the uprisings was made outside the area and communicated through this conference. In addition, Anthony Short, the official historian of the Emergency in Malaya, argues that with the increasing pressure from the British government in Malaya on the Communist agitators, especially with the change of the trade union legislation to weed out all but genuine workers from the leadership, the Communists had no alternative but to turn to violence. That is, normal legal and security measures were threatening the gains and the future of the Communist party in Malaya.

[12] Lennox A. Mills, *Malaya, A Political and Economic Appraisal*, Minneapolis, 1958, p. 53, material quoted from the Straits Budget of June 20, 1957.

More important, however, was the Communist failure to establish any liberated areas, forcing them to carry on their struggle only as guerillas. In this they learned an important qualification of the Mao Tse-tung blueprint for revolution. The countryside can encircle the towns with effective guerilla action only if liberated areas can be established with sufficient regular troops to engage a significant segment of government field forces.

It was clear, however, that the guerilla forces were far too powerful for the Malayan security forces alone. There seemed to be an endless stream of supplies and information for the guerillas. For this the Communists had organized an extensive supply force, known as the Min Yuen. The base of support lay in the Chinese community. By extortion and by winning sympathy with both ideological and personal appeals, the Communists obtained money from wealthy Chinese and food and information from the squatters.[13]

The 500,000 Chinese squatters, wresting a living from the edges of the Malayan jungles, posed the greatest problem for the government. Both their numbers and their dispersion made it impossible to control them as a source of supply for the guerillas. In 1950 General Briggs, director of Emergency operations, set in motion his plan to resettle these squatters. By the end of 1953 the resettlement was generally completed, as approximately half a million squatters were removed from the edges of the jungle and resettled in over 500 New Villages, surrounded with barbed wire and provided with guards. People could enter and leave at will except during curfew hours, but they could not take food, medicines, or other supplies out with them. Movements of food by road were curtailed and rationing was established. In addition, the New Villages were provided with electricity, schools, water supplies, and other modern amenities. In some cases they were also provided with land for farming, though this was not always possible. Even today, with the fences down and the security regulations a thing of the past, the major need of the New Villagers is for land.

---

[13] Han Su-yin's *And the Rain My Drink*, Boston, 1956, is a sensitive account of the Chinese position in the Emergency. Lucien Pye's *Guerilla Communism in Malaya*, Princeton, 1956, is also of interest in that it illuminates some of the political thinking, and the personal considerations, that led some Chinese to join the insurgents. Pye's work is defective in its general research design, however. He interviewed in depth over 70 surrendered enemy personnel. Unfortunately he reported no interviews with Chinese who had not joined the insurgents, thus failing to provide a control group. Anyone familiar with the Chinese of Malaya must find the personality and political sketches of Pye's surrendered enemy personnel not uncommon for the rest of the Chinese population. Thus, though his information is generally enlightening, it really tells us nothing substantial about why these men joined the insurgency.

At the end of 1951 the British High Commissioner, Sir Henry Guerney, was ambushed and killed on his way to Fraser's Hill, a resort station near Kuala Lumpur. His loss was felt both as a deep blow to government and the people and as a great victory for the insurgents. In the three years he had been in Malaya, Sir Henry had made considerable progress in identifying the Emergency as an ideological, economic, and political struggle as well as a military one. His successor, General Gerald Templer, provided a pattern of leadership that is still deeply ingrained in Malaya. Templer was an extremely forceful man who used widely, but well, the almost dictatorial powers he held. With a loathing of red tape and excuses, he was strong in his demand for results and in his impatience with incompetent staff. One of his great admirers was a young Malay civil servant from Pahang, Abdul Razak, who later emulated Templer's leadership techniques in implementing Malaya's rural development program.

By the time General Templer left Malaya in 1954 the main military threat of Communism had been broken. The resettlement plan was effective in denying supplies to the insurgents. Estates and mines were guarded by a corps of special constables, whose later resettlements caused the new nation a great deal of concern. Commonwealth forces had come in great numbers and the police were considerably augmented and gained great skill in carrying the attack to the insurgents. Soon police and army units were laying ambushes for the insurgents.

Of equal importance were the moves to self-government that were gaining momentum during the early stages of the Emergency. This political progress was effective in taking the force from the Communists' claim to be the liberators from the colonial yoke. Local elections were held for the first time, local leaders exercised quasi-ministerial functions, and plans were under way to hold national elections in 1955. Shortly after the new government came to power in 1955, a general amnesty was declared for all surrendered guerillas, and an offer of negotiation was made by the new Chief Minister, Tungku Abdul Rahman. The Tungku and the leader of the Malayan Communist Party, Chin Peng, met in the small town of Baling, together with Singapore's Chief Minister, David Marshall, and Tan Cheng-lock, the acknowledged leader of the Chinese in Malaya. The meeting proved fruitless because the Tungku demanded complete surrender with a promise of fair treatment, and Chin Peng demanded that his party be made legal and the guerillas given freedom of action. Nonetheless the Tungku did obtain the promise that when independence was achieved the Communists would cease the struggle.

Chin Peng: "As soon as these two Governments [Singapore and the Federation] have self determination in internal security and defense matters, then we can stop the war immediately."

Tungku: "Is that a promise? When I come back from England that is the thing I am bringing back with me."

Chin Peng: "That being the case, we can straightaway stop our hostilities and also disband our armed units." [14]

The Tungku did return from England with a promise of independence and with immediate control over internal security. Appeals were broadcast to the Communists to honor their promise, but prospects of an unconditional surrender apparently could not be accepted. The Emergency was ended unilaterally by the Malayan government on 31 July 1960. Minor operations are still (1963) being carried on against the remnants of the guerilla forces in the jungles on the Malayan-Thai border, but Malaya itself is quite free from insurgent terrorism.

The significance of the Emergency lies in three things. In the first place, it demonstrated the futility of violent, nonconstitutional means to advance group interest precisely at the time when constitutional means were proving effective. Thus it helped to push Malaya along the road to a parliamentary democratic system. Second, it served to weaken the ideology of the economic left and thus to strengthen Malayan commitment to a free market economy.[15] Finally, it made an issue of national loyalty, especially among the Chinese. The emergence of an independent Malayan state would have done this in any case, but only a military threat to the country, especially one that was internal and divided people along ethnic lines, could push the issue into a dominant position demanding an active commitment to the country on the part of the immigrant groups. The Emergency probably speeded rather than retarded the acquisition of independence in Malaya. By posing as liberators from the colonial yoke, the Communists gave Malayan nationalists an opportunity to strengthen their position by offering the colonial government a peaceful alternative that would divest that government of its unpopular imperialist role, while at the same time protecting its general position in the area. British acceptance of this argument was facilitated by the government's long-standing preference for the Malays and desire to protect them against the

---

[14] Report by the Chief Minister of the Federation of Malaya on the Baling Talks, Kuala Lumpur, Government Printer, 1956, p. 11.

[15] There have been, however, forces working in the opposite direction without the stigma of illegitimate political activity attached to them.

economically more aggressive Chinese. Nonetheless, it is much to the credit of British statesmen that they recognized the legitimacy of the demands for independence and acceded to those demands in a rational manner, sometimes even more rapidly than Malayan nationalists themselves desired.

THE ECONOMY

The Malayan economy currently manifests two basic characteristics. Along with the continuation of the old colonial economy can be seen the beginnings of a radical change in the entire economic structure. It is difficult at this point to see which of these two characteristics is most important. Pessimists tend to concentrate on the former, optimists on the latter. However, the direction of the larger political and economic forces both within and outside Malaya seems to argue that sustained radical change is inevitable. This view is generally accepted in this study. A more profound question, however, is whether this change can continue and be successful while maintaining the organizational integration of the Malayan economy with that of the West. That is, will the radical change entail a strong reaction against Western enterprise, as it has in Indonesia, or will it be worked out without extreme reactions and involve only the gradual erosion of the power of specific Western enterprises? It seems certain that the functional alignment of the economy with the new independent state must involve the weakening of the power of Western enterprises in Malaya. This is the larger political and economic problem for the country. It bears on our study indirectly in that one of the major forces behind the current rural development program is the desire to engage in rapid development while avoiding an open clash with Western enterprises.

Tin and rubber have remained Malaya's major industries. From 1955 through 1960 rubber accounted for about 25 percent of the gross domestic product,[16] and tin accounted for about 5 percent. In the same period the replanting of rubber accounted for an average of about 22 percent of gross domestic capital formation at current prices. In 1962 Malayan exports totaled M$ 2,625,900,000 (M$ = Malayan dollars). Crude rubber accounted for 52 percent of this and tin for 24 percent. Both figures fluctuate with world market prices, but they still consistently account for 70 to 80 percent of Malayan exports. Rubber continues to dominate Malaya's agricultural scene, with approximately

---

[16] In constant prices at factor cost. These and subsequent national income account data are taken from Federation of Malaya, Department of Statistics, *National Accounts of the Federation of Malaya, 1955–1960*, Kuala Lumpur, 1963.

4 million of the total 5.5 million cultivated acres. The latest census (1957) shows 480,000 males, or about 30 percent of the male labor force, engaged directly in plantation agriculture.[17]

It seems probable that the absolute, if not the proportionate, value of the rubber industry will increase for another decade at least. A forecast made by the Economic Planning Unit envisages that between 1962 and 1970 total production of rubber will increase from 750,000 to 1,249,000 tons. Though the price is expected to fall in the same period from M$ 0.75 to M$ 0.55 per pound, the increase in production will be sufficient to provide a net increase in the total value of the industry.

The economy is still very much outwardly oriented. Between 1955 and 1960 export earnings averaged about 50 percent of GNP at current prices.[18] Imports during this period have amounted to about 43 percent of GNP, but this fluctuates much less than export earnings. In 1962 at least 57 percent of imports were products of modern industrial economies, including refined petroleum, chemicals, manufactured goods, and machinery. These are the signs of the continued colonial, or export, character of the economy. It is a typical exporter of primary products and an importer of manufactured products.

Behind this continued dominance of the export character of the economy, however, can be seen unmistakable signs of change. Tin and rubber have undoubtedly lost some of their dominance, but it is difficult to say to what extent this change has occurred. According to the 1954 mission of the International Bank for Reconstruction and Development,

By Asian standards, the Malayan economy has reached a relatively advanced stage, not only in the level of per capita income, but also in structure. . . . Accordingly, further economic development will undoubtedly follow a broader and more varied pattern than prevailed until fairly recent times.[19]

Unfortunately the national income accounts cannot be used to measure sectoral change in the past decade or more. Comparable series do not exist for more than five years at a time. The most recent series, 1955–1960, is not comparable with that for the five years pre-

---

[17] A few of these are in oil palm or coconut plantations, but the great majority are in rubber.

[18] Since primary commodities with fluctuating prices make up the bulk of exports, the proportion of national income can vary as much as 10 percentage points in one year.

[19] International Bank for Reconstruction and Development, *The Economic Development of Malaya*, Baltimore, 1957, p. 20.

ceding because of the inclusion of Singapore in the earlier series. These two series can be taken together to indicate rough changes in total economic activity, but they cannot be used for sectoral analysis, which is necessary to evaluate the change in the structure of the economy. The most recent series is not for a long enough period to show secular changes, especially given the extreme sensitivity of the indicators to external market conditions over which the economy has no control. The latter series, for example, shows no change in the proportion of the total product provided by any of the nine sectors listed. Other indicators suggest, however, that this is a result of the insensitivity of the national income accounts rather than a real lack of change in the economy.

The most direct evidence of change available lies in the changing distribution of the labor force between 1947 and 1957.[20] A summary of this change is given in table III-1.

This table indicates both continuity and change in the economy. The continuity is seen in the stable percentages in rubber, mining, manufacturing, commerce, and transportation. The changes are in the decline of peasant agriculture, especially in rice where there was an absolute as well as a percentage change, in the absolute decrease in domestic servants, and in the increase in construction and government services. In broader terms, this shows a decrease in the primary sector, balanced by increases in both the secondary and tertiary sectors. Even within the primary sector the change is in the direction of modernization, for there is a shift from rice to rubber, from a product of lower value to one of higher value, and from a less advanced to a more advanced technology. All of these changes are generally associated with increased per capita product.

Within the manufacturing sector itself, the changes are also those associated with increased per capita product. The labor force in the total sector increased at the same rate as the total labor force. Within the sector, however, the largest proportionate and absolute change recorded was a decline in attap and rattan manufacture, which is essentially a handicraft industry. Textiles and basic metals showed slight proportionate and absolute declines. All other categories showed

---

[20] There is always a danger in using just one intercensal period to analyze change. Either or both the censuses may be biased by some short-range change and totally distort secular changes that are taking place. In the Mayalan case, the 1947 census was distorted by the Japanese war and occupation, the 1957 census by the Emergency and the advent of independence. Caution is thus urged in accepting the following analysis. We shall attempt to use a number of different independent indicators. To the extent they all point in the same direction, we can be more confident of our general evaluation.

TABLE III-1

CHANGING INDUSTRIAL DISTRIBUTION OF THE MALE LABOR FORCE
IN MALAYA 1947–1957

	1947		1957	
	(000)	(percent)	(000)	(percent)
Total male labor force	1,436.5	100	1,602.8	100
Peasant agriculture	509.4	36	413.0	26
Rice	333.2	23	264.9	16
Plantation agriculture	384.2	27	430.5	27
Rubber	342.3	24	384.1	24
Mining	39.4	3	49.0	3
Manufacturing	99.9	7	113.2	7
Construction	13.1	1	62.5	4
Utilities	4.5	---	11.2	1
Commerce	156.1	11	176.6	11
Trans-communication	64.5	4	73.3	5
Services	159.9	11	258.7	16
Government	66.1	5	91.9	6
Domestic	20.2	1	10.1	1
Military, Police	23.4	2	95.9	6

SOURCE: Federation of Malaya, *Population Census*, 1957, Vol. 14, p. 31.

increases, with footwear, wearing apparel, general engineering and machinery, woodworking, and furniture showing the largest proportionate and absolute gains.

The little that is known about the value of the manufacturing sector also indicates both change and continuity.[21] The four largest industries are rubber milling off estates, rubber latex processing, coconut oil mills, and large rice mills. With the exception of latex processing, these are industries associated with the old colonial export economy. In the survey of 1,600 establishments, these four industries accounted for 52 percent of gross sales, 24 percent of the total value added, and employed 21 percent of the full-time employees. These are also the industries most affected by fluctuations in world prices, because they have a very high purchases-to-sales ratio, or a very low proportion of value added to gross value.

In the three years 1959–1961 the general trend of manufacturing in the Federation was an increase in total value from 1959 to 1960, and

[21] Federation of Malaya, Department of Statistics, *Survey of Manufacturing Industries*, Kuala Lumpur, 1962. This gives adjusted results of the 1959, 1960, and 1961 surveys.

a decrease from 1960 to 1961. This corresponds exactly with the
changes in the rubber price for the period. The Singapore rubber price
per pound of smoked rubber sheet was M\$ 1.02, M\$ 1.08, and M\$ 0.80
in those three years.[22] However, the trend for the entire sector was
established primarily by the big four export industries. The trends for
other industries, those generally associated with the modern national
economy, showed an increase.

The big four showed decreases in both gross value and net value
(value added); all other industries showed increases. The six modern
national industries with more than 1,000 employees (rubber products,
tobacco, soft drinks, biscuits, structural clay, and basic metals) all
showed continued increases throughout the three-year period. The
downturn of the rubber price that brought an absolute decrease in
value to the big four colonial export industries brought only a decrease in the rate of growth of the modern national industries oriented
to the home market. Besides, the export industries showed a general
decline in their proportion of the net value of all industries: 46, 45,
and 39 percent for the three years. It is important to note that this
proportion declined slightly between 1959 and 1960, despite the substantial upturn in the rubber price over those two years. In general
it appears that the industries oriented to the home market are growing
steadily and are capturing a larger and larger share of the total manufacturing activity.

Malaya's pattern of external trade also gives some indication of the
change in the economic structure. During the past decade the volume
of exports and imports increased steadily, except for a slight drop in
1957 to 1958. Since the general price index has remained fairly constant the value of both imports and exports has also shown a general
increase, though the terms of trade appear to be turning against
Malaya.

The change in the trade pattern is seen in imports rather than
exports. Since 1953 all commodity categories in exports have continued at about the same proportion, with the exception of *crude
inedibles except fuels* (primarily rubber) and *manufactured goods*
(primarily tin blocks). The general trend has been for a decline in the
former and an increase in the latter. This does not indicate any change,
however, except in the price of rubber. When rubber prices are high,
crude inedibles increase in value, and consequently decrease the
proportionate value of manufactured goods. These two categories are
those of the old colonial export economy; taken together they have

---

[22] Federation of Malaya, Department of Statistics, *Rubber Statistics Handbook,
1961*, Kuala Lumpur, 1962, p. 7.

averaged 88 percent, with fluctuations from 85 to 91 percent, of total exports in the ten years from 1953 to 1962.

The pattern of imports does, however, show some indication of real change. Table III-2 shows a proportionate decrease in food imports,

TABLE III-2

PROPORTIONATE VALUE OF IMPORTS INTO MALAYA 1953–1962

Year	Total (M$ millions)	Food (percent)	Crude inedibles (percent)	Machinery and transport equipment (percent)
1953	1,451.4	39	7	12
1954	1,319.1	32	10	11
1955	1,524.9	31	11	11
1956	1,751.0	30	11	13
1957	1,814.4	29	11	13
1958	1,657.5	32	11	13
1959	1,739.3	29	11	14
1960	2,150.6	25	16	15
1961	2,230.5	23	14	20
1962	2,447.4	23	14	20

SOURCE: Federation of Malaya, Department of Statistics, *Monthly Statistics of External Trade, December 1962*, Kuala Lumpur, 1963.

balanced by a slight increase in crude inedibles and a larger increase in machinery and transport equipment, especially after 1958. All other categories show no change.

These three separate sources, the industrial distribution of the labor force, surveys of manufacturing industries, and the pattern of external trade, all point to some changes in the structure of the economy. Though the economy is still dominated by tin and rubber and though it is still largely externally oriented, it appears to be moving in the direction of a modern, diversified, internally oriented economy. Thus the predictions of the World Bank team in 1954 appear to have been borne out. Many would argue that the changes do not proceed rapidly enough and that government should increase its concern for industrialization. There is some movement in this direction, though it is as yet not very strong. Pioneer industries legislation gives up to a five-year tax moratorium, the tariff structure is slowly being reworked to provide greater protection and stimulation for local industry, and new institutions for the mobilization of capital are slowly gaining momentum. The movement is admittedly slow, partly because government interest in rural development has been far greater than in industrialization during this period. This slowness and the piecemeal manner of industrial stimulation are important indications that the radical change in the structure of the economy is occurring in a context of continual organizational integration with Western economies, rather than in a violent reaction against Western enterprises.

One of the most crucial problems in the future of the Malayan economy is that of natural rubber. The three most important variables are the cost of Malayan labor, the yield from Malayan rubber, and the competition of synthetic rubber. All three point to a radical change in, if not an eventual decline and demise of, the natural rubber industry. The general economic growth of Malaya can be expected to exert upward pressures on the cost of labor. This pressure will undoubtedly be transmitted to the rubber industry through the National Union of Plantation Workers, one of the strongest unions in Malaya today. Labor costs are already more than half of the total production costs. Against these rising costs are the declining costs of synthetic rubber. The recent developments in stereo-regular rubber means that the competition between synthetic and natural rubber is now primarily one of price, and in this competition the capital-intensive synthetic certainly has a long-term advantage. Against this can be set the marked secular increase in consumption of both synthetic and natural rubber, and the large increase in yields following the use of high-yielding strains of trees. Thus Malaya might have ten to thirty more years of major earning power with natural rubber, but the economy of replanting when the current trees have been exhausted is questionable.

Another type of readjustment in the industry is possible, however— a move in the direction of greater smallholder participation, associated with the weakening of the dependent state and the emergence of the independent state. Government land schemes are designed to open about half a million acres of new land by the end of 1965, providing eight to ten acres of land for selected Malayan settlers.[23] It is probable that at least half of this will be rubber land. In addition, there has been some fragmentation of estates into rented smallholdings, especially since independence. This latter development is currently deplored by Malayan intellectuals,[24] but it may represent a natural adjustment of the structure of the industry to a more competitive market. It seems likely that greater smallholder participation would have oc-

[23] See Federal Land Development Authority, *Annual Report for the Period July 1, 1960 to June 31, 1961*, Kuala Lumpur, 1962.
[24] See Ungku Aziz, *The Subdivision of Estates in Malaya 1951–1960*, Kuala Lumpur, 1963, *passim*.

curred earlier had Malayan smallholders not been prevented by government from opening more land for rubber, and had they not been discriminated against in favor of the estates. The estate costs may be too high and too fixed to allow the industry to adapt itself to changing market conditions. In addition, the pressure of rising labor costs is largely a pressure on estate labor. The smallholder, especially if he has a diversified farm, may be in a far better position to meet strong international competition. This will be more certain if the smallholder is supported by research and extension facilities that give him services commensurate with what he pays for them, which has not been the case in the past.[25]

In the long run, however, there can be little doubt that Malaya's economic development will be influenced by the diminishing importance of rubber in the total economy. Therefore, one of the questions this study must raise at some point is the extent to which the development organizations of government can and do take cognizance of this necessary broader change in the economy. To what extent are government and its specialized agencies concerned with industrialization, and what political and organizational forces determine both the quality and the quantity of government's concern? We shall argue in the final pages of this study that the characteristics of the new emerging system may be unsuitable for that system's adjustment to the exogenous force of the world rubber market, and may therefore present a very serious source of strain in the system in the coming decades.

THE SOCIETY

It is impossible to say with any precision to what extent, or whether or not, the Malayan society is becoming less plural and more national in its basic groupings. There are essentially no data on Malayan values that would admit of even an educated guess on the degree of national consciousness that exists on any issue. There are no studies of voting, opinions, or attitudes on which the assessment of consensus might be made. There are, however, a few sets of data that can provide some information on the degree of ethnic concentration in specific areas of behavior. These are objective indicators and tell nothing about individual or group positions. However, since these are the only types of data that exist, we shall begin with an analysis of some of them, then

[25] See P. T. Bauer, *A Report on a Visit to the Rubber Growing Smallholdings in Malaya, July–September 1946*, London, 1948, in which he argues persuasively that the Rubber Research Institute has provided far more service to estates than to smallholders, despite the fact that smallholders have paid approximately half the cost of the Institute through the export tax on their rubber.

proceed to a discussion of certain impressions—perhaps the only possible reaction of observers of the Malayan scene.

The best data available showing ethnic concentration of behavior are those of the industrial distribution of the labor force for the years 1947 and 1957. The industrial classifications used in these two censuses are not completely comparable, but they are sufficiently close for our use. As is generally the case, the larger categories are closer than the smaller ones, in part because changes in definitions and errors in classification of individuals will generally cancel each other if the category is large enough to form an easily identified unit. Thus the analysis that we use tends to keep to the larger categories except where we can be fairly certain that the smaller ones have been similarly treated in both censuses.[26]

In analyzing the industrial distribution of the labor force we are interested primarily in the extent to which any ethnic group is concentrated in specific activities to the exclusion of other groups, and the degree to which this has changed over the period of the two censuses. We have constructed a simple index of concentration for each of the industrial categories. This was done by simply taking the difference, d, regardless of sign, between the proportion of an ethnic group in a given industry and its proportion in the total labor force. For each industrial category we have measured the difference d for each of the three major ethnic groups. The sum of these three differences is the single index of concentration. Thus in a given industry, if each ethnic group is represented in a proportion equal to its representation in the total labor force, the index will be zero. On the other hand, if all the workers in one industry are provided by one ethnic group alone, the index will be some higher value. A complete table, showing the industrial distribution of the labor force for 1947 and 1957 is given in Appendix III-I. Table III-3 shows only the single index of ethnic concentration for each of the industrial categories used.

On the whole there appears to be a decrease in ethnic concentration or ethnic specialization in Malayan industries. The only two categories that showed an increase were peasant agriculture and commerce. Peasant agriculture is the only industrial category that showed a decrease in the absolute number of workers. All ethnic groups have moved out of peasant agriculture, but the Chinese and Indians have moved out

---

[26] It must be admitted that the degree of certainty established on comparability is not very systematic. It involves far too much individual decision based on other impressions to be really objective. Nonetheless, this must be accepted if we are to have any attempt at systematic analysis at all.

TABLE III-3

INDEX OF ETHNIC CONCENTRATION IN SELECTED INDUSTRIES
IN MALAYA 1947 AND 1957

Industries	1947	1957
I. Peasant agriculture	41	62
II. Plantation agriculture	23	21
III. Mining	62	53
IV. Manufacturing, utilities, construction	65	51
V. Tertiary total	33	23
A. Commerce	62	66
B. Transportation	26	23
C. Services	26	13
Government	54	33
Unweighted average of I, II, III, IV, VA, VB and VC	43.5	41.5
(Excluding I: Peasant agriculture)	(44.0)	(36.8)

more rapidly than the Malays, causing the index to rise. The changes in commerce are very small and actually show a move in the direction of a reduction of Chinese exclusive participation in the industry. The Malays slightly increased their proportion in commerce from 13 percent in 1947 to 14 percent in 1957. The Chinese dropped from 70 percent to 66 percent and the Indians increased from 16 percent to 18 percent. The index increased because the Malay increase was less than the Malay increase in the total labor force, and the Chinese decrease was less than the Chinese decrease in the total labor force. That is, Malays are entering commerce, but not as rapidly as they are growing in the total labor force.

The decrease in plantation agriculture may indicate a move of considerable significance. It was caused essentially by a strong increase of Malays in the industry and an actual decline in the numbers of Chinese. It may be argued that plantation agriculture affords a stepping stone for the more economically backward Malays into the modern economy—a stepping stone that has already been used by the Chinese and Indians.

Thus to the extent that the last two censuses accurately reflect changes in ethnic industrial specialization, the objective base of the ethnic plural society is withering away and being replaced by an objective base that provides for national groupings.

Three other sets of demographic data also allow for a measure of ethnic concentration similar to that used above. These are the urban

TABLE III-4

INDICES OF ETHNIC CONCENTRATION IN URBAN AREAS

Urban areas	1947	1957
Places of 1,000 or more	56	54
Places of 10,000 or more	60	57

See Appendix III-II for data used in computation of the indices.

data, the ethnic distribution in each state of the Federation, and literacy data. The indices of concentration are shown in tables III-4, III-5, and III-6.

The urban indices of ethnic concentration decreased during the decade, regardless of whether 1,000 or 10,000 is used to define urban places. It is, of course, impossible to say how significant is this decline of indices, but it should be noted that it results from two different types of urbanization, which acted differentially on the major ethnic groups. In places of 1,000 or more, the absolute growth of the Chinese population was approximately 900,000. This included the roughly 500,-

TABLE III-5

INDICES OF ETHNIC CONCENTRATION IN THE STATES OF MALAYA

	1947	1957	Change
"Old" Federated States			
Negri Sembilan	16	16	none
Selangor	45	41	−
Perak	24	21	−
Pahang	11	13	+
"Old" Straits Settlements			
Malacca	6	8	+
Penang	47	42	−
"Old" Unfederated States			
Johore	1	0	−
Kedah	38	35	−
Perlis	59	57	−
Kelantan	86	83	−
Trengganu	84	82	−
Average for all states	37.8	36.2	−

See Appendix III-III for data used in computation of the indices.

TABLE III-6

INDICES OF ETHNIC CONCENTRATION IN LITERACY

(Showing males 15 years and over, literate
in Malay, in English, and in any language.)

Type of literacy	1947	1957
Literate in Malay	102	90
Literate in English	32	29
Literate in any language	11	6

SOURCE: 1947: M. V. Del Tufo, *A Report on the 1947 Census of Population*, Tables 52–77. 1957: *1957 Population Census*, Table 9. See Appendix III-IV for the data used in computation of the indices.

000 squatters who were resettled into New Villages, which were generally between 1,000 and 10,000 in size. This forced urbanization undoubtedly added to the more natural process of urbanization that would have occurred among the Chinese in any event, but it is not possible to distinguish the magnitude of the two forces. On the other hand, the roughly 300,000 increase in the Malay urban population resulted primarily from natural increase and migration stimulated by the more normal economic and political developments of the country. Thus it seems quite likely that without the forced relocation of the Chinese under Emergency conditions, the degree of ethnic concentration would have further decreased in urban areas.[27]

The measure of concentration in the states shows the same general downward trend. In table III-5 the states have been grouped as the old Federated States, the Straits Settlements, and the Unfederated States. Today it is generally conceded that the old Federated States and Johore are economically more advanced than the old Unfederated States. It can be seen here that in both periods these more advanced states, with the exception of Penang, have lower levels of concentration than the economically less advanced. In all states but Penang and Pahang the index of concentration dropped. It cannot be said that the movement has been strong. In most cases the change is the result of a 1 or 2 percentage point difference in the ethnic composition. Thus it may be argued that the stability is more important than the change. However, it does appear significant that nine of the eleven states

[27] To give some idea of the magnitude of changes involved, we might assume that without the forced relocation, perhaps 300,000 of the 500,000 Chinese would have become urban dwellers. This reduces the total urban population by 200,000 and changes the ethnic composition of the urban areas. Under these assumptions the index of ethnic concentration would be 51 rather than the 54 actually observed.

showed a decrease in the index. Further, it must be remembered that
this change took place during the Emergency, with its pervasive restrictions on economic activities and geographic movements. Since the
last census the Emergency has ended and there has been a great increase in public investment in all forms of communications facilities,
especially in the rural areas. If the economic advance of the states has
been previously associated with reductions in their ethnic imbalance,
it can be postulated that the next census will show a much greater
equalization of population distribution.

It will be possible to test this hypothesis of economic advance and
ethnic geographic equalization using the deviant cases of Kelantan and
Trengganu. These two states were won by the Pan Malayan Islamic
Party in the 1959 elections and have consequently had very weak programs of public investment. Trengganu was won back by the ruling
Alliance Party in 1961, resulting in a great increase in public investment. Thus we should expect the 1967 census to show the most rapid
declines in the index of concentration in the Alliance-controlled states,
a lesser decline in Trengganu, and a very weak decline, if any at all, in
Kelantan.

In table III-6, languages have been arranged in the order of their
significance for modern Malayan communication. It is the stated intent
of the government to make Malay the national language of the state.
Most literate Malays are literate in the Malay language. To the extent
that Chinese and Indians become literate in Malay, the index of ethnic
concentration will decrease. Also to this extent will there be a single
national medium of communication. English has been and continues
to be the major language of communication in the modern sector:
government and urban business. It provides a medium of communication especially for the elite and therefore especially in the area of modern policy decisions. Though English is highly important at this level,
it is less important than Malay as a means of communication within
which a new national consensus can emerge. Literacy in any language
is here considered least important for national consciousness because it
operates in two potential directions. On the one hand it can signify
increases in ethnic identity, in ethnic exclusiveness, and hence pose a
threat to the development of a national society. On the other hand, we
would argue quite generally that literacy extends the boundaries of
an individual's community and opens him to influences of the wider
world. This offers at least the possibility of building a new identity
based on national boundaries.

The most encouraging change in the ethnic concentration index in
literacy is its decrease in the Malay language, an indication that both

Chinese and Indians are becoming literate in Malay. Subsequent census data should show a very rapid decline in this index because Malay is now a compulsory language in all schools. Even without this force, however, in the period 1947 to 1957, Malay was becoming more a means of communication within the new emerging state. With only slight increases in total Chinese and Indian males 15 years and over, these two groups tripled and doubled, respectively, the number of males who were literate in Malay.

TABLE III-7

PERCENT OF MALAYAN CHINESE AND INDIANS BORN IN MALAYA

	1921	1931	1947	1957
Chinese	20.9	29.9	63.5	75.5
Indians	12.1	21.4	51.6	65.0

SOURCE: *1957 Population Census*, Vol. 14, p. 15.

In place of origin and sex ratios, Malaya's population shows evidence of becoming more and more a settled, national population. The Chinese and Indians are losing the objective criteria of aliens as the proportion born in the country increases rapidly (table III-7). In addition, the sex ratios of both immigrant ethnic groups are rapidly approaching unity (table III-8).

TABLE III-8

INDIAN AND CHINESE SEX RATIOS IN MALAYA
(Females per 1,000 males)

	1911	1921	1931	1947	1957
Chinese	215	371	486	815	928
Indian	320	424	514	687	714

SOURCE: 1911–1947: *1947 Population Census*, pp. 57–58. 1957: *1957 Population Census*, Vol. 14, p. 51.

These are, of course, only objective indicators. Whether or not a plural society can be associated with a viable national state depends in the final analysis upon how the different groups are defined by one another. Even today a large proportion of those defined as Malays are immigrants from Indonesia, and are of more recent origin than many

Chinese. Nonetheless, these Indonesian immigrants are defined socially and legally as Malays, and therefore as part of the indigenous group. On the other hand, the old "Straits Chinese," many of whom speak no Chinese and have been in Malaya for generations, are socially defined as Chinese, and legally defined as non-Malays. The strength of Malay sentiments supporting this type of definition can be seen in various public statements in which Chinese are defined as guests and Malays as hosts.[28] It is also evident in repeated attempts of the Pan Malayan Islamic Party and other Malay chauvinists to have the Constitution stipulate that the country belongs to the Malays. It is impossible to say whether or to what extent these definitions are changing. It can be expected, however, that a change in objective criteria will facilitate a change in definitions. It can also be expected that education, the major institution for socializing members of the national society, will play a major role in whatever redefinitions will follow.

Just as the plural character of the society and the articulation between the dependent state and the ethnic plural society could be clearly seen in the educational institution, so can the efforts to build a national community. Unfortunately there are no studies of the impact of education on national consensus, and given the current sensitivity over "communal issues" it is doubtful that any such studies will be made in the near future. Thus it is only possible to examine official policy and to see the extent to which the policy of the independent polity differs from that of the dependent state.

In 1951 the British colonial government in Malaya began to take a greater interest in the country's educational requirements.[29] Consistent with the colonial pattern, the government called in an Oxford scholar, L. J. Barnes, to investigate and report upon the education *of the Malays* in Malaya. There was still no recognition in policy of the necessity of building a national education institution. Barnes considerably overstepped the terms of reference of his committee and made a series of wide-ranging recommendations calling for the establishment of a national educational institution using only Malay and English as media of instruction. He argued that the transition to this system could be made voluntarily, with parents sending their children to the new national schools because they would be superior to the

---

[28] See pp. 114–115 for a good example of this type of statement in a somewhat heated parliamentary debate.

[29] In part this was merely an extension of the secular trend of increasing social services. However, it also represents an increase in the rate of change in the secular trend, which was brought about by the Emergency. The problem of the Chinese squatters forced upon government the recognition that the war was a war for men's minds as well as for their bodies.

old ethnic schools. At the same time, he ended his report with a strong statement equating Chinese and Indian acceptance of this type of institution with loyalty to the country.

We have set up bi-lingualism in Malay and English as its [the education policy's] objective because we believe that all parents who regard Malaya as their permanent home and object of their undivided loyalty will be happy to have their children educated in these languages. If parents were not happy about this, their unhappiness would properly be taken as indication that they did not so regard Malaya.[30]

This report was presented during the Emergency when there was real and legitimate concern about the loyalty of the Chinese to the new Federation of Malaya. However, the equation of the willingness to give up their schools with loyalty of Malayan Chinese to Malaya was at best an ill-advised formulation. Such an equation might easily be accepted by a community that had never held formal education in high value, or by one that had not itself built an extensive educational institution. This could never be said of the Chinese, however. They have always placed more value on education than have the Malays, a point that was acknowledged in the Barnes report, and they had built many schools with their own resources in active pursuit of that value.

Public reaction to the Barnes report was immediate and vehement. Newspapers contained daily letters and articles praising and vilifying Malay and Chinese cultures. The Chinese community felt a direct threat to its way of life, its language, and its culture. The sense of insecurity was heightened by the knowledge that they had had no voice in the Barnes committee. In overstepping his formal terms of reference, Barnes had also gone considerably beyond the competence of his committee to deal with its problem. There were no Chinese members on the committee, no views were heard from Chinese educators as such, and no information was sought on the Chinese schools in Malaya.

Partly in reaction to the communal passions aroused by the Barnes report, the colonial government called two Chinese educators, W. P. Fenn from the United States, and T. Y. Wu from the United Nations, to study the education of Chinese in Malaya.[31] The Fenn-Wu report gave due respect to the great efforts the Chinese had put forth to advance their own education, but it also called for considerable reform in that education. It was noted that Chinese schools used texts, syllabi,

---

[30] Federation of Malaya, *Report of the Committee on Malay Education*, Kuala Lumpur, 1951, p. 24.
[31] See *The Report of a Mission Invited by the Federation Government to Study the Problem of Education of Chinese in Malaya*, Kuala Lumpur, 1951.

and teachers from mainland China. The teaching methods were out-dated and the curriculum was suited to an older China rather than to modern Malaya. A program was recommended to provide Malaya-oriented syllabi and textbooks for the Chinese schools.

An education ordinance of 1952 effected something of a compromise, but left the major problem unsettled. Educational benefits were increased slowly, with government protesting that the prosecution of the Emergency and the requirements of economic development were of higher priority in claims on government resources.

As soon as the new quasi-independent government was elected to power in 1955, it set about to provide a national educational policy for a national educational institution. One of the strongest, and the most dynamic, of the Malay political leaders, Dato Abdul Razak (later Tun Abdul Razak, Deputy Prime Minister, Minister of Defense, and Minister of Rural Development), became the first Minister of Education. Razak immediately established a committee to study the education problem and to provide recommendations for a policy.

The terms of reference of the committee were in striking contrast to those of the previous colonial committees. The independent committee was to examine the education system and recommend changes to "establish a national system of education acceptable to the people of the Federation as a whole which will satisfy their needs to promote their development as a nation, having regard to the intention to make Malay the national language . . . whilst preserving and sustaining the growth of the language and culture of other communities in the country." [32] The membership of the committee included eight Malays, five Chinese, and two Indians, all of whom were elected members of Parliament.

The Razak committee advanced a plan that was implemented and appears to be generally acceptable to all ethnic groups in Malaya. Primary education, free to all children from 1962, is now in four streams: English, Malay, Chinese (Mandarin), and Tamil. Regardless of the medium of instruction used, Malay and English will be taught. Any school will teach Chinese or Tamil as languages if the parents of fifteen or more children request it. Secondary education is only in Malay and English. Other languages are taught as subjects, but are not used as media of instruction. Examinations will be only in English and Malay at the end of secondary school. All schools are either completely aided government schools, or completely unaided private

---

[32] *Report of the Education Policy Committee* [The Razak Report], Kuala Lumpur, 1956, p. 2. Substantially the same phrase was included in sect. 3 of The Education Act of 1957.

schools. The independent schools must adhere to the curricula and language teaching of the government schools, but they may use whatever language they choose as the medium of instruction. In all schools the texts and curricula have been given a Malayan orientation.

This new school system has been in operation for only a few years, since about 1959 or 1960; it is impossible to be precise about dates. In two respects it represents a radical change from past systems. It is a unified national and nationally oriented school system, and its aim is mass education. At the time of writing essentially all of the primary-age school children are in school. The number in secondary schools is growing rapidly, though there is still an almost magical attachment to the older British standard of sending only 30 percent of the primary school graduates on to secondary school.

Table III-9 gives some indication of the quantitative developments

TABLE III-9

TOTAL SCHOOL ENROLLMENT AND POPULATION AGE 5–15 IN MALAYA

| | 1947 | | | 1957 | | |
	A Enrollment (1949)	B Population 5–15 (1947)	A as percent of B	C Enrollment	D Population 5–15	C as percent of D
Malay	238,590 (250,000)	649,410	37 (39)	439,462 (488,000)	805,000	54 (61)
Chinese	202,769 (240,000)	522,346	39 (46)	392,244 (536,000)	641,019	61 (83)
Indian	38,743 (50,000)	126,911	31 (39)	48,821 (97,000)	165,050	29 (59)
English	62,266	—	—	242,171	—	—
Total	547,370	1,298,667	42	1,122,710	1,633,865	69

SOURCES: 1949 enrollment: Federation of Malaya Annual Report, 1949, pp. 84 ff. 1957 enrollment: Federation of Malaya Annual Report on Education for 1957, pp. 60–64. This is the last annual report on education issued by the Ministry. The figures in parentheses include an estimate of the students by ethnic group in English schools. The estimate used for both years was 60 percent Chinese, 20 percent Malay, and 20 percent Indian.

of the school system between 1947 and 1957. This table must be used with caution. Note that the left-hand column is schools, not the ethnic background of the students. The great majority of the children in Malay schools are Malays, but not all of them; the same provisions apply to the other groups as well. All three ethnic groups are represented in the English schools, estimated at 60 percent Chinese, 20 percent Malays, and 20 percent Indians—at best only a rough approximation. The enrollment includes all students at all levels and is not drawn only from the age group 5 to 15 years. That age group is used merely as a ratio base to give some idea of the magnitude of the problem and the extent to which it is being met.

All ethnic groups have approximately doubled their numbers in school, though the numbers in the 5 to 15 age group have increased by only about 25 percent. English schools are still probably the most national of all schools, though they were not by any means as exclusively national in 1957 as they were in 1947. At the earlier date these exclusively national schools contained only about 10 percent of students. At the later date, when the other schools were being reoriented in a national direction, the English schools had about 25 percent of all students.

Again, these are only objective indicators, though they undoubtedly have more political and social impact on the plural society than do the pure demographic indicators. The policy changes manifested in the Razak Report do in fact represent the political implications of the national plural society. They represent government's awareness of the ethnic divisions as a threat to the existence of the state. In addition, they represent an attempt to create a national consciousness through the major socializing instrument of the state, its school system.

Although it is true that a crucial problem for a plural society is the way one group defines another, it is more important to note the political implications of whatever definitions exist. These are far more important than the intensity with which the divisive definitions are held, though the two are probably not unrelated. In the education policy can be seen a clear indication of government's determination to create a national consciousness, even in the face of powerful and contrary ethnic sentiments. The education policy did provide a point of focus for opposition groups both within the Alliance Party and outside of it. Those within the Party were ejected and those outside the Party were without influence. In the natural growth of the Alliance Party one sees an effective accommodating mechanism for a plural society in a modern national state. This accommodation worked because the party has always made maximum efforts to resolve any issue defined in the party as a "communal issue." [33] The education issue was one of the most severe and open of the communal issues of the emerging system. Nonetheless it was resolved in a national rather than a

[33] See Margaret Clark, *The Malayan Alliance and Its Accommodation of Communal Pressures, 1952–1962, passim.*

communal direction, despite the existence in the Alliance of strong demands to the contrary. This resolution, then, reflects some of the political implications of the divisive, ethnic definitions in Malaya's plural society. It can be argued that government policy is such as to minimize the divisiveness of those definitions. In part this is done by defining communal sentiments as illegitimate and not allowing them a full and open hearing.[34] In part this is done by compromise and bargaining, as each of the three main communal sentiments are represented in the Alliance executive committee. Thus government's insistence upon maintaining a viable national state encompassing a plural society is the most important key to the political implications of that plural society.

This account is by no means exhaustive. It has been possible to do no more than to suggest what now appear to be the major characteristics of the new social system that is still in the process of formation in Malaya. The dependent polity was brought to an end largely as the result of forces exogenous to the system. Its place was taken by a state, still in the process of formation, that is best described as an independent parliamentary democratic polity. The political and military forces operating in Malaya in the post-war period were such as to strengthen the commitment of Malayan leaders to an open parliamentary system. This, they found, could bring them the most rapid control over their own affairs, a discovery that was reinforced by the failure of violence to achieve the same ends.

With this major political change, the economy and the society of the old colonial system became increasingly untenable. With Malayan labor and Malayan consumers represented in the centers of decision-making, there has been a demand for an economy that can provide a better and more secure life for the indigenous population. This is essentially a demand for a modern industrial economy oriented more strongly than was the colonial economy to the indigenous laborer and consumer. Though the data on the emerging economy are incomplete and only suggestive, they do point to the development of characteristics that will be functionally attuned to the independent parliamentary state.

The political change also made the old ethnic plural society untenable. A modern national state is based upon a degree of consensus that cuts across major ethnic or regional lines and sees in the state a major point of reference, a major sense of identity, a major focus of loyalty, and a major arbiter of conflict. As with the economic change,

[34] The rules of order of the Dewan Ra'ayat, or House of Representatives, forbid any member to make any statements that might arouse communal sentiments.

the social changes of the new Malayan nation can be seen only vaguely in the scant data available. Yet these, too, point to the untenability of the ethnic plural character of the society and to the emergence of a national, plural rather than totalitarian, society.

It is not the argument of this chapter that this new system has already emerged with firm characteristics. Rather, it has been the aim to draw attention to those elements of the old system that became centers of serious strain in the new polity. We have also tried to suggest the major directions in which the social system is moving, given the rather limited objective data that are available.

The remainder of this study will be taken up with an analysis of one major pattern of the new changes, the attempt to stimulate economic development with complex organizations. Since this pattern of change is at the center of the political process, generated by the new organs of the new state, it illuminates some of the major forms of adjustment involved in the alignment of the economy and society with the new state. That is, this large-scale attempt to use the central administration to stimulate economic development provides a clear view of some of the major points at which the old economy and society experienced severe strains, and the specific mechanisms of adjustment that have been fashioned to relieve those strains. It will show how closely articulated with the still emerging polity are the adjustive forces in the economy and society. The economic and social changes reflected in this study of complex organizations and economic development in a new state are *functions* of the new polity. They are not simply effects of the political change, that then may react on further political change. They are seen here in a fully functional, or synchronic sense. The major political change was *accompanied* by at least forces for change in the economy and the society, and as these forces of change manifested themselves, they were accompanied by further changes in the polity. We shall attempt to show this in some detail in the main body of this study.

APPENDIX TABLE III-I

ETHNIC COMPOSITION AND INDEX OF ETHNIC CONCENTRATION IN SELECTED MALAYAN INDUSTRIAL CATEGORIES, 1947 AND 1957

Categories		Malays	1947 Chinese	Indians	Total (000)	Malays	1957 Chinese	Indians	Total (000)
Total Labor Force	%	44	40	15	(1461.7)	47	36	15	(1635.1)
Peasant agriculture	%	70	27	13	(508.0)	78	19	1	(413.0)
	d	*26*	*13*	*2*	*41*	*31*	*17*	*14*	*62*
Plantation agriculture	%	39	33	27	(381.0)	48	28	23	(430.0)
	d	*5*	*6*	*12*	*23*	*1*	*12*	*8*	*21*
Mining	%	14	71	14	(39.4)	22	62	13	(49.0)
	d	*30*	*31*	*1*	*62*	*25*	*26*	*2*	*53*
Manufacturing Utilities, Construction	%	19	71	6	(124.8)	23	61	13	(186.9)
	d	*25*	*31*	*9*	*65*	*24*	*25*	*2*	*51*
Tertiary total	%	27	48	23	(409.2)	33	42	18	(540.9)
	d	*17*	*8*	*8*	*33*	*14*	*6*	*3*	*23*
Commerce	%	13	70	16	(156.1)	14	66	18	(176.6)
	d	*31*	*30*	*1*	*62*	*33*	*30*	*3*	*66*
Transport	%	29	44	24	(59.2)	36	39	22	(73.3)
	d	*13*	*4*	*9*	*26*	*13*	*3*	*7*	*23*
Services	%	38	33	28	(188.3)	44	28	17	(258.7)
	d	*6*	*7*	*13*	*26*	*3*	*8*	*2*	*13*
Government	%	54	11	30	(104.9)	61	18	16	(181.4)
	d	*10*	*29*	*15*	*54*	*14*	*18*	*1*	*33*

NOTES: *d* is the difference, without sign, between each ethnic group's proportion of a given industry and its proportion of total labor force. The total of the three values of *d* for each industry is the single index of ethnic concentration in that industry. The index numbers are shown in italics.

Absolute figures are shown in the total column for the entire labor force and for each industry. In some cases the exclusion of Europeans and others makes the total of the three ethnic groups as much as 5 percentage points below 100 percent.

Data are taken from the 1947 census, table 78, pp. 443–5; and from the 1957 census, Vol. 14, table 11, pp. 102–110. Table 6.5, p. 31 of Vol. 14 shows a comparison of the 1947 and 1957 industrial distribution of the population. As these categories have been adjusted to be comparable, it would have been preferable to use that table. However it was not detailed by ethnic origin, thus it could not be used for this analysis. In addition, a discrepancy makes table 6.5 somewhat suspect. This table understates the 1957 labor force by 40,000: 33,000 males and 7,000 females. Compared with table 6.5, the figures we have used here are almost identical for both agricultural categories and for mining. For other categories, the differences are somewhat larger. Our figures are 6 percent higher for manufacturing, 10 percent lower for both commerce and transportation, and 5 percent lower for services. If these discrepancies are not ethnically biased, however, they will not affect this analysis at all. We were unable to determine the source of the discrepancies.

APPENDIX TABLE III-II

ETHNIC COMPOSITION AND INDICES OF ETHNIC CONCENTRATION IN URBAN AREAS
(Total population)

1947 Places of		Malays	Chinese	Indians	Total
1,000+	N (000)	a	a	a	1,301
	%	21	62	14	100
	d	31	25	4	56
10,000+	N (000)	a	a	a	907
	%	19	63	15	100
	d	31	25	4	60
Total population	N (000)	2,428	1,885	531	4,908
	%	50	38	11	100
1957 Places of					
1,000+	N (000)	604	1,704	286	2,668
	%	23	64	11	100
	d	27	27	0	54
10,000+	N (000)	a	a	a	1,646
	%	21	63	13	100
	d	29	26	2	57
Total population	N (000)	3,125	2,334	707	6,279
	%	50	37	11	100

SOURCE: *1957 Population Census*, Vol. 14, pp. 5 ff.
a Indicates that absolute figures were not given in the census publication. Percentages were given and can be used to calculate the absolute numbers, but only to the nearest hundreds.

APPENDIX TABLE III-III

Ethnic Composition and Indices of Ethnic Concentration in the States

(Total population)

State		1947 Total (000)	Malays	Chinese	Indians	1957 Total (000)	Malays	Chinese	Indians
Negri Sembilan	N (000)	268				364			
	%	100	41	43	14	100	42	41	15
	d	16	8	5	3	16	8	4	4
Selangor	N (000)	711				1,013			
	%	100	26	51	20	100	29	48	20
	d	45	23	13	9	41	21	11	9
Perak	N (000)	954				1,221			
	%	100	38	47	15	100	40	44	15
	d	24	11	9	4	21	10	7	4
Pahang	N (000)	250				313			
	%	100	54	39	6	100	57	35	7
	d	11	5	1	5	13	7	2	4
Malacca	N (000)	239				291			
	%	100	50	40	8	100	50	42	8
	d	6	1	2	3	8	0	5	3

(Continued on next page)

APPENDIX TABLE III-III (Continued)

ETHNIC COMPOSITION AND INDICES OF ETHNIC CONCENTRATION IN THE STATES
(Total population)

State		1947				1957			
		Total (000)	Malays	Chinese	Indians	Total (000)	Malays	Chinese	Indians
Penang	N (000)	446				572			
	%	100	31	55	13	100	29	57	12
	d	47	18	27	2	42	21	20	1
Johore	N (000)	738				927			
	%	100	50	38	11	100	50	37	11
	d	1	1	0	0	0	0	0	0
Kedah	N (000)	554				702			
	%	100	68	21	9	100	68	21	10
	d	38	19	17	2	35	18	16	1
Perlis	N (000)	70				91			
	%	100	78	17	2	100	78	17	2
	d	59	29	21	9	57	28	20	9
Kelantan	N (000)	449				506			
	%	100	92	5	1	100	92	6	1
	d	86	43	33	10	83	42	31	10
Trengganu	N (000)	226				278			
	%	100	92	7	1	100	92	7	1
	d	84	43	31	10	82	42	30	10
Total population	N (000)	4,908				6,279			
	%	100	49	38	11	100	50	37	11

SOURCE: *1957 Population Census*, Vol. 14, p. 3.

APPENDIX TABLE III-IV

ETHNIC COMPOSITION AND INDICES OF ETHNIC CONCENTRATION IN LITERACY
(Malayan males, ages 15 and over)

1947 Literate in:		Malays[a]	Chinese	Indians	Total[b]
Malay	N (000)	335[c]	8	6	352[c]
	%	95	2	2	100
	d	51	39	12	102
English	N (000)	26	44	26	103
	%	25	43	25	100
	d	19	2	11	32
Any language	N (000)	342	410	132	903
	%	38	45	15	100
	d	6	4	1	11
Total males	(000)	696	644	221	1,585
15 years +	%	44	41	14	100

1957 Literate in:					
Malay	N (000)	514	24	12	559
	%	92	4	2	100
	d	45	33	12	90
English	N (000)	57	86	45	225
	%	26	39	20	100
	d	21	2	6	29
Any language	N (000)	515	471	171	1,204
	%	43	39	14	100
	d	4	2	0	6
Total males	(000)	855	676	248	1,834
15 years +	%	47	37	14	100

[a] Includes "Other Malaysians" in the 1947 census. In the 1957 census Malays and Other Malaysians are grouped together as Malaysians.

[b] Includes "Others," not shown in this table.

[c] The 1947 census does not give literacy rates in Malay for Malays and Other Malaysians. We have here assumed that almost all Malays and Malaysians who are literate in any language are literate in Malay. The 342,000 literate in any language has been rounded downward to 335,000 to eliminate possible cases of Malays literate only in another language than Malay. The total non-Malaysians literate in Malay was 17,000, giving a grand total of 352,000 persons literate in Malay.

SOURCES: 1947 data from the 1947 Census, tables 52–69. 1957 data from the 1957 Census, Vol. 14, table 9.

IV

FROM CUSTODY TO DEVELOPMENT: GOAL CHANGES IN THE GOVERNMENT OF MALAYA

The goals of government in Malaya can best be understood by analyzing the change of goals as Malaya moved from dependent to independent status. This is more than an analytical convenience. To a large extent the goals of the new independent government are a reaction to specific elements in the goal structure of the old colonial government. Goal change is inherent in the nationalist argument, providing distinctiveness and legitimacy to the new indigenous leaders. In addition, the analysis of goal change provides an understanding of the subtle play of forces, of argument, conflict, interest articulation, and accommodation, that are the dynamic elements of a new independent polity. It is important to gain some understanding of these dynamic elements if we are to understand the role the new development organizations of the new government play in the larger pattern of social change experienced by the emerging social system.

Identification of the goals of government presents certain problems. A problem common to goal identification in any organization is the fact that public or stated goals are often different from actual or operative goals. The former can be identified in public policy statements, the latter in allocations of personnel and financial resources. Although the operative goals reflect what the organization is actually doing, we do not argue that they are more important than the public goals. It is necessary to analyze both. Public goals are often important indicators of the general world views of the organization's elites, and they also reflect in part the organization's adjustment to its external environment. Both are important in determining the organization's selection of means appropriate to goal achievement and therefore affect the content of the operative goals as well.

Second, identifying the goals of government is a somewhat special problem because governments tend to carry all types of goals: order must be maintained, certain goods and services are produced, and new entrants into the society must be socialized. In the modern state, specialized organizations are generally created to achieve these specific goals. The problem, therefore, is not determining what are the goals of government, but which goals are dominant.

Finally, the complexity and the long-term nature of the goal structure of governments make it necessary to distinguish between broad long-term goals and more specific, often short-term, goals. The broad goal of maintaining order over the long run may be subverted by an immediate campaign quelling disorder in a fashion so repressive as to create the basis for a more general rebellion. The achievement of broad economic goals may be subverted by limited programs that obstruct an over-all increase in human productivity. And establishing new and more effective mechanisms of culture transmission may well destroy the culture being transmitted. The revolutionary result of education programs is a phenomenon experienced by almost every colonial power.

Thus in this chapter we shall attempt to identify the change in broad, long-term, dominant goals of government. The next chapter will identify the specific and more short-term goals of the specialized development organizations established in the process of changing its broader goals.

In the decade of the 1950's, as Malaya achieved independence, the goals of government changed from *custody* to *development,* or from a dominance of order goals to a dominance of output and cultural goals. This broad change in the general orientation of government and its leaders resulted primarily from the emergence of new men of power. The over-all change in orientation included five specific changes:

1. There was a change from an emphasis on a balanced budget to an emphasis on an expanding economy.
2. There was a change from an unstated emphasis on urban development, or development for the modern sector, to a stated and actual emphasis on rural development, or development largely for the uplift of the Malays in the traditional sector.
3. Social services, especially education, moved from a position of

low priority to one of high priority, and were partially redefined
as elements of investment rather than consumption.

4. There was an increased demand for, and finally the creation of,
   new organizations competent to plan for and stimulate the development of the economy.

5. There was a change in the character of protest from *nationalism*
   and *communalism* to *communalism* and *class interest*.

These changes can best be seen in government's major forum, the
Legislative Council of the Colonial Government, and the House of
Representatives (*Dewan Rayaat*) of the Independent Government.
Speeches and public statements, especially those concerned with the
allocation of resources, the budget, identify both the public goals of
government and the general theories or world views that dictated
means to achieve these goals. In addition, the actual allocation of
financial resources, in the budgets and development plans, identify the
actual goals of government.

FROM A BALANCED BUDGET TO AN EXPANDING ECONOMY

In the budget speeches of Financial Secretaries and Finance Ministers,
one sees clearly a change in public goals. In the first half of the decade
the Financial Secretaries constantly emphasized the government's
commitment to balancing the budget. In every year but one, 1952,
government estimated a deficit, but it was always careful to state its
commitment to balancing the budget. Deficits were required by the
exigencies of the Emergency. The largest deficit was for 1954, estimated
at M$ 222 million (the realized deficit for that year was actually only
M$ 92 million). Of that deficit, M$ 200 was occasioned by the heavy
requirements of the Emergency. As in other years, government apolo-
gized for the deficit, arguing that without the demands of the Emergency it would be possible to achieve a balanced budget.

Even in 1955, when the economic and military situation was easing
and government planned for a deficit of M$ 149 million (but realized
a surplus of M$ 65 million), it defined the road ahead as the "battle
of the gap." The battle would be to match increases in government
services with increases in government revenues. The 1955 budget, the
Finance Secretary claimed, was a step in the direction of closing that
gap, but it was a long hard road, which "every right thinking man
must appreciate."

The first three budget speeches for the decade were very brief, each being less than 1,000 words, and were presented before a Legislative Council that was only beginning to be a forum for the discussion of resource allocation. A more lengthy statement of the budget was presented to the newspapers for publication before the budget sessions: government was making its statements to the general public, not to the body that would theoretically pass upon its decisions. In 1953 the Finance Secretary began the policy of making a lengthy budget speech, which was then followed by a full-dress debate on Government's decisions. This was in accord with the general process of political development in Malaya, in which institutions of the modern independent state were being fashioned.

Almost immediately upon taking control of the Legislative Council in 1955, the indigenous leaders began to emphasize new goals in their budget speeches. The first of these speeches was made in 1956 for the budget of 1957[1] by the new Finance Minister, Col. H. S. Lee of the Malayan Chinese Association. Lee argued that this budget was designed to carry out the Alliance manifesto. "In that manifesto we set ourselves two pillars of economic and financial policy, namely a basically sound economy and a balanced budget. We have based our plans on an expanding economy. In order to achieve it, we accept for the time being the deferment of our second aim. We are budgeting for a deficit in 1957."[2]

He argued further that the deficit planned was not a deliberate policy but was based upon the policy of achieving an expanding economy. For this public investment was required. Further, the balance at which Lee aimed was not a yearly balance, but a balance over the trade cycle, a balance that "will give us a surplus in the good years to offset the deficits which may still arise when the state of our trade is unfavorable to us."[3]

For the following years to the end of the decade, and beyond, the Finance Ministers, H. S. Lee, and Tan Siew Sin from 1959, made the same appeal. An expanding economy was more important than balancing the budget.

The budget debates also reflect this change in public goals, but they

---

[1] The speech presenting the 1956 budget was made by the outgoing British Finance Secretary for the indigenous government, which had been elected to power only three months previously. The budget was titled a temporary standstill budget made to fill the time it would take for the new government to translate its policies into budgetary directives.

[2] Proceedings of the Legislative Council (hereinafter referred to as *Proceedings* for both the colonial Legislative Council and the independent Dewan Raayat or lower house), 7 November 1956.

[3] *Ibid.*

provide an additional insight into the subtle changes that lay behind that change with the emergence of indigenous Finance Ministers. Both governments found substantial support for their goals in the legislative body, but the extent and character of dissent changed radically.

In the early part of the decade the European unofficial members of the Council led the attack on deficit financing with studied eloquence. They supported the goal of a balanced budget and constantly criticized the deficits, government's irresponsibility and lack of reality. In discussion of the great deficit budget for 1954 (M$ 222 million planned deficit), Mr. J. C. Mathison led the attack with great vigor.[4] The budget represented financial suicide. The Emergency could not be blamed, for it accounted for only M$ 200 million of the planned M$ 222 million deficit. Government had not learned the lesson of taking care of the pennies and letting the dollars take care of themselves. The country needed development, but this required primarily the influx of capital from abroad. The only way to stimulate this influx was to balance the budget, maintain financial stability, and refrain from engaging in threats of increased taxation. Following this attack the budget was accepted, but only after Mathison recorded what appears to have been the only formally dissenting vote on a budget during the entire decade.

Mathison's attack was followed by others, but the line of attack shows considerable difference between European and indigenous members. Of the eight European members, three took part in this debate. All three argued strongly against the deficit. Of the 39 indigenous members 24 took part in the debate, and of these 14 argued against the budget; 10 argued essentially for an increase in government services or for a change in allocation patterns. Even the 14 antideficit debaters differed from the Europeans in their attack. They followed the Europeans in demanding financial responsibility, but differed in the means to this end. The European members argued only in a general way that economies could be effected, but the indigenous members made more specific suggestions. They saw the possibility of effecting economies by getting rid of high-salaried expatriate government officers, with their home leaves and expensive houses with parquet flooring, and staffing more of the administration with local people.

Of the indigenous members who debated without attacking the deficit, the most sophisticated arguments came from Dato (now Tun) Abdul Razak and Tan Siew Sin. Razak argued that it was proper that government services be extended. Attention should certainly be paid to costs, but it was more important to extend services to the rural areas and to increase the total productivity of the nation. Tan Siew Sin

---

[4] *Ibid.*, 26 November 1953.

supported Razak's argument, and demanded more assistance to rubber replanting, but he also argued that some expenditures should be curtailed during the current slump.

The new indigenous government planned deficits for every year from 1956 through 1960 to stimulate development through public investment. During this period no criticism was raised in the legislature against the deficit budgeting. Even the European members, who remained in the legislature through the independence of 1957 until the first fully independent elections of 1959, voiced only support for the new government. Cognizant of the extremes to which nationalist sentiment could carry a new nation, they were not anxious to rouse such sentiments. Even more, they could be thankful—the collective sigh was almost audible—that the new government showed such responsibility and rational commitment to public investment as it did.

A simple but very significant change in the organization of development financing is also revealing of the change in government goals. Until early 1958 development loans had to be authorized by the legislature in specific bills that included a schedule of projects, and their costs, for which loan monies were to be spent. Thus the utilization of the funds was fixed by law before the loan could be sought on the money market. On 30 April 1958 the Finance Minister, H. S. Lee, introduced the Federation of Malaya Development Fund Bill. This established a development fund into which monies from various sources could be placed, including budget surpluses and borrowed funds. Money could be taken from this fund for any development projects approved by the legislature. This would make development financing more flexible and would give the legislature greater control over development expenditures. Lee's closing remarks on this bill are worth quoting at length.

The changes for which this bill provides are changes in *methods* of financing development expenditure. But they have a wider context. They imply in the dispensation with detailed loan schedules, a major break-away from financial practices of dependent territories, and they will provide flexibility in the use of funds, subject always to control of the House, which practical necessity and sovereign status alike require. They will not in themselves make more or less money available for development in the Federation. But insofar as they demonstrate that this Government is taking necessary and proper measures to regulate its arrangements *for the use of development finance* they assist in maintaining conditions favorable to investment of such finances in the Federation, an objective which, as the House is aware, is and will remain a cardinal principle of our policy.[5]

---

[5] *Ibid.*, 30 April 1958 (my italics).

Finally, in the movement of the national debt we can see part of the congruence of public and operative goal change in the two governments. In 1950 the total public debt of the Federation of Malaya was M$ 289.3 million. In 1961 it had reached M$ 1.6 billion, more than a fivefold increase. The sharpest periods of growth were in 1951 to 1954, when the debt grew by 133 percent, from M$ 305.6 million to M$ 706.9 million, and 1957 to 1961, when the debt grew by 62 percent, from M$ 976.5 million to M$ 1.6 billion. In the first half of the decade the debt was consistently slightly less than the actual yearly Federal revenues. In the second half of the decade it was consistently about 30 percent higher than actual yearly Federal revenues.

The composition of the debt also changed significantly during this period. Table IV-1 shows long-term domestic debt and external debt

TABLE IV-1

Long-Term Domestic Debt and External Debt in the Total Public Debt of the Federation of Malaya, 1946 to 1961

(in percent)

	1946	1947	1948	1949	1950	1951	1952	1953	1954	1955	1956	1957	1958	1959	1960	1961
Domestic	63	66	66	49	45	47	44	50	45	48	39	52	53	58	58	61
External	31	25	24	43	30	38	28	25	34	38	36	32	28	26	25	24

SOURCE: See Statistical Appendix, Table IV-VI.

as changing proportions of the total debt. In the first half of the decade both categories fluctuate somewhat erratically. In the second half a clearer pattern emerges in the increasing proportion of the debt provided by domestic sources.

While publicly committed to balancing the budget, the colonial government was willing to increase the national debt for the purpose of prosecuting the Emergency. This it did in a rather erratic and *ad hoc* manner. The independent government was committed to stimulating development, it was willing to mortgage the future of the country for that development, and at the same time it was increasingly mobilizing local resources to finance that development.

In the budget speeches, changes in the national debt, and fiscal policies for controlling development expenditure and in the public debates around these issues can be seen a consistent picture of the

changing goals of the Malayan government. The change largely re-
volved around independence, and resulted primarily from the emergence of new men of power. The colonial Finance Secretaries displayed
a commitment to a balanced budget that bordered on the religious.
It was more than a mere means for attaining economic stability; it
was a daily visible symbol of that stability and of fiscal responsibility.
A Finance Secretary who could balance the budget was at least a good
technician. One who could do it in the face of severe economic or
military pressures on the state was more than a competent technician,
he was something of a hero. The Finance Secretary who could realize
surpluses and build up reserves of the state was almost qualified for
sainthood. The state of the total economy mattered little, nor was
there much thought given to the use of reserves, other than that they
were good safeguards for a rainy day. They could be called upon, of
course, during a military emergency; Malaya distinguished itself by
purchasing a cruiser for the British navy during the first world war.
This was a legitimate use of reserves. To deplete them for the building
of schools or for stimulating the growth of the indigenous sectors of
the economy would be considered sheer folly.

At the same time, it cannot be said that the Finance Secretaries did
not desire the development of the Malayan economy. Quite the contrary. They often expressed a strong desire for such development—to
provide more revenues so that social services could be increased. However, their economic theories totally supported their commitment both
to the balanced budget and an expanding economy. They understood
that economic development requires capital investment, and their view
of investment was orthodox and narrow. They also knew that Malaya
was an underdeveloped economy which, by definition, meant that
there was a shortage of local investment capital. Thus development
required the influx of foreign capital, which they saw primarily going
into expansion of primary production. For their part the way to
achieve this influx was to balance the budget, thereby demonstrating
the stability and responsibility of the government, and to keep taxes
low, thereby lowering the costs and raising the incentives for foreign
investors. This meant, of course, that the only economic policy the
country could have would be fiscal policy, with its narrow but rational
year-by-year orientation to government revenues and expenditures.

The new men of power were in substantial disagreement with the
Finance Secretaries on almost all these points. The Finance Ministers
of the independent government wanted economic development, but
they had different ideas as to what this meant and how it was to be

achieved. They saw development as total development of all sectors of
the economy. Where the secretaries and the European members of
Council had often remarked that Malaya would always be an agricultural country, the ministers hoped for the expansion of other types of
economic activities. They thought of industrialization, though not exclusively and not with the same fierce commitment shown in India,
China, or Soviet Russia. Though they agreed in general on the value
of fiscal responsibility, they considered other factors more important in
stimulating development.

The ministers well understood that capital investment was needed
for development, but they took a broader view of that investment and
of investors than did the secretaries. To them investment included
public as well as private investment. The ministers also saw greater
potential in local investors than did the secretaries. They understood
that to attract investors it was necessary to show that the economy was
developing rapidly and that government was committed to a program
of further development. These conditions would draw out the capital
of local investors and induce them to risk their wealth in ventures that
would increase the general wealth of the nation. They realized that
the confidence of the entrepreneur is based not alone on a conservative
fiscal policy and low taxes, but upon a more general atmosphere of
growth and the image of a potential for increasing wealth.

These differences are easily understandable from a sociological point
of view. Whether we examine the general social positions of these two
groups of leaders, their organizational settings, or the political forces
in which they were involved, we can find significant organizational
supports for both the conservatism of the secretaries and the progres-
siveness of the ministers. The secretaries were well-trained bureaucrats.
They occupied social positions totally different from those of the
entrepreneurs, thus they were not able to think like entrepreneurs. In
the bureaucracy they achieved recognition for such things as balancing
the budget, a tidy office, maintaining accountability, and avoiding
uprisings. In their political positions they were insulated from the
masses who might make demands upon government. The desires of the
governed in Malaya had to travel to London and back in order to
pierce the insulation of the bureaucrats. This is not to argue that these
men were thoughtless and insensitive or lacking in a sense of responsibility for the governed. Though the bureaucracy had its share of racists
who could feel more empathy for stray animals than for the "Asians,"
and manifest this in a flurry of activity in forming and supporting such
organizations as the Royal Society for the Prevention of Cruelty to
Animals, it was also well endowed with good human beings. The point

is not one of personalities, but of positions in the social structure. Most of the social forces under which the colonial officer operated supported his commitment to narrow and conservative fiscal policies.

The same forces operated, though in an opposite direction, for the new Ministers of Finance. It need not be argued that they were better or more altruistic men. They were, however, in a complex of social positions that supported their commitment to an expanding economy. In the first place, these men were successful businessmen and politicians rather than bureaucrats. They were the real entrepreneurs, even more so than the ordinary British businessman in Malaya, who has been more of a manager in a large bureaucracy than a real entrepreneur himself. The Finance Ministers and the close core of planners they represented were of families who had come to Malaya with nothing and had amassed great fortunes for themselves by the force of their own diligence, luck, and entrepreneurial skill. Thus their view of the investor who would provide growth forces for the Malayan economy was in large part a self-image. Their positions in the organization were the same. They were heads of successful firms, often based upon extended family ties. They received recognition by making profits, by being successful in business.

Finally, they were politically in a position of great vulnerability to the demands of the masses. They had been elected to office and were part of a party that had been elected to office. To be sure, some of them came from constituencies that were so safe as to make the candidate well insulated from mass demands. Even in these cases, however, the candidate was a part of a party that had to win a majority if the candidate was to gain a position of power.

All of the forces inherent in these social positions tended in the direction of a progressive economic policy. Public investment could provide votes by creating jobs and visible symbols of government's concern for the voter. Development of the total economy meant more profits, more income, for the entrepreneurs as well as for the masses. The existence of a national debt or budgetary deficit was not something that bothered either the voters, or most of the new elite; thus it could be easily accepted.

The wealth of evidence thus points to a radical change in at least the public goals of government. We have also seen some evidence that there was a change in the operative goals as well. Before turning to an analysis of the actual allocation of financial resources for a more complete view of actual goals, we must consider two other basic elements in the Malayan government's goal change: the issue of urban or rural development, and the issue of social services.

FROM URBAN TO RURAL DEVELOPMENT

Much of rural Malaya is urban. The rubber estates and the tin mines are essentially extensions of the modern urban culture. Rural development in Malaya refers primarily to development for the traditional, economically backward, Malay peasant sector.

It should come as no surprise that the colonial government acted more vigorously in the development of this extended urban sector than in the development of the traditional Malay sector.[6] Nor was this really an issue of debate until the post-war nationalist movement began to fashion new aspirations in the new organizations of Malayan life.

The character of the debate over rural development was established at the opening of the new Legislative Council in 1948. In his opening address the British High Commissioner, Sir Henry Gurney, promised that the Government would attend to the needs of the rural people.[7] He was referring at this time to projects the Department of Agriculture had programmed for the following year. From that time onward, throughout the first half of the 1950's, the Government gave constant expression, especially in budget speeches, to its commitment to raise the economic life of the rural peoples. But just as constantly, Government followed these promises with the observation that the Emergency required great resources that otherwise might have gone to rural development. The Emergency, quite naturally, had first priority.

As Malays began to find their voice in the new forum they became increasingly vociferous in their demands for more development in the traditional Malay sectors. And they became increasingly impatient with the apology provided by the requirements of the Emergency.

In every Council session from 1948 on, Malays rose to request more attention to the rural areas. They demanded more roads, more schools, more assistance to cottage and small-scale industry, more attention to the east coast states, more attention to the Malays. The demand was persistent and ubiquitous. In the great deficit budget debate of 1953

---

[6] The colonial government did attempt to stimulate the development of rice cultivation. Whatever the motive for this investment, it was functional for the export economy, as increased local rice production would have contributed to lower food costs and thus to lower labor costs. It is important to note, too, that this was attention to rice production, not attention to the rural sector as a whole. Finally, this attention may have been dysfunctional for the development of the Malay rural sector, for the rice policy aimed at keeping Malays in small-scale traditional rice production and out of the more lucrative rubber industry, often against a decided preference for the latter. See above, pp. 29–31.

[7] *Proceedings*, 21 November 1948.

half of all Malays taking part in the debate, or one-quarter of all debaters, requested more assistance for the rural areas. Even in the first budget debate of the newly elected government, in 1955, nine elected Malay back-benchers took part in the debate and eight asked for more rural development.

Malay impatience with the Emergency apology also mounted in the early years of the 1950's. In the great deficit budget debate of 1953, a Malay member argued, for example, that the large deficit "should not be taken as an excuse to retard the proposed plans for raising the economy of the Malays, especially in the kampongs." [8]

This impatience was spurred by that most divisive of all forces in modern Malaya, racial antagonism. By 1952 the resettlement of Chinese squatters in the New Villages had progressed sufficiently to become a powerful racial issue in the debate on rural development. In the budget debates at the end of 1952, a Malay member gave an almost passionate expression to this issue. He argued that the loyal Malays who were rising up in force to fight the Communist insurgents were being neglected in their *kampongs*. All Government's efforts were bent toward assisting the Chinese in the New Villages. Red tape could be cut in their behalf, to provide them with all the amenities that had always been denied to the Malays in the kampongs. He observed that these amenities could be given to the Chinese with the argument that it was necessary to win their loyalty; the same amenities were denied to the Malays with the argument of insufficient funds. The member ended his speech with the poignant question, "What price loyalty?" [9]

With an elected legislature and with independence the demand for more rural development increased rather than decreased. Their numbers and their positions as elected representatives gave the Malays in the Council increased courage to speak for their cause. They were no longer restrained by the sophisticated and well-turned arguments of the European members supporting a balanced budget.[10] They increased the demand for improvements. They argued that the people expected great things of *Merdeka* (independence) and it would be morally and politically wrong to disappoint them. The expectations were often naive, and often far greater than the Government could possibly have met. Nonetheless, they existed and were given constant expression in this new forum.

---

[8] Tuan Sheikh Ahmad, J. P., unofficial member of the Legislative Council, *Proceedings*, 25 November 1953.

[9] Dato Haji Mohammed Eusoff, *Proceedings*, 20 November 1952.

[10] As we have seen, the European members fell silent after the elections of 1955. In the face of an elected indigenous government, the appointed members withheld the criticism they had bestowed so lavishly upon the colonial government.

Where the colonial government had qualified its promises of rural development with the demands of the Emergency, the new elected government placed its emphasis upon a more unqualified promise of rural development. The Alliance Party manifestos for the 1955 and the 1959 elections promised more for the little man, more for the rural areas, more for the previously neglected Malays, and land for the landless. In 1955 the emphasis upon rural development shared a place with the promise of independence. In 1959 it held top priority.

Organizational growth for the commitment to rural development also reflected the change in government's goals. This will be considered in detail later; here it is sufficient to note the broad pattern of changing emphasis. In 1950 and 1951 the Rural and Industrial Development Authority (RIDA) was formed, giving the first major manifestation of government's increasing concern for rural development. RIDA was small, had a small budget, and was politically almost impotent. In 1956 the Federal Land Development Authority (FLDA) was formed, redeeming the newly elected government's promise to provide land for the landless. FLDA soon became a politically and financially powerful organization. The major move in the direction of increased rural development, however, came in 1959 with the formation of a new Ministry for Rural Development. With the Deputy Prime Minister as its head, the new ministry brought the commitment to rural development to the center of the state. In general we see here an increasing organizational commitment to rural development that paralleled the general development of public goals.

THE CHANGING PRIORITY OF SOCIAL SERVICES

The colonial government displayed an ambivalent attitude toward education, health, and welfare. On the one hand these services had some intrinsic value, and in any event were considered the proper responsibility of a beneficent, if paternalistic, government. In addition education and health had some instrumental value. Education could produce clerks for the bureaucracy, thus reducing the costs of local administration. Health was earlier and more clearly seen as instrumental, since the control of infectious disease was useful to the plantation economy and made life more pleasant for the civil servants. Mosquito and malaria control were among the earliest and most common activities of the colonial government, though local leaders may not have agreed with the pace and areal specialization of these activities.

On the other hand, such social services were largely considered a cost to the economy. They gave no direct returns as did mines and plantations. When economic development became a major public goal in the post-war period, social services were accorded a low priority. Economic development required *investment*, whereas social services— health and education—were defined as items of *consumption*. Malaya's federal accounts were, in addition, divided into broad categories of *economic*, including agriculture, public works, and the like, and *social*, including education, health, and welfare.

Thus, conceptually the stage was set. If economic development were the goal, consumption in social services would have to be retarded in favor of investment in economic sectors. This would increase total productivity, income, and revenues, thus enabling both the government and the economy to pay for the desired increase in social services. Finance secretaries and European members of council often expressed the view, along with criticisms of deficit financing, that education was certainly of value, but the country could have only as much of it as it could afford.

The colonial government began to change its definition of education as a result of the Emergency. In 1951 Lord Lyttleton, Secretary of State for the Colonies for the new Labor Government in England, visited Malaya and announced a new six-point plan for the prosecution of the Emergency. The third point called for an increase in education, including adult education. The aim was to win the war of ideas against Communism. Lyttleton noted that this would be a long-term investment, but that, "even at the beginning the children who go back to their parents from school are living evidence of another way of life set against that which is being whispered to them from the jungle." [11] Even ignoring the fact that this was education primarily for the Chinese, Lyttleton's definition of education as investment was still a means to the maintenance of order.

The Alliance manifesto, with which it contested the 1955 elections, made great promises of increased education for all people, but especially for those—the Malays—who had previously been neglected in this respect. When the Alliance came to power in 1955 it immediately set about redeeming this pledge to the electorate. In the 1955 budget address of the new Chief Minister, Tungku Abdul Rahman, the goal change emerged. The government would have liked to balance the budget, but some things were more important. Education was one. For the following year 8,000 new places would be provided in schools.

[11] *Straits Times*, 12 December 1951.

The government had pressed the Department of Education to do everything possible to achieve this increase, even to building schools with makeshift jungle materials if necessary. The Department indicated that it would not be necessary; existing schools could be used in the afternoons. It would be possible to make room for all children over seven years of age who might otherwise not have had schools available to them.

Almost immediately a powerful new committee, headed by the Deputy Chief Minister, Dato Abdul Razak, was created to provide the new state with a national education policy. The rapid and effective work of the committee enabled the Finance Minister to translate a new educational policy into fiscal directives when he presented a supplementary budget during 1956.

This new budget raised the total planned deficit from M$ 50 million to M$ 146 million. The Finance Minister observed that this could not continue, but it was currently necessary to provide for the economic development the country needed. He noted that a large part of the supplementary estimate was for education (M$ 21 million), arguing that it was vitally necessary for the schools to increase their output of technicians and administrators needed for the country's growth. Thus, in the Minister's first opportunity to present a coherent statement of the new government's fiscal policy, he defined education as an item of investment for economic development.

In the debate the supplementary budget was accepted without criticism and acclaim was given the estimates for education. Earlier in the year the Razak report on education had been debated in Council. This, too, met with universal acclaim and an expressed recognition of the need for more education. There was no talk of economizing, no suggestion that the country was spending more than it could afford. Even the European members who had previously argued against expenditures on education either remained silent or praised the diligent and rational work of the Razak committee and the new Minister of Education. The debates and policy statements since 1956 have not changed this picture of new priorities and new definitions for social services.

Health and social welfare have been of less public importance than education, both because they have constituted less of a popular demand and because they have not contained the divisive ethnic issue that attached to education. Nonetheless, though less dramatic, the changes in goals and priorities have been roughly similar to the changes in education.

THE ORGANIZATION OF PLANNING
AND COORDINATION

The change in public goals was accompanied by a change in the organization structure for the planning and coordination of development. As did the other changes, this emerged first as a voice of protest in the colonial Legislative Council and was later manifest in actual change under the independent government.

In the early part of the decade there was an undercurrent of dissatisfaction with the way government was expressing its concern for economic development. Various indigenous councillors rose to request new forms of planning and coordinating agencies. Officials in Council normally answered these requests with observations that things were well as they were.

Typical of this type of exchange was a discussion in March 1954.[12] An indigenous councillor, Mr. Heah, asked for the creation of an Economic Affairs Advisory Committee. Mr. Spencer, the Economic Adviser, answered that there were already sufficient committees for this purpose and he was hesitant to add another. Heah persisted, noting that such a committee would help the officials to come in closer touch with public opinion, would provide for the "formation of long-term plans for the public benefit," and for the "solution to many problems of an over-all basis." Spencer resisted the suggestion that he was not close to public opinion or that current plans were not for the public benefit, and observed that Mr. Heah's suggestion was too vague to be acted upon and could be more appropriately discussed privately.

Other similar requests appeared constantly—for long-term planning, for collecting data on resources and on the economic condition of the people, and for coordinating existing development services. Although enthusiastic about planning, the councillors were uninformed of the magnitude and complexity of the tasks they wished accomplished. However, they did demonstrate a highly appropriate criticism of the state of the economy and government's acceptance of responsibility for changing the economy. Official reaction was that of a government concerned with balancing the budget and prosecuting the Emergency. It was neither sympathetic to the dissatisfactions of the councillors, nor was it willing to understand what the councillors wanted.

Official reactions in Council were not, however, the whole story. While the officials were chafing at the unsophisticated criticism of

---

[12] *Proceedings*, "Oral Answers to Questions," 31 March 1954.

indigenous councillors, they were also drifting toward a more rational organization for development planning. Significantly, much of the impetus for this drift came from outside Malaya. One could be impervious to local demands, but one could scarcely oppose the ground swell of interest in economic development that was encompassing the world, especially given its intellectual pedigree registered in British centers of learning. Nor could one be impervious to the external funds made available for development plans.

In 1950 the colonial government created an Office of the Economic Advisor to the High Commissioner. Technically directly under the High Commissioner, this office was actually subordinated to the Financial Secretary. Further, its primary concern was for trade; economic development was added almost as an afterthought. Trade, with its well-organized reporting services and good statistics, would certainly have been the dominant concern of the Office but for the necessity of creating a development plan in response to information that Malaya could receive approximately £ 5 million for economic development through the United Kingdom's Colonial Development and Welfare Act. The impetus resulted in the first plan for Malayan economic development, a draft development plan drawn up in 1949–1950 and revised in 1952.[13] This was no more than a hurried compilation of departmental projects, which even included some major projects for which firm estimates were not then complete. The latter were included in the 1952 revision.

This impetus for development planning was largely vitiated, however, by the exigencies of the Emergency. Financial and human resources were fully committed to the war and could not be lavished on attempts to change the economy.

This need not have been so. It was the result of an unbalanced development of leadership. Local leadership was competent in political organization: it could mobilize mass following, build local organizations to deliver the vote, and argue persuasively for greater indigenous control. Far from retarding this political development, the Emergency probably facilitated and hastened it, but only because there existed local leadership with the competence to formulate political goals and to design means appropriate to the achievement of those goals. Such leadership in economic affairs was lacking, largely because of the lack of higher education in Malaya and the consequent lack of economists

---

[13] Federation of Malaya, Office of the Member for Economic Affairs, The Treasury, *Progress Report on the Development Plan of the Federation of Malaya 1950–1952,* Kuala Lumpur, 1953, *passim.* This contains the only record I have been able to obtain of the plan prepared in 1949–1950.

with both professional competence and social vision. That independence and not economic planning was achieved, despite popular sentiment in support of both, argues that the critical variable in translating popular sentiment into effective policy was leadership with specific competence.

Under the popularly elected government in 1956 a new Economic Advisory Committee to the Cabinet was formed with a Secretariat headed by the former Economic Adviser, Mr. Spender. This specialized organization was asked to draw up the First Five-Year Plan for scheduled talks with the government of the United Kingdom on financing development in Malaya.[14]

The external stimulus for planning in the early period is clear in the financing procedures as well as in the formal instructions carried out. The 1950 Draft Plan envisaged that about 75 percent of the capital would come from abroad, leaving only 25 percent for domestic financing. The 1952 revision was silent on the source of financing, but the planners apparently counted on about the same ratio of foreign to domestic capital. By 1956 this orientation changed considerably—the First Five-Year Plan envisaged that roughly 80 percent of capital requirements could be met from domestic sources.[15] The Second Five-Year Plan looked to domestic sources to provide about 60 percent of the capital requirements in the public sector and about 75 percent in the private sector.[16]

The organizational significance for specialized development planning seen in these changes was manifest in the recession of 1957–1958. The recession brought a conflict between the new Secretariat and the new Finance Minister over who should control development expenditures. Naturally, both claimed legitimate control on grounds of rationality, but their objectives illustrate the organizational impact on values and attitudes. The Finance Minister argued for cutting back development expenditures to conserve resources and reduce the deficit, whereas the Economic Secretary argued for continued development expenditures on the grounds that this was necessary to transform the old export economy into a more productive and modern one. This argument is the more remarkable because it was the indigenous Minister of Finance who argued for retrenchment, after only recently arguing for increased public investment for economic development. The more

---

[14] Federation of Malaya, *Report on Economic Planning in the Federation of Malaya in 1956*, Kuala Lumpur, 1957.

[15] *Ibid.*, Appendix II.

[16] Federation of Malaya, *Second Five-Year Plan, 1961–1965*, Kuala Lumpur, 1961, p. 3.

progressive argument, to increase public investment despite the recession, was made by Dato (previously Mr.) Spencer, who had previously advocated budget balancing.[17]

The Economic Secretariat was the direct forerunner of the current
Economic Planning Unit, headed by a highly competent economist
from the United Nations, and staffed by an increasing number of
qualified local economists.

The problem of coordination has been less one of a shortage of
qualified personnel and more a problem of organizational structure.
The developments in this area are the central concern of the remainder
of this study. Here we need note only the general lines of development.
Specialized development agencies were established in the Rural and
Industrial Development Authority and the Federal Land Development
Authority. This specialization reached its peak in 1959 with the formation of the Ministry of Rural Development, which essentially brought
the high power and the evaluative competence needed to coordinate
existing services and to increase the development-stimulating work of
the bureaucracy.

THE ALLOCATION OF FINANCIAL RESOURCES:
BUDGETS AND DEVELOPMENT PLANS

Policy statements provide a picture of the public or stated goals of an
organization. To gain insight into the actual or operative goals, it is
necessary to analyze the actual allocation of the organization's resources. Financial resources are the most useful for this type of analysis
because they are the least specific, the most generalized, form of resource. Equipment is designed for a special function; human resources
are trained for specific functions, though these may, of course, vary in
their degree of specificity. On the other hand, financial resources can
be used for essentially all functions, and their use can be shifted easily
and rapidly. In addition, financial resources are available in standardized and quantifiable units: two dollars spent for roads is twice as
much as one dollar spent for education. The returns may differ considerably, but the allocation pattern shown is rather unambiguous.

The allocation of Malaya's financial resources is organized primarily
around annual government budgets and longer term development
plans. The latter are centrally constructed and can be used almost
exactly as given in official reports. These are summarized in table IV-4.
Since Malaya is a federated nation, annual budgets are prepared for
both federal and state governments; smaller units are of no real im-

---

[17] Information from personal interviews.

TABLE IV-2

SUMMARY OF PERCENTAGE ALLOCATIONS OF COMBINED ACTUAL FEDERAL, STATE, AND DEVELOPMENT EXPENDITURES. FEDERATION OF MALAYA, 1950–1962

	1950	1951	1952	1953	1954	1955	1956	1957	1958	1959	1960	1961	1962
Total expenditure (M$ 000)	399	614	756	873	810	817	853	928	1106	1077	1133	1380	1658
Percentages:													
Economic	17	18	18	19[a]	17	17	18	15[a]	20[a]	21[a]	20[a]	21	24
Agriculture	2	2	2	2	2	2	2	4	4	3	4	4	4
DID	1	1	1	1	1	1	2 }	1	6	6	4	4	3
C-I	—	—	—	—	—	—	2	1	—	—	1	1	3
RD	—	—	1	1	1	1	1	1	—	—	1	1	3
PWD	14	15	14	16	13	13	13	10	11	11	12	12	14
Social	14	15	15[a]	15	15[a]	17	33	33[a]	20[a]	21[a]	23[a]	22	23
Education	7	8	9	9	11	11	21	22	14	15	16	15	16
Health	7	7	7	6	5	7	12	10	7	7	7	7	7
Combined Economic-Social	31	33	33	34	28	34	53	48	40	36	36	36	40
Military	22	29	27	32	29	26	23	23	20	18	16	16	13
Combined Economic-Social-Military	57	62	60	66	62	60	75	81	61	61	60	59	61

SOURCE: See table IV-I in the Statistical Appendix to this chapter.
[a] Components do not equal totals due to rounding.
Agriculture—includes Fisheries, Forestry.
DID—Drainage and Irrigation Department.
C-I—Commerce and Industry (mostly rubber replanting grants, after 1957).
RD—Rural Development (RIDA, 1952–1957, Ministry of Rural Development 1960 onward).
PWD—Public Works Department.
Military—includes military, police, prisons.

portance. Thus for the annual budgets, it is necessary to combine state
and federal accounts to gain a clear picture of the allocation of the
total resources available to government. Tables IV-2 and IV-3 show
the movement of total actual expenditures, the percentage breakdowns,
and indices of absolute figures by expenditure categories for these
combined budgets in the period 1950 to 1962. The raw data for all
tables appear in the Statistical Appendix to this chapter.

TABLE IV-3

INDICES OF ACTUAL ABSOLUTE EXPENDITURES BY MAJOR CATEGORIES
(1950 = 100; in million Malayan dollars)

Year	Total	Order	Economic	Social
(1950)	(399)	(89)	(63)	(55)
1950	100	100	100	100
1951	154	198	178	164
1952	189	227	214	211
1953	218	310	263	235
1954	203	259	224	231
1955	204	244	214	258
1956	213	221	244	518
1957	232	236	227	556
1958	277	250	365	404
1959	269	221	360	431
1960	283	200	387	480
1961	345	244	444	553
1962	415	247	635	698

See table IV-IV in the Statistical Appendix to this chapter.

The most striking change that these tables show is the rapid increase
in total spending. It grew more than fourfold, from M\$ 399 million in
1950 to M\$ 1,658 million in 1962. The growth was not, however, con-
stant throughout the thirteen years. The rapid growth at the beginning
of the decade brought spending to a peak in 1953. This year was followed by a three-year plateau. In 1956 growth began again and continued moderately until 1958. The next two years showed another
plateau, followed by a period of very rapid growth starting in 1960.

The composition of expenditures also shows a gross change during
the period: proportionate expenditures on Order declined while those
on Economic and Development categories increased. The weighted

TABLE IV-4

MALAYAN DEVELOPMENT PLANS 1950–1960

Sector	1950–1955			1956–1960		1961–1965	
	Plan	Revised plan	Actual	Plan	Actual	Plan	Actual
Total public investment (M$ 000)	214.7	855.9	730	1148.7	1006.7	2150.0	2651.7
Percentages:							
Economic sector	73	89	n.a.	82	83	74	73
Agriculture	7	2	n.a.	17	17	12	9
Drainage and irrigation	13	5	n.a.	5	4	5	4
Land development	1	15	n.a.	1	2	9	5
Transportation, Public works, and Communications	35	36	n.a.	20	23	20	27
Utilities	n.a.	26	n.a.	19	24	19	20
Industry	1	0.2	n.a.	1	1	1	2
General government	n.a.	n.a.	n.a.	12	7	4	6
Social sector	27	10	n.a.	18	14	23	16
Health	8	2	n.a.	4	1	7	4
Education	16	6	n.a.	8	6	12	9
Social welfare	1	1	n.a.	(included in Health)			
Labor	0.5	0.1	n.a.	(included in Health)			
Housing	1	1	n.a.	6	7	4	3
Defense	n.a.	n.a.	n.a.	n.a.	3	4	12

For amounts and notes see table IV-V in the Statistical Appendix to this chapter.

mean of Order expenditures was 28 percent for the first six years, 1950–1955, and 20 percent for the following seven years. For Economic and Social expenditures the weighted mean was 33 percent in the first six years and 39 percent in the last seven.

Indices based on 1950 absolute expenditures to show the relations between growth in total expenditures and changes in the expenditures in major categories are given in table IV-3. In the first period of rapid growth, 1950–1953, all categories of expenditures grew together, with Order showing the most rapid growth. During the plateau of 1954–1956 there were a decline in expenditures on Order, the relative stagnation of expenditures on Development, and the rise of expenditures in Social categories. The second total growth period, 1956–1958, saw the growth of all categories again, with Development growing most rapidly, Order growing only moderately and Social growing rapidly at first, but then cut back rather drastically in the last year. During the

second plateau there was a further decline of Order expenditures, relative stability in Development, and a new spurt of growth in Social
categories. The final spurt of total growth showed rapid increase in
Economic expenditures, substantial but less rapid growth in Social
expenditures, and stagnation in Order expenditures.

The proportionate expenditures in subcategories (table IV-2) help
to specify further the character of the changing composition of resource allocation. Agriculture, Drainage, and Rural Development all
grew moderately from relatively low proportions along with the growth
in the total Economic category of expenditures. The most rapid growth
took place in Commerce and Industry, where expenditures were largely
in the form of grants for replanting and new planting of rubber. Public
Works remained the largest single category of Economic expenditures.
It grew rapidly to the peak year of 1953. After an initial cutback in
both absolute and proportionate expenditures in 1954, Public Works
continued to grow in absolute terms throughout most of the period,
but not until the latter part of the period did it begin to grow again
in proportionate terms.

The over-all growth in Social expenditures was the result of the
growth of absolute expenditures in Health that matched the growth
in total expenditures, and a more rapid growth in Education expenditures. Thus Health maintained a steady proportion around 7 percent,
and Education climbed from 7 and 8 percent to 15 and 16 percent,
with a very large two-year spurt to over 20 percent following the first
federal elections.

Total planned development expenditures in the public sector show
a rapid increase in the three plans covering the period. The ratio of
actual to planned expenditures also shows a constant increase during
that period. The first Draft Plan achieved about 85 percent of actual
to planned expenditures. The First Plan achieved about 88 percent,
and the Second Plan, extending beyond our period, achieved about
123 percent of planned expenditures.

The sectoral distribution of investment shows in the first place a
consistently high emphasis upon Economic investments, taking 70
to 80 percent of planned and actual expenditures throughout. The
level of achievement in these sectors shows some parallel with the
composition of budget expenditures. Transportation, Public Works,
Communication, and Utilities consistently do better than expected,
given the over-all rate of achievement. The Social sector has both a
lower proportion of investment and less success in the achievement of
investment targets. And within this sector, Education fares better than
Health and Social Welfare.

On the whole, this pattern of resource allocation gives firm support to the proposition of goal change in over-all government activity. The change in public goals was followed rather faithfully by the change in operative goals. The colonial government was concerned for order and bent its major efforts to the maintenance of order. The new independent government was concerned with stimulating development and turned its major efforts in that direction. Objections to this analysis can be raised and qualifications to the data must be made. On the whole, however, these are not damaging to the analysis, and even often support it.

In the first place, the expenditures categories used only give a rough approximation of goals. The major inaccuracies, however, actually tend to understate the extent of goal change. For example, public works and land development expenditures under the British were primarily directed toward the creation of military and police installations, the building of strategic roads, and the relocation of Chinese squatters. Under the independent government the same categories of expenditures reflect the construction of rural roads and schools demanded by the voters, and the settlement of landless agriculturalists in new development projects.

In the second place, the Malayan economy is heavily influenced by world market conditions over which the Malayan government has no control. The most significant manifestations of this influence, for this analysis, are the high rubber prices that resulted from the Korean boom early in the decade, and the recession of 1957–1958. We have already seen that all categories of expenditure increased along with the total in the first period of growth, from 1950–1953. Certainly the rapidity of this growth was made possible by the rapid growth of rubber prices. It seems safe to infer, however, that since this was a period of intense military threat, the greatest benefactor of the boom was expenditure for development and social activities. Without the boom, the growth of military expenditures would greatly have outstripped those for development and social ends.

On the other hand, the severe cutback in social and development expenditures as a result of the 1957–1958 recession indicates that the actual commitment to the new goals was not so great as the public commitment. Although the new men of power could accept more easily than their predecessors the principle of deficit financing to stimulate development, they nonetheless reacted almost instinctively (for organizations, not individuals) to the recession by ordering a retrenchment of spending. As Ministers of Finance rather than critics of the colonial government, they could not accept with equanimity the drop

in revenues with the continued increase in expenditures. It is understandable that such a blast of cold air from an inhospitable world
market undermined somewhat the confidence of the new leaders, especially since they had just assumed power. That this was a temporary
condition, one that could be removed with greater experience in operating a modern government, was demonstrated after 1960; though
rubber prices fell, development expenditures skyrocketed.

Finally, one can point out that the colonial government was faced
with a severe test of strength in the insurgency. By the time independence was granted, the insurgency was largely defeated, the military
threat had passed. In addition, the independent government could
continue to count upon strong external assistance for its military
needs. That is, in large part the goal change reflects a simple change
in the objective situation of the state. The colonial government had
to restore order, not only maintain it. The independent government
was granted freedom from such an onerous task.

This objection points to the necessity of seeing not only what freedom and resources exist, but how they are used. Given both the freedom from a military threat and the rich revenues from rubber and
tin, a number of possibilities were opened to the new government. It
could increase its own independent military capacity; it could balance
its budget and increase its reserves; or it could actively stimulate development through public investment. That it chose the latter indicated a goal change.

THE CHANGING CHARACTER OF PROTEST
ARTICULATION

Expressions of protest and conflict associated with the colonial situation and the ethnic diversity of Malaya have appeared in many of the
issues discussed above. It is now useful to focus upon that protest itself
and the manner in which it was articulated to understand better the
social changes that preceded the formation of the Ministry of Rural
Development. The specific relevance of this protest articulation lies
first in the unifying or nation-building functions of the struggle taking
place in government and manifest in the change of goals, and second,
in the rules or shared expectations that emerged during the conflict
and in the direction given to government actions.[18]

Under the colonial government various protests were expressed in a
nationalist form. Malay reaction against the Malayan Union, in defense

---

[18] In the emphasis upon the functional aspects of conflict, this section draws heavily
upon Lewis Coser, *The Functions of Social Conflict*, Glencoe, 1959, *passim*.

of their traditional rulers and their privileged position, took the form of a modern political party capable of protecting its interests in a parliamentary government. This led easily and naturally in a nationalist direction as greater self-rule, then independence, became feasible. From 1948 to 1950 Malayans learned to play the roles of parliamentary critics. Dato Onn's objection to the Loan Bill of 1949 was an example of early nationalist protest against foreign rule.

During the establishment of the Member system, the government coopted the most vocal leaders of the opposition and thus for a time undercut the nationalist protest. Government was even in the enviable position of pressing for parliamentary reforms more rapidly than suited the European appointed members of the Council. Though these members agreed in principle with increased indigenous representation and responsibility, they thought the time unpropitious. They argued that the highest priority should be given to the prosecution of the Emergency and they feared that the introduction of politics into the Council would divert time and resources from that goal.

National sentiments were again given leadership when the Alliance emerged and won elections in 1952 and 1953. The conflict was now between rival indigenous leaders for popular support. Dato Onn's position as a coopted member of Government put the Alliance members in the advantageous position of being able to kill two birds with one stone—the colonial government and their chief rival, Dato Onn himself. The personal, party, and national aspirations of these energetic men could be achieved by the use of nationalist goals.

The sentiments that the Alliance leaders were able to mobilize and capitalize upon at this time were by no means weak and scattered. They were, however, highly varied. Council debates were constantly punctuated with Alliance protests against the higher class, status, and power positions of the foreign rulers and managers.

Even the internally divisive communal and class sentiments could be turned to the support of the nationalist protest as articulated by the Alliance. When Dato Haji Mohammed Eusoff raised his poignant question, "What price loyalty?" in 1952,[19] his anti-Chinese sentiments could be turned against the colonial government that was neglecting loyal Malays while providing for the Chinese. In the same manner the call for rural development was a criticism of the colonial government for neglect of the Malays. The Malayan Chinese Association also expressed ethnic sentiments when it criticized Dato Onn and the government for obstructing its privately organized welfare activities.

One form of class and ethnic sentiment was being expressed violently

---

[19] See above, p. 99.

from the jungle in the insurgency, while another form found a more legitimate outlet in class protests in the Council. Labor leaders could criticize the colonial government for using the insurgency as an excuse for curtailing labor organizations and holding back from labor its legitimate share of profits.

The most important function of this articulation of protest and conflict was to define the essentially national boundaries of the group. It gave the new leaders a unique identity as men of the nation and at least partly overshadowed the more divisive ethnic identities. It served to strengthen the unity of the protesters, and even to create unity where none had previously existed, as in the new Alliance Party. It provided an important safety valve for deep and pervasive protests in the society, some of which had been given expression in the insurgency. Perhaps most important was a more substantive and less analytical function. The protests, many of which were dangerously divisive to the society, were focused upon a conflict which involved only a mild struggle and which was almost certain to end successfully for the new leaders.

The nationalist conflict was successfully resolved in the Federal election of 1955 and in independence in 1957. The time was one of confidence, hope, and the desire for activity. There was an impatience to get on with the job, to see a rapid development and modernization of the new nation.

Even this positive sentiment, however, blew to life the flames of ethnic divisiveness. An elected Councillor, E. T. Lee, rose late in 1956 in a debate on the new budget to present a forceful plea for more rapid development. Overestimating the degree of unity in the Council, and probably in the nation, he observed that the Chinese had developed through hard work; only hard work would produce the growth the nation wanted; the Malays would have to give up their carefree ways and to work hard for the betterment of the nation.

His observation was made in the spirit of brotherly constructive criticism. He even attempted to dredge up nationalist sentiments by referring to the old spoon-feeding of the Malays by the British. To no avail. The observation was essentially an invidious ethnic distinction and was taken as such by the Malays. Raja Musa rose to react:

As a Malay I think it would only be polite that I should refrain myself from expressing unsolicited views on the weaknesses and shortcomings of other races. But I feel that other people, who have been and continue to be guests of the Malays in this country have got every reason to be grateful that we have been peace-loving, hospitable and friendly to everyone. I do not like to say further than that because as a Malay I should not be impolite.[20]

This was one of the very few expressions of Legislative Council conflict between Malay and Chinese. The infrequency of such conflicts should not, however, be taken as an index of unity, but rather as an indication of the precariousness of the new relationship.[21] No one actually knew how well Malays and Chinese would act together in running their own nation. The legislature indicated the precariousness of this new relationship by forbidding any utterance intended to increase or having the effect of increasing communal tensions.

Even before there was a written rule to this effect, there was an unwritten understanding that communal sentiments were not to be expressed in the Legislature. The conflict expressed in the above exchange has thus an additional significance. Like the periodic communal riots that occurred, it served to remind the members that divisive ethnic sentiments had not been exorcised by independence, but had only been given legitimate expression. Now a new and equally effective form of articulation was needed if their energies were to be channeled in a constructive and nonviolent manner. In the manner of one of Simmel's paradoxes of Conflict,[22] this outbreak of ethnic sentiment served to make known the relative power of the divisive sentiments on both sides and thus to provide one requisite for preventing conflict.

The new articulation of sentiments of protest took the form of development activity. The new men of power would use the resources of government to provide more of the good things of life for all Malaya's people. Malay sentiments could be expressed in the demand for more rural development. Chinese sentiments could be assuaged by protecting established economic interests and working out an effective national educational policy. Both were activities in which success was relatively easy to achieve.

Thus on both sides of the colonial situation, the form taken by the articulation of protest fit comfortably with the dynamics of goal change.

---

[20] *Proceedings*, 12 November 1956. It is important to note the value agreement expressed in this exchange. Lee argues that (1) Malays are lazy and improvident, and (2) these values are dysfunctional for economic development. In accepting this as "weakness and shortcomings" of the Malays, Raja Musa was essentially expressing agreement on both points. Here we see the emergent consensus on definitions of the situation on the ethnic frontier.

[21] Coser, *op. cit.*, pp. 81ff.

[22] *Ibid.*, pp. 133 ff.

The new leaders found a means of mobilizing popular sentiments against the custodial goals of the colonial government, which in turn helped to define a new set of goals for the independent government. And those new goals were also supported by and could in turn contain the sentiments of protest that are an inherent part of the society.

STATISTICAL APPENDIX

Tables

IV-I.   Combined Federal, State, and Development Actual Expenditures for Select Categories, Federation of Malaya, 1950–1962

IV-II.   Actual State Expenditures, Federation of Malaya, 1950–1962

IV-III. Actual Federal Development Expenditures, Federation of Malaya, 1957–1962

IV-IV.   Indices for Combined Actual Federal, State, and Development Expenditures by Major Categories, Federation of Malaya, 1950–1962

IV-V.   Planned and Actual Public Investment Under the Development Plans, Federation of Malaya

IV-VI.   National Debt, Federation of Malaya, 1947–1961

APPENDIX TABLE IV-I

Combined Federal, State and Development Actual Expenditures for Select Categories
Federation of Malaya 1950–1962
(in million Malayan dollars)

Categories	1950	1951	1952	1953	1954	1955	1956	1957	1958	1959	1960	1961[a]	1962[b]
Total	399	614	756	873	810	817	853	928	1,106	1,077	1,133	1,380	1,658
Agriculture[c]	7	11	16	16	15	16	20	37	39	37	50	49	65
Drainage and Irrigation	5	7	9	11	11	11	13	7	61	69	50	52	50
Commerce and Industry[d]	—	—	4	5	8	4	7	6	4	4			
Rural development[e]											13	17	47
Public works	54	94	106	134	107	104	114	93	126	117	131	172	238
Education	28	48	67	78	91	86	182	206	150	160	179	211	262
Health and Social welfare	27	42	49	51	36	56	103	100	72	77	85	93	122
Military and Police	89	176	202	276	231	217	197	210	223	197	178	217	220

source: For all years except 1962 the sources are Federation of Malaya, *Financial Statement* for the respective years. For 1962 the draft copy of the *Financial Statement*, prepared by the Economic Planning Unit, was used.

[a] The expenditures in individual categories will be slightly inflated due to double counting. The 1961 Financial Statement of the Federation of Malaya gives expenditures *including grants to states*. The grants could be subtracted from the total, but not from the individual categories of expenditures. The total amount involved—grants to states—was about M$ 64 million in that year, or about 6 percent of total expenditures. This is the maximum overstatement that will appear in the individual categories. The actual overstatement will be considerably less than this, however, because we have not used all categories of expenditure for either State or Federal Allocations. See note a in Appendix table IV-II.

[b] Figures for the individual states were not available at the time of writing. See note a of Appendix table IV-II for the estimates made for state expenditures.

[c] Includes Agriculture, Fisheries, Forestry, Veterinary.

[d] This is primarily expenditure in grants for rubber replanting.

[e] Rural Development: primarily for RIDA, listed under various departments or Ministries during the period 1952–1959. From 1960 this includes the entire expenditure of the new Ministry of Rural Development.

APPENDIX TABLE IV-II

ACTUAL STATE EXPENDITURES, FEDERATION OF MALAYA 1950-1962

(in million Malayan dollars)

	1950	1951	1952	1953	1954	1955	1956	1957	1958	1959	1960	1961	1962
Total	109	160	207	240	251	252	273	281	162	176	195	240[a]	240[b]
Agriculture[c]	3	5	7	7	8	10	10	9	11	11	12	15	26
Drainage and Irrigation	4	6	8	10	10	10	12	12	10	11	19	10	—
Public works	28	37	48	60	59	56	61	62	65	67	65	54	55
Education[d]	25	41	53	65	71	72	80	82	—	—	—	—	—
Health and Social welfare	17	26	34	34	36	38	40	48	...	...	2	2	2

[a] State figures for Kedah, Kelantan, and Trengganu were not available at the time of writing. Estimates were made for these three states using essentially the 1960 figures. This will result in a slight understatement of the actual expenditures, but this will be very small in absolute terms and negligible in proportionate terms. These are among the less affluent and less populous states of Malaya. In 1960 their combined actual expenditures amounted to only about 15 percent of the total of all state expenditures.

[b] State figures for 1962 were not available at the time of writing. Estimates were made using the 1961 figures unchanged. This will give an understatement of expenditures, but the amount of understatement will be very small, and negligible in proportionate terms.

[c] Includes Forestry, Fisheries, Veterinary, and Drainage and Irrigation Department.

[d] Until 1957 Education was a State subject. In that year it became a Federal subject with all expenditures emanating from the Federal Ministry.

APPENDIX TABLE IV-III

Actual Federal Development Expenditures, Federation of Malaya 1957–1962[a]
(in million Malayan dollars)

Sector	1957	1958	1959	1960	1961	1962[b]
Total	26	140	142	141	265	415
Agriculture[c]	1	7	5	5	18	29
Rural development	—	—	—	7	9	35
Public works	6	32	25	39	99	151
Commerce and Industry	—	45	52	46	49	47
Education	2	15	10	14	27	43
Health and Social welfare	2	1	3	5	10	31
Military and Police	6	7	6	11	23	25

[a] Before 1957 development expenditures were not shown separately in the Financial Statements. The new accounting procedure began in 1957, but was not complete in that year. Thus the figures for 1957 considerably understate the allocation of financial resources to "development."

The Interim Review of Development in Malaya, December 1963 presents separate actual development as follows:

	1955	1956	1957	1958	1959	1960
M$ Million	97	147	168	140	142	141

It was not possible to obtain departmental breakdowns of expenditures for the years 1955, 1956, 1957. From 1958 onward, all sources of data are consistent in figures and reporting categories.

[b] Source for the 1962 data was a draft copy of the Financial Statement then in preparation.

[c] Includes Cooperatives, Drainage and Irrigation, as well as Forestry, Fisheries, and Veterinary.

APPENDIX TABLE IV-IV

INDICES FOR COMBINED ACTUAL FEDERAL, STATE, AND DEVELOPMENT EXPENDITURES BY MAJOR CATEGORIES FEDERATION OF MALAYA 1950–1962

Categories	1950	1951	1952	1953	1954	1955	1956	1957	1958	1959	1960	1961	1962
Total													
(M$ million)	399	612	756	873	810	817	853	928	1,106	1,077	1,133	1,380	1,658
Index	100	154	189	218	203	204	213	232	277	269	283	345	415
Economic													
(M$ million)	63	112	135	166	141	135	154	143	230	227	244	280	400
Index	100	178	214	263	224	214	244	227	365	360	387	444	635
Social													
(M$ million)	55	90	116	129	127	142	285	306	222	237	264	304	384
Index	100	164	211	235	231	258	518	556	404	431	480	553	698
Order													
(M$ million)	89	176	202	276	231	217	197	210	223	197	178	217	220
Index	100	198	227	310	259	244	221	236	250	221	200	244	247

SOURCE: Computed from Table IV-I.

APPENDIX TABLE IV-V

PLANNED AND ACTUAL PUBLIC INVESTMENT UNDER THE DEVELOPMENT PLANS,
FEDERATION OF MALAYA, 1950–1965
(in millions)

Sector	1950–1955 Plan	1950–1955 Revised (1952)	1956–1960 Plan	1956–1960 Actual	1961–1965 Plan	1961–1965 Est. actual[a]
Total (public)	214.7	855.9	1,148.7	1,006.7	2,150.0	2,651.7
Economic	156.4	766.8	936.0	832.9	1,599.0	1,930.8
Agriculture	14.8	17.9	190.6	172.5	254.3	229.6
Drainage, Irrigation	28.8	38.5[b]	60.0	38.3	100.0	108.5
Land development	2.9	133.0	15.0	16.7	191.0	129.8
Transportation	5.9	126.6	222.5	206.5	362.0	524.9
Public works, Plant and equipment	67.7	180.9	13.0	23.6	68.7	63.6
Communications	34.4	45.9	63.3	51.6	72.9	112.8
Utilities	—	221.6	214.5	238.6	402.0	535.4
Industry	2.0	2.5	15.8	12.1	27.0	59.1
General	—	—	141.3	73.0	88.1	167.1
Social	58.3	89.1	212.7	138.8	491.0	413.6
Education	35.0	51.1	95.4	60.9	260.0	236.5
Health	16.9	18.5	50.0	12.7	145.0	101.9
Social welfare	2.9	8.7	—[c]	—[c]	6.0	5.8
Labor	0.5	0.8	—	—	—	—
Housing	3.0	10.0	67.3	65.2	80.0	69.4
Security	—	—	—	35.0	93.0	307.3

SOURCES: *Progress Report on the Development Plan of the Federation of Malaya, 1950–1952.*
Kuala Lumpur, 1953. *Report on Economic Planning in the Federation of Malaya in 1956,*
Kuala Lumpur, 1957. *Federation of Malaya Second Five-Year Plan 1961–1965,* Kuala
Lumpur, 1961.

[a] Federation of Malaya, First Malaysia Plan 1966–1970, pp. 28, 29.

[b] Excludes M$ 10.6 million for major schemes not included in the plan. See page
119 of the 1952 report.

[c] Included in Health.

APPENDIX TABLE IV-VI

National Debt, Federation of Malaya, 1946–1961

(in million Malayan dollars)

Type of debt	1946	1947	1948	1949	1950	1951	1952	1953	1954	1955	1956	1957	1958	1959	1960	1961
1. Treasury bills	7.2	17.3	20.0	22.2	46.6	48.4	69.3	88.9	95.0	10.6	87.6	51.3	71.5	94.6	112.9	106.0
2. Treasury deposit receipts	—	—	—	—	—	—	45.0	49.1	49.2	99.3	144.4	99.5	124.4	104.4	140.2	140.2
3. Long-term domestic debt	93.3	119.7	127.5	127.5	127.5	142.0	177.5	260.9	321.0	362.2	349.8	509.7	577.6	743.7	843.7	963.1
4. Total domestic debt	100.5	137.0	147.5	149.7	174.1	190.4	291.8	399.0	465.2	472.1	581.6	660.5	773.5	942.7	1,096.8	1,209.2
5. External debt of the federal government	46.2	46.2	46.2	115.2	115.2	115.2	115.2	131.3	241.7	286.2	321.1	316.0	308.1	334.2	359.6	373.3
6. Total public debt of the federal government	146.7	183.2	193.7	264.8	289.3	305.5	407.0	530.2	706.9	758.2	902.8	976.5	1,081.5	1,276.8	1,456.3	1,582.5
7. External debt of the public authorities	—	—	—	—	5.5	19.2	27.8	40.5	50.1	60.7	60.7	60.7	60.7	69.1	77.4	91.6

source: Federation of Malaya, Ministry of Finance, The Treasury.

V

THE EMERGENCE OF AN OUTPUT
GOAL IN RURAL DEVELOPMENT

In the gradual process of changing its goals during the 1950's, the Malayan government engaged in a series of new, organized activities in the attempt to stimulate economic development. The most important of these were the Rural and Industrial Development Authority (RIDA), the Federal Land Development Authority (FLDA), a Community Development Program, and finally the Ministry of Rural Development.

The Rural and Industrial Development Authority was formed in 1950 as Malaya's first nationally organized attempt to stimulate development in the rural areas. RIDA activities originally included (a) the provision of physical improvements to rural areas; (b) changing the structure of the rural economy through the provision of rural credit and marketing, and technical assistance; (c) fostering in the rural people a spirit of self-reliance and initiative. By the end of the decade RIDA's records revealed that the organization had primarily concentrated upon the provision of physical improvements.

In 1956 the Federal Land Development Authority was formed to open new agricultural areas and to provide land for the landless. In the original recommendation, it was envisaged that FLDA would foster the value of self-help by giving priority to those people who had already shown a desire to help themselves. In its operations FLDA at first required that the settlers demonstrate their commitment to the value of self-help by clearing their own land, building their own houses and planting their own crops. Pressures on FLDA to speed up operations, and problems of settler control, forced the organization to abandon the use of settler labor. Today FLDA uses contractors to clear the land, build the houses, plant the crops, and provide the first three months' maintenance on the crops. In the selection of settlers, since no systematic attempt is made to evaluate the applicant's attitudes or values, no direct support is given to the value of self-help.

Between 1953 and 1958 various forms of community development programs were discussed and launched by government. Adhering to the universal *Community Development* formula, the programs aimed at organizing rural people to play a decisive role in their own development. After 1958 community development in Malaya became a political issue in the struggle for power between the Minister of Agriculture and the Deputy Prime Minister, who also formed the new Ministry of Rural Development in 1959. In 1960 community development was absorbed into the Ministry of Rural Development and its ideology and aims were abandoned.

Since 1960 the Ministry of Rural Development has been in the vanguard of the organized attempt to stimulate the growth of the rural economy. The Ministry has concentrated its efforts on the provision of social overhead capital and physical improvements and has achieved considerable success in this field. In the past three years the Malayan countryside has experienced a wave of new construction including new roads and bridges, new schools and health centers, village wells and community halls, and the opening of new agricultural land. The Ministry's chief success thus lies in providing a powerful wave of new construction that reaches to the remotest rural areas.

Malaya's organized efforts to stimulate the development of its rural sector manifest three major orientations, each corresponding to a type of organizational goal:

1. *Output goal:* the production of amenities, building up the rural infrastructure, or providing aids and assistance to rural people.
2. *Cultural goals:* community development; changing the values of the rural people by increasing their participation in their own uplift; reconstructing the rural community.
3. *Mixed Output-Cultural goals:* changing the structure of the rural economy through the extension of credit, technical assistance and rural education, cooperatives, farmers' associations, and extension work. These are mixed goals in that in one specific organization there is a combination of an attempt to create a new culture, to change the economic or social structure or small parts of it, and to produce some service or amenity.

Taken as a whole, Malaya's organized development effort has experimented with all three types of goals, but the period 1950 to 1960 has seen the *progressive weakening of cultural and mixed output-cultural goals and the growing dominance of pure output goals.* This chapter will trace briefly this emergence of a dominant goal. Somewhat more attention will be given to RIDA, whose longer history and more complex set of activities make the process of experimentation and emerging goal dominance quite clear. The operations of FLDA and the Ministry of Rural Development will be described in more detail in a later chapter. Here we are concerned only with analyzing the goal commitments that had emerged as dominant by the time the Ministry was established.

THE RURAL AND INDUSTRIAL DEVELOPMENT AUTHORITY (RIDA)

In a letter to Dato Onn bin Ja'afar early in 1950, the British High Commissioner, Sir Henry Guerney, set out the original case for RIDA.[1] An organization was needed that would stimulate the development of the rural Malays, whose economic backwardness presented a serious obstacle to the future economic development and political stability of the new nation. Malay poverty was due, Sir Henry argued, to deficiencies in organization. These deficiencies kept productivity low and allowed others to take a larger share of what wealth was produced. The rural producer needed a more modern and scientifically based mode of production and a more extensive control of all stages and factors of production.

In the ensuing years other British officials echoed Sir Henry's views and added another argument. Malay poverty was also due in part to a dysfunctional Malay value system. One aim of RIDA would be to exorcise the *tidapa* ("it doesn't matter") spirit of the rural Malay population. This would require training Malays "to use equipment without breaking it up . . . [and] to instill . . . the desire to get ahead . . . ."[2]

Dato Onn held slightly different views of the causes of rural poverty.[3]

---

[1] Sir Henry Guerney, "Government Proposal for Improvement of Social and Economic Well-being of Malays," Kuala Lumpur, 19 May 1950, mimeographed.

[2] Speech by D. C. Horton, RIDA Secretary, reported in the *Straits Times*, 5 August 1952.

[3] These can be found expressed in official RIDA reports and in public statements of Dato Onn as reported in local newspapers. Such views will normally be complex and dynamic and at times contradictory. What follows is my own interpretation, based on as exhaustive a reading of his statements as I was able to make.

The deficiencies in organization that Sir Henry noted resulted essentially in the exploitation of the rural Malays by Chinese and Indian merchants and moneylenders. The dysfunctional value system was a reflection of the distintegration of village life, brought about largely by the paternalism of colonial rule. People had lost the old cooperative spirit and self-reliance of the traditional village and now looked to government to satisfy all their needs.

The Rural and Industrial Development Authority was established to attack this problem of rural poverty. Dato Onn was appointed its first Chairman, and hopes were raised for an early victory.

The tasks given to RIDA reflected the wide range of goals it was to carry. RIDA would engage in specific projects of providing physical improvements to the rural areas. By doing this only on a self-help basis, it would resurrect the old spirit of self-reliance in rural communities, show the rural people how to organize for their own benefit, create a new value system by rewarding energy and initiative, and incidentally foster communal harmony by showing the races the advantages of working together. RIDA would also inject a new technology into the rural population by training, extension schemes, and by bringing modern machinery into rural production. It would restructure the old exploitative market system by providing credit and market services. And above all, it would tend to coordinate all the diverse activities of government and people at all levels to produce a team moving to the planned and coordinated objective of reconstructing village life and raising the living standards of the rural people.[4] RIDA would carry output, cultural, and mixed output-cultural types of goals.

As an organization, RIDA was set outside the normal structure of the government bureaucracy, but responsible to a cabinet position.[5] At the top RIDA was governed by the "Authority," a rather unwieldy body containing technical officers and a representative from each state.[6] Below the Authority and its central executive offices were state development boards, followed by district, then *mukim* and village de-

---

[4] See Federation of Malaya Legislative Council Paper No. 10 of 1951, "Scheme for the Reorganization of the Rural and Industrial Development Authority, Federation of Malaya."

[5] At the outset RIDA was under the Member of Home Affairs, a cabinet position held by Dato Onn. In 1954 it became a semiautonomous Authority, still under Home Affairs. In 1956 a cabinet reorganization eliminated the Member for Home Affairs and placed RIDA under the Ministry of Natural Resources. Having been defeated in elections, Dato Onn resigned his Chairmanship of RIDA. Finally, in 1959, RIDA became the responsibility of the new Ministry of Rural Development.

[6] Dato Onn attempted to reduce the size of the Authority by having states represented collectively by two or three members. That he was unsuccessful in this testifies to the powerful centrifugal force of federalism in Malaya.

velopment boards and committees. At state and district levels, RIDA provided separate development officers to perform the planning and coordination of government services, the central function of the organization.

Organizational character derives more from the work performed than from the formal structure and stated goals. Thus a full understanding of RIDA can only be gained by observing the kind of work it actually performed, and especially by noting the pattern of change in the performance over the decade. For this we can analyze the annual reports of RIDA,[7] a formal evaluation by D. E. M. Fiennes carried out in 1956,[8] together with the reactions of the RIDA Chairman to the Fiennes report,[9] and finally interviews carried out among RIDA officers in 1961/2.

The all-important coordinating function was soon abdicated. At the outset RIDA had difficulties with state governments, who felt development was properly a state rather than a federal function. It also had difficulty with government agencies at all levels, which had their own set of priorities and their own ideas on how projects should be scheduled. RIDA could claim neither greater expertise in stimulating development nor greater power over existing agencies. The real problem lay in its political impotence. Although Dato Onn was perhaps the most influential indigenous person in government, he was essentially powerless. He was in a position only to request and persuade, not to order, government officers. RIDA did learn to get along with federal and state government agencies, but only by going its own way. Fiennes could report in 1956 both that relations were on the whole good, and that the development boards did little more than assist RIDA officers in processing requests of local people for direct assistance.[10]

RIDA's cultural goals were put into action through self-help schemes, community development schemes, and training. At the outset, RIDA would assist only those who were willing to help themselves. This meant specifically that RIDA assistance would come on a dollar-for-dollar matching basis, with RIDA contributing materials and technical assistance and the local people providing labor. The first reports made

---

[7] These appear as semiannual reports in Legislative Council Papers (hereinafter referred to as Legco Papers), numbered by paper and year, through 1953. From 1954 on RIDA published annual reports of its activities.

[8] Federation of Malaya, *Report on the Rural and Industrial Development Authority, 1950–1955*, by D. E. M. Fiennes, Kuala Lumpur, 1957.

[9] Legco Paper 15 of 1957, "Directive to the Rural and Industrial Development Authority," Kuala Lumpur, 1957. The paper contains a point-by-point answer from the RIDA Chairman to Fiennes' report. This is followed by the High Commissioner's directives to RIDA.

[10] D. E. M. Fiennes, *op. cit.*, pp. 4 and 8.

some attempt to give a cost value to the labor provided locally. This was soon discarded as accounting and organizational difficulties emerged. In the face of these RIDA allowed "a portion" of cost to be contributed locally.[11] Then local contributions for one scheme could be credited against another in which RIDA provided almost the total value of goods and services required. A further retreat was made in 1954 when RIDA admitted that self-help in either cash or kind would be acceptable.[12]

This provided the deathblow to RIDA's commitment to the value of self-help. If cash could be substituted for labor in local contributions, RIDA would have no opportunity to instill new values and organization into the rural people. Further, the allowance indicated an adjustment to a unique rural labor market. Apparently peasants could employ their time more productively in ways other than working on RIDA self-help projects. From this point on, RIDA continued to give only general expression to the value of self-help. The actual labor mobilized in this fashion, and the value-changing opportunities it would provide, ceased to be an important part of RIDA's work.

Community development schemes began almost immediately with projects to construct community halls. It was hoped that these would provide meeting places in which local initiative and racial harmony would be engendered. After a rash of hall construction in 1951 and 1952, RIDA asked Ungku Aziz, of the Department of Economics at the University of Singapore,[13] to survey the rural scene and make recommendations on future location and scheduling of hall construction. Professor Aziz found that the halls themselves were superfluous. They were unused and were being allowed to fall into disrepair. RIDA then cut back its activities drastically. In future reports, however, it continued to give emphasis to the value of social betterment and reconstruction of village life. Occasionally it pursued this value by constructing playing fields, parks, and park benches.

RIDA's training program was originally aimed at providing a wide range of technical skills and leadership capacities. Schools were to be located throughout the country and traveling teams could work from these centers. Most training programs were extremely short-lived, and training as a whole came to be dominated by a commercial college located in a suburb of Kuala Lumpur. The college has actually had considerable success in training Malay secondary school graduates in

---

[11] Legco Paper 84 of 1953, paragraph 223.
[12] Legco Paper 17 of 1954, p. 4.
[13] Now Professor Ungku A. Aziz, Chairman of the Department of Economics, University of Malaysia, Kuala Lumpur.

commercial subjects, enabling them to pass British examinations and to find good positions in foreign firms in the major cities.

Cultural goals have been subverted by output goals. Self-help withered away in RIDA's concern for building. Village reconstruction and social betterment were pursued through the construction of rural improvements. Even the training program worked most successfully at removing young people from the rural scene and giving them the skills to work in urban commercial enterprises.

The mixed output-cultural goals were to be pursued through the provision of technical assistance and machinery, through creating new rural enterprises, planning for over-all development, and especially through the extension of credit. The history of technical assistance is little more than a dreary chronicle of small projects of short duration and little lasting impact. A hand railway in a major rice scheme was found to be impractical after it was installed. Tractor stations were set up only to find that the old buffalo was more economical; the tractors were more useful to, and finally transferred to, the Public Works Department. Fertilizer was distributed to peasants who resold it or found it uneconomical unless heavily subsidized. Fish ponds were promoted as were small chicken runs, neither with any real success. In all cases RIDA operated enthusiastically for a year or so, then discontinued in the face of difficulties and went on to a new project.

Rural enterprises managed directly by RIDA were created for rubber milling, transportation, fruit canning, boat building, and domestic handicrafts. All have been plagued with problems of management and have generally been run at a deficit. The net loss from these direct managed projects was at least M$ 3 million over the decade. This was from a total gross expenditure on the projects of about M$ 9.8 million.[14]

Economic planning was emphasized after 1957, but soon became the exclusive preserve of the far more functionally located and technically competent Economic Planning Unit in the Office of the Prime Minister.

Credit activities began with large loans to newly formed cooperative organizations in the major rice growing areas. The peasant would be freed from the moneylender by the provision of RIDA credit at terms that would not be usurious. It was soon discovered that RIDA resources were insufficient to provide credit for rice production, and RIDA *cum* cooperative organization was not able to control credit sufficiently to see that it was used productively. This large-scale credit was turned over to the central cooperative bank and RIDA began its long-term attachment to small loans for small producers.

---

[14] See the account of RIDA expenditures in the Appendix to this chapter.

By the end of 1953 80 percent of all loans were under M\$ 3,000 and 49 percent were under M\$ 1,000.[15] A census taken in 1962 of the 758 RIDA-assisted manufacturing industries showed that 87 percent of RIDA manufacturing loans were for less than M\$ 3,000 and 53 percent were for less than M\$ 1,000.[16] Over all, the small-loan program has been a major part of RIDA's work. Approximately one fourth of all RIDA expenditures during the decade have been for loans. Administering this program has taken a major share of officers' time, so that we may estimate 40 percent of administrative costs attributable to loans, bringing the over-all allocation to the loan program to about 40 percent of all RIDA expenditures.[17]

The commitment of time and resources to small loans for small producers reflects RIDA's view of the world. We saw this first in Dato Onn's view of the cause of rural poverty. The rural people were exploited by moneylenders and merchants: capitalists. It came out again in the exchange between Fiennes and the Chairman in 1956. Fiennes recommended more loans in the M\$ 10,000+ category. These could be more carefully supervised, and they were more likely to succeed because they were for projects to which a producer was fully committed, not simply to backyard chicken projects whose success or failure would not make much difference to the individual.[18] The Chairman argued only that it was RIDA's special province to help the small people. He also argued that all loans brought training in modern business practices.[19] Fiennes, by inference, disagreed. The large number of small loans left administrators with no time to do more than process applications. Fewer larger loans would have left time for technical assistance.

The exchange shows an important lack of agreement in basic orientations. Fiennes was arguing for larger loans, which could have been granted to small producers. The Chairman argued for small producers, implicitly equating the size of loan with the size of the producer.[20]

---

[15] Legco Paper 17 of 1954.

[16] Federation of Malaya, RIDA, *Census 1/62 of RIDA Assisted Manufacturing Industries in the Federation of Malaya, Period Covered, 1 June 1951 to 31 May 1962*, compiled by Eric D. Manning. This was the first systematic attempt RIDA has made to analyze its loan program.

[17] See the RIDA account in the Appendix to this chapter.

[18] D. E. M. Fiennes, *Report on the Rural and Industrial Development Authority, 1950–1955*, p. 13.

[19] Legco Paper 15 of 1957, p. 3.

[20] This betrays a narrow emphasis upon loan security in the program. Large loans are only for large or wealthy producers, because only they can provide the necessary security. RIDA has publicly denied this emphasis upon security, but interviews with field officers indicate that security has been an overriding concern, largely because there was insufficient time or competence to analyze probable returns.

The connotations of large and small were left unstated at this time.

In personal interviews with the RIDA Chairman in 1961 a more complete picture of the determinants of the loan policy emerged. RIDA wanted to help the small producers. Helping large producers would only create a new class of rural (Malay) capitalists, and that would not solve the problem of poverty, because exploitation would continue to exist. RIDA loans were almost designed explicitly to keep rural producers small, for RIDA would assist "only up to a point." The logic of this reasoning is less than impeccable. If the producer being helped by RIDA "only up to a point" were successful in increasing his productivity beyond that point, by virtue of being bigger, he would be a new rural capitalist. That RIDA helped him only part way would not make him less a capitalist, nor less exploitative, if that is what capitalists do. Operating policies less often hang on impeccable logic than upon more deep-seated views of the world, however. RIDA's mildly anticapitalist orientation, its definition of capitalist by size, and its equation of size of producer with size of loan dictated a firm policy of concentrating its activities on small loans.

The goal implications of this policy are directly apparent. Small loans meant that RIDA loan officers had opportunity to do little more than process written applications, without time to investigate applicants personally. They had even less time to survey the rural scene to determine where loan capital could be most effective. Given the state of RIDA loan records, it was impossible for loan officers to locate successful borrowers to assist them in increasing their productivity further. Far from using credit to create a new organization of production and marketing, RIDA has been concerned simply with giving out loans.

Mixed output-cultural goals have also been subverted by output goals. Technical assistance was given out, but there was little competence to evaluate its impact in other than dichotomous success-failure terms. Generally observing the latter, RIDA simply withdrew from the activity. Enterprises were created and maintained by subsidies largely because they were there. No real attention was paid to evaluations of their impact. Aspirations for planning and field evaluation died when the larger macroeconomic aspects of national planning were developed under the Economic Planning Unit. And the loan program works primarily at processing applications in order to grant loans, rather indiscriminately of their impact on the rural economy.

Output goals were pursued through the construction of amenities and physical infrastructure in the rural areas. Unable to coordinate the activities of the technically competent agencies of government, RIDA gradually built up its own small public works department. RIDA tractors could be found building rural roads, bridges, and water systems. RIDA monies and personnel were set to work in construction. Fiennes could complain in 1956 that neither the loan nor the improvement programs ranked high in the list of original priorities, and that concentration on these programs had resulted in administration costs out of proportion to their economic effect.[21] He recommended flatly that minor village works should no longer be undertaken by RIDA. By this time, however, RIDA's experience in construction had been too extensive to be given up lightly. Through 1955 some 28 percent of total expenditures had been directly in this activity. If about 40 percent of administrative costs are added to this, the proportion becomes just over 50 percent of financial resources allocated to construction. The Chairman replied to Fiennes' suggestion with the observation that "it is the unanimous and considered opinion of State Development Officers . . ." that RIDA should continue in this activity.[22]

In his last instructions to RIDA, in 1957, the High Commissioner took Fiennes' advice and directed RIDA to reduce its construction activities at the rate of 25 percent per year from 1958 through 1961 and thereafter to cease these activities altogether. Table V-1 shows the

TABLE V-1

RIDA EXPENDITURES ON DEVELOPMENT SCHEMES
(Village construction projects)

Expenditures	1951	1952	1953	1954	1955	1956	1957	1958	1959	1960
Amount (M$ 000)	226	1,389	1,808	2,834	1,890	1,305	860	652	1,139	302
Percent of total expenditures	56	45	28	37	30	27	21	19	28	8

SOURCE: See account of RIDA expenditures in table V-I, the Appendix to this chapter.

movement of RIDA expenditures for construction projects throughout the decade. The data indicate that the High Commissioner's instructions were followed somewhat for the first year.

After 1960 RIDA relinquished all responsibility for construction, but for reasons other than those noted above. Some indication of the

[21] D. E. M. Fiennes, *op. cit.*, p. 22.
[22] Legco Paper 15 of 1957, p. 5.

reasons can be seen in the sharp upturn of construction in 1959, an election year. Construction was removed from RIDA's concern by the new government after its Rural Development Program started. This was done not because rural construction was unimportant, but because it was too important to be left in the hands of an essentially impotent organization. Further, with the extreme power of the Rural Development Minister, the coordination of relevant state and federal agencies, which RIDA was forced to renounce, could be effected.

RIDA's broad attack on rural poverty through the carrying out of a variety of goals was subverted. Output goals emerged gradually as dominant for the organization and even its most specific type of output activity, rural improvement construction, was essentially taken over by the powerful new Ministry of Rural Development after it was formed in 1959.

COMMUNITY DEVELOPMENT

The Malayan government made two ill-fated attempts to launch Community Development programs during the 1950's. The first developed from the joint efforts of a British District Officer in Perak and Dato Onn and his Rural and Industrial Development Authority. Characteristically the program began with a conference, in Taiping, Perak in 1953. Also characteristically, a foreign expert was in attendance, toured Community Development efforts after the conference, and made a series of observations and recommendations. Finally, and still characteristically, a Legislative Council Paper was presented setting forth government's commitment to the broad principles and value of Community Development. Dato Onn wanted more, but the exigencies of the Emergency took precedence. Community Development faded away.

Such a forceful idea was not to be permanently denied, however. It sprang to life again in 1957 in the breast of the new Minister for Agriculture, Aziz bin Ishak. Aziz was moved by the successful experiments he saw in Ceylon and India, and he pressed for their replication in Malaya. Again, a conference was called. This time, however, the conference was held in the capital with the Prime Minister and the Deputy Prime Minister in attendance and giving key addresses. Foreign experts were called upon. Responsibility for Community Development was given to an existing organization already charged with the resettlement of special constables, a group of para-police guards enlisted during the Emergency. Funds were allocated, but largely unspent. In 1959 responsibility for Community Development was transferred to the Office of the Prime Minister, thence to the new Ministry of Rural

Development. More money was allocated; less was spent.[23] In 1961 a formal cabinet decision announced the termination of the Community Development Programs.

There was not sufficient work done under either of these attempts to give a definite character to the organization of the programs. We can see only a potential character, a view of the problems to be solved and the ways to solve them, in the public statements called forth by the programs. On the one hand the program in Malaya shared a view of the problem with other formally designated Community Development programs in the world. The fundamental aspect of the problem is found in the lack of initiative in the rural population. There is neither the desire nor the ability for local communities to organize themselves for their own betterment. Community Development seeks to engender such desire and to create the organizational skills to satisfy the desire. This implies a minimum of government activity. It may send organizers, multiple-purpose workers, and leaders, but it must not do for the rural population what that population can do for itself.

Two other dimensions of this potential character are of importance for Malaya; one marks consensus, the other marks cleavage, especially between British and indigenous officers. On one point all were in agreement. Community Development was almost exclusively for the Malays. No one appeared to think the rural Chinese or Indians needed assistance in developing initiative. British officers spoke to Malays. At the 1958 conference the Prime Minister used Community Development synonymously with *kampong* development. Only at the close of his remarks, in an almost parenthetical manner, did he call attention to the New Villages (almost totally Chinese) and the new land development schemes (mixed).[24]

Cleavage is introduced by a consideration of the reasons for Community Development's exclusive concern for the Malays. British officers found the reasons in Malay character. Malays were considered lazy, improvident, and lacking in an achievement orientation. In this they differed markedly from Chinese and Indians. G. S. Rawlings, the first Commissioner for Community Development and previously British

---

[23] In 1957 Community Development was first recorded as a separate entry in the FOM Financial Statement. M$ 829 was spent for an experimental course in Community Development under the Ministry of Agriculture. In 1958 a total of M$ 47,000 was allocated, of which only M$ 30,000 was spent. In 1959 the allocation climbed to M$ 660,000, of which M$ 100,000 was actually spent. In the final year, 1960, M$ 750,000 was allocated but actual expenditures dropped to only M$ 57,000.

[24] Federation of Malaya, *Report on the Conference on Community Development,* Kuala Lumpur, 1958, p. 10. This report contains also the other key speeches of the Deputy Minister and the Minister of Agriculture.

Adviser in Kelantan, a man who (allegedly) knew the Malays well and (apparently) admired them dearly, presented a rather typical sugar-coated form of the argument. Rawlings knew the Malay as proud, courteous, naturally aesthetic, and willing to toil long and hard for his friends, but "unlike almost everyone else in the modern world, he is not obsessed with the need to exert himself more than will provide for his quite modest wants." [25] Community Development was only for the Malays, because only the Malays needed a change of values.

The Prime Minister's speech during the 1958 conference typifies the Malay view of the problem. He began by arguing that old values and ways of life had to be changed. The future life of the nation would depend upon this. But for him this carried very different programmatic implications. The rural people needed a new deal. Government would close the gap between rural and urban living and stop the drift to the towns by providing the rural areas with the amenities the towns had long had in abundance. Existing government organization was insufficient. More coordination of specialized agencies was required. A national program was needed. At the local level coordination should be organized along the lines of the state and district war executive committees that had successfully prosecuted the Emergency. At the national level the program must be directed by the most powerful leaders; the Deputy Prime Minister himself was suggested.

Thus in a speech proclaiming the value of Community Development, the Prime Minister laid down the principles and goals that were crystallized the following year in the formation of the Ministry of Rural Development. As Malays saw it, the real change required was not so much in the rural population itself as in the orientation, activity, and organization of government.

Malays disagreed with British officers on the nature of the problem and the causes of rural poverty. For the British it was a dysfunctional value system; for the Malays it was past government neglect. In addition, this orientation reflects the impatience of the new men of power. They rejected the notion, inherent in Community Development, that change could be achieved only slowly. They had just come to power over a wealthy and well-established government. They were anxious to get on with the job, to use the new powers they had to produce the things the existing organization was already capable of producing. This was essentially a rejection of the cultural goal of Community Development and an embryonic commitment to output goals.

----

[25] G. S. Rawlings, "First Steps in Community Development in Malaya." Paper prepared for a seminar on Home Economics and Other Programmes Related to the Needs of Malayan Families, Kuala Lumpur, 1958, mimeographed.

THE FEDERAL LAND DEVELOPMENT
AUTHORITY (FLDA)

The Federal Land Development Authority was created by a Federal Ordinance on July 1, 1956.[26] The need for the organization was conceived to lie in two obstacles to land development in the Federation; one was administrative, the other cultural.[27]

There was a great demand for land in Malaya, and sufficient land to meet that demand. The obstacle lay in the land administration, which was neither properly staffed nor organized to process applications and to allocate land in an orderly manner.[28] In addition, land was a state matter to be administered by state governments, which on the whole have had less developed bureaucracies than the federal government. The new organization would help to overcome this administrative obstacle by providing financing and technical assistance for developing large new settlements. Tracts of two to five thousand acres would be developed in single settlements, complete with planned villages that could be provided with an entire range of modern public utilities and services. Given state prerogatives in land matters, however, the FLDA would really only be a lending agency, with additional functions of providing technical assistance. Each state would organize its own land development boards to control and administer the actual development.

The other obstacle lay in the culture of indolence and poverty. Malayan farmers were poorer than they needed to be, but not because of an absolute shortage of land; they did not do a full day's work. *Padi* planters did not use off seasons productively and rubber tappers did not use afternoons profitably.[29] Too often land or tapping rights are rented out. "What could be a good living for one family becomes poverty for two families; both the families and Malaya suffer." [30] The

---

[26] Federation of Malaya, Legislative Council, Principal Ordinance Number 20 of 1956, 1 July 1956.

[27] Clear expositions appear in two major policy statements: Federation of Malaya, *Report of the Working Party Set up to Consider the Development of New Areas for Land Settlement in the Federation of Malaya*, Kuala Lumpur, 1956; and Federation of Malaya, FLDA, *No Need to Be Poor, A Policy Statement*, Kuala Lumpur, 1956. The latter was written by FLDA's first Chairman, D. E. M. Fiennes.

[28] The large demand was caused in part by population growth and in part by the great backlog of applications that had built up when the Emergency essentially brought a halt to land allocation.

[29] Rubber is tapped in the early morning, usually beginning at first light and ending about noon.

[30] D. E. M. Fiennes, *No Need to Be Poor*, p. 3.

new organization would overcome these cultural obstacles by selecting only those with drive and initiative to be the new settlers.

Settler selection would be both difficult and highly important. No single test would be adequate because both appropriate skills and appropriate values were required. Sons of farmers would probably be the most successful because of their past experience; proper values would be more difficult to determine. Settlers could always be found in overcrowded districts, but if applications resulted from the energy of district officers rather than from the energy of the applicants, the schemes would probably fail. The world was littered with such settlement failures. The best sign of proper values might be for the applicant to have saved some money toward a land application. On the other hand, "as a negative test, it can be safely said that any applicant for land who has no savings but has a watch and a fountain pen will be a failure as a pioneer settler. Malaya needs people who want their own farm more than they want a watch or fountain pen." [31] Here was an appeal for carriers of the Protestant Ethic.

With these modern Calvinists as raw material, the tasks of land development would not be overwhelming. The settlers would be allowed to start fertilizing their land with the sweat of their own brows from the very beginning. They were to clear the approximately eight acres of jungle land for main crops, plant and maintain the rubber, clear house and catch-crop land, and build their own houses. And the projects provided them with the opportunity to work in the close, warm relationship of traditional cooperation, or *gotong royong*. All would work to help all. Government would do its part by providing technical assistance, utilities and services such as water, roads, and schools, and a subsistence allowance for the first two years.

The states began almost immediately to create the necessary land development boards. Kelantan opened the first federally assisted projects at Ayer Lanas in 1957. By the middle of that year development boards had been created and begun planning in Kedah, Malacca, Trengganu, Johore, and Negri Sembilan. Pahang took a different approach, which presaged later developments. As the largest and least densely populated state in the Federation,[32] it was concerned less with excluding than with including others in its land development. It began negotiations to turn over a large tract of land in Bilut Valley directly to FLDA for development. Other states' plans were to be exclusively

---

[31] *Ibid.*, p. 2.

[32] Pahang has an area of 13,873 square miles, about 25 percent of the land area of Malaya, and a population density of only 22.6 persons per square mile. Trengganu is next lowest with 55; Penang is highest with 1,438. The average population density for all of Malaya is 129 persons per square mile.

for state residents; the Pahang project would be for all citizens of the Federation.

The opening of projects went ahead gradually, building up speed as it went. At the end of 1959, when the Ministry of Rural Development was created, FLDA was financing eleven operating projects, one of which it managed directly.

Two sets of forces pushed land development in the direction of increasing centralization, in which FLDA would play an increasingly direct role. In the first place, state governments did not have the quantity or quality of staff required to move ahead rapidly in the development process. With its specialization, FLDA was proving to be more highly qualified to direct that development. Essentially only the legal prerogatives and the jealous concern of the states in land matters kept FLDA chained to its original formal status as a loans board, and there was as yet no Federal organization with sufficient power to abrogate state prerogatives and free FLDA to exercise its full capacities.

In the second place was the thorny problem of settler control. In the hands of the states, settler selection was more political than agriculturally rational. Further, since the state boards held the ultimate sanction of allocation and removal, and since the subsistence allowance was a grant and was not tied to performance, the project managers had essentially no utilitarian powers over the settlers. Their powers were essentially social or normative.

At the same time the nature of the physical task demanded more than normative controls. Even the original working party estimated that one man-year would be required to clear and plant two acres of rubber land, making a requirement of four years just to create the basic eight acre rubber plot. In addition, time was required for clearing and planting the two acres designed for catch crops and for building a house. The settlers were sometimes not healthy enough, and often insufficiently skilled for the strenuous task of clearing the jungle. Finally, there were settlers who wished to make frequent visits to their home villages, and fishermen who came to the projects only when the monsoons closed the seas to them and who wished to return to fishing when the weather cleared.

FLDA moved rationally, but to the end of developing land, not of changing values. To speed the process of development and cut the elapsed time before the land would come into production, FLDA used contractors and heavy equipment on its directly managed project in Bilut Valley. Gradually contractors took over more and more of the tasks until they were clearing the land, planting the rubber, providing the first three to six months' maintenance, clearing the village land,

and building the settlers' houses. This would cut the time, by almost half, before the land would be productive, and it would greatly reduce the time FLDA would have to provide subsistence allowances to the settlers.

The selective process has moved in the same rationalizing direction. The focus has been on skills and need rather than upon values. Points are given in a rating system that favors young men with farm backgrounds and large families. The demand for land was too great, and the cost of fountain pens and watches too low, to allow for a clear and easy distinction between the energetic and the nonenergetic.

The original dream, Fiennes' dream, of using the FLDA to bring forth good Malayan Calvinists to open the land and to increase the wealth of the state has partly miscarried. The demand for land, the vulnerability of government to that demand, the capacity of the specialized organization and the slowness of others, together with the distinctive views of Malayan leaders on the causes of poverty, all led the FLDA in the direction of a major goal change. The original commitment to a mixture of cultural and output goals gradually gave way to an almost exclusive commitment to output goals. FLDA emerged in 1959 concerned largely with opening new land and getting settlers on that land. The major obstacle to the full achievement of its output goals lay in state prerogatives and the Authority's political impotence in the face of the rest of the slow-moving bureaucracy.

By the end of the decade Malaya had undergone a major change. The country had gained increasing self-rule and finally independence. This brought to power a new leadership with a new orientation to economic development. The passive and conservative orientation of the old colonial leaders gave way to the more active stimulating orientation of the new independent leaders. But the development of specialized organizations to give life to this new orientation was as yet incomplete. The organizations that did emerge experimented with specific goals and showed a pervasive and powerful drift toward almost pure output goals. It still remained, however, to find an organizational instrument powerful enough to reshape the existing bureaucracy toward the achievement of this type of goal. The task that lay ahead was that of coordinating the diverse elements of the existing bureaucracy, of creating an instrument that could give life and work to the forces manifest in the general orientation of the new government. This is the task the new Ministry of Rural Development performed with such skill. And it is to the actual performance of that task that we must now turn our attention.

APPENDIX TABLE V-I

RURAL AND INDUSTRIAL DEVELOPMENT AUTHORITY EXPENDITURES 1951–1960

(in thousands of Malayan dollars)

Sector		1951	1952	1953	1954	1955	1956	1957	1958	1959	1960	Total
Total expenditures[a]	$	698[b]	4,005	8,543	8,543	7,277	6,054	6,033	4,892	4,846	4,561	55,272
	%	100	100	100	100	100	100	100	100	100	100	100
Administration[c]	$	130[d]	672[d]	1,337[d]	1,808	2,597	1,823	1,616	1,592	1,760	1,938	15,273
	%	18.6	16.9	15.8	21.4	35.6	30.1	26.6	32.6	36.3	42.5	27.6
(Salaries)	$	(61)[e]	(472)[f]	618	(757)	(801)	(877)	(920)	(906)	(921)	(944)	7,277
	%	(8.6)	(11.8)	(7.3)	(9.0)	(11.0)	(14.5)	(15.3)	(18.5)	(19.0)	(21.8)	(13.1)
Training	$	—	—	—	—	217	430	524	415	423	415	2,424
	%	—	—	—	—	3.0	7.1	8.7	8.5	8.7	9.1	4.5
Physical amenities	$	226[g]	1,373[g]	2,669[g]	2,834[g]	1,890	1,305	860	651	1,148	302	13,268
	%	32.4	34.5	31.6	33.5	26.0	21.6	14.3	13.3	23.7	6.6	24.0
(Community halls)	$	(73)	(214)	(65)	—	—	(16)	(9)	—	—	—	(377)
	%	(10.5)	(5.7)	(0.8)	—	—	(0.3)	(0.1)	—	—	—	0.7
Direct managed projects gross expenditure[h]	$	62[i]	686[i]	2,235[i]	1,290	1,342	915	619	795[j]	788[k]	1,031[l]	9,763
	%	8.9	17.1	26.4	15.3	18.5	15.1	10.3	16.2	16.3	22.6	17.6
(Direct managed projects revenue)	$	(20)	(240)	(906)	(849)	(1,128)	(854)	(598)	(621)	(745)	(832)	(6,793)
Loans granted	$	279[m]	1,264[m]	2,212[m]	2,521[m]	1,232[m]	1,580[m]	2,413	1,439	727	874	14,541
	%	40.0	31.5	26.2	29.8	16.9	26.1	40.0	29.4	15.0	19.2	26.3

N. B.: The aim here is to show the actual financial outlay for RIDA activities during the period; this is *not* a series of balance sheets for the organization. For this reason the annual income amounts have been omitted. Income statements would be somewhat confusing to this analysis, especially since the projects fund is a fund that must be conserved and can be drawn upon. Thus, it can be argued that in the projects fund, income equals outlay plus interest. A rough income-expenditure balance can be drawn up for the entire period, however. RIDA received a total of M$ 50 million in grants from the Federal government. It earned M$ 11 million in interest and revenue from its loans and direct managed projects. It drew a total of M$ 7.6 million from its authorized M$ 10 million loan fund, and received approximately M$ 11.4 million in loan repayments (which did not revert to the M$ 10 million fund, but became a part of RIDA's projects fund). The grand total of income—or money received and available for allocation—was M$ 80 million. Direct actual expenditures show M$ 55 million, to which can be added approximately M$ 23 million in what must be called savings—reserve funds, etc. This gives a grand total of expenditures of M$ 78 million. The two million discrepancy between income and outlay is due to rounding and the exclusion of minor items.

Unless otherwise noted, the data from each year are taken from the annual or semiannual reports from that year.

ᵃ This shows the actual expenditure on RIDA activities. It excludes allowances for depreciation, and other paper transfers, most of which are included in the M$ 23 million described above as "savings."

ᵇ Legislative Council Paper 24 of 1951, P. 4, notes that "about ⅛ of this [M$ 5 million grant] was spent in 1951." This is approximately M$ 625,000. The figure shown here is larger because of the inclusion of some salaries (see n. f) not directly paid by RIDA, and part of the estimated capital costs (see n. e), which were not shown in the RIDA reports until 1953.

ᶜ Includes the cost of salaries and allowances for staff, other expenses classed as "administration" in the reports, and capital costs under the administration and schemes fund—largely office buildings and quarters.

ᵈ No breakdown of capital costs by projects is shown until 1953. On December 31, 1953 fixed capital in the administration account was valued at M$ 680,600. The estimated allocation of this for the three years is as follows:

1951	M $ 70,000 (*ca.* 10 percent)
1952	M $200,000 (*ca.* 30 percent)
1953	M $410,600 (*ca.* 60 percent)

ᵉ This figure is presented in the Federation of Malaya Financial Statement for 1951 as "Member for Home Affairs, emoluments and personal allowances." The actual salary costs of RIDA should undoubtedly be higher than this, and all of this specific allocation for Home Affairs should not be attributed to RIDA. However, since RIDA officers at this time were generally on loan from other departments, it is impossible to arrive at a better estimate of salary costs.

ᶠ This is an estimate arrived at by using the 130 staff members (average of 107 for the first half of the year and 154 for the second half) for 1953, multiplied by the average cost per staff member for 1954 and 1953—M$ 6,500. This is a crude estimate, but is undoubtedly more accurate than the M$ 149,500 reported as emoluments and allowances under the Member for Home Affairs, the only other direct source of information on RIDA finances.

ᵍ Source: annual report for 1956.

ʰ Includes capital and operating costs in the projects, but not depreciation costs or allowances.

ⁱ Operating costs are shown directly in the reports. Capital costs were obtained by taking the difference between given capital value at the end of 1952 and 1953.

ʲ Includes M$ 24,900 listed as miscellaneous expenses under the project fund. This category first appeared in 1955, but did not include amounts greater than M$ 1,000 until 1958–1959.

ᵏ Includes M$ 2,500 listed as miscellaneous.

ˡ Includes M$ 132,000 listed for the Small Industries Services Institute. This might be included under training, although it was conceived largely as a revenue earning project.

ᵐ Source: annual report for 1954.

VI

THE MINISTRY
OF RURAL DEVELOPMENT:
ACTIVATING THE BUREAUCRACY

FIRST MOVES: THE RED BOOK

Shortly after it was returned to power in the elections of 1959, the Alliance Government announced (7 October 1959) the creation of a new Ministry of Rural Development. This was to be the organizational stimulant behind a new and coordinated drive for development of the rural areas. The high priority of this drive was made explicit by placing the new Ministry within the portfolio of the Prime Minister and giving its active control to the Deputy Prime Minister, Tun Abdul Razak.

In the months that followed the October announcement, government provided through speeches and policy statements a picture of the rationale, the aims, and the means to be employed by the new Ministry.[1] Government argued that the majority of the people live in rural areas and that it is the responsibility of any democratic government to serve the majority. Economically, Malaya was viewed as an agricultural country. National development depended on agricultural development, hence the rural producers must be given pride of place in government's development programs. In addition, the rural areas had in the past been neglected and had not received amenities equal to those of the towns. The development of a stable national state required

---

[1] What follows is distilled from newspaper accounts and government press releases from the period 7 October 1959 to May 1960.

that this imbalance be redressed. Finally, the Communist insurgency had been put down, but the poverty on which Communism feeds had not been eliminated. Therefore the struggle against Communism now had to be carried on a new front. Poverty was to be attacked with all the military precision and sense of urgency that had produced a successful struggle against the Communist insurgents.

Two general aims were made explicit. Government would lend all its efforts to providing the rural people with the improvements and other resources needed to ensure development, and it would call upon the rural people to cooperate and participate in their own uplift. To achieve these ends the new Ministry would coordinate the activities of all technical and administrative units throughout the country to mobilize the state's resources for investment in the rural sector. To gain the cooperation of the people, the new Ministry would provide them with the incentives, the organizational avenues, and the literate skills required to enable them to take a full part in their own uplift.

The two underlying motives of rural development and its new Ministry, implied in most of government's statements, were recognized and made explicit in a newspaper editorial comment in December.[2] The editor observed that continued rule of the Alliance Government, and of the democratic institutions to which it was committed, would be determined by the Government's ability to fill the peasants' pots. Government's sincerity and ability would be measured in the number of schools, roads, and health centers built, the wells dug and the utilities provided, and the amount of new land opened. Significant reservations about the new state are implied in this private editorial comment, which could be somewhat more candid than could the Government itself. First, the rule of democratic institutions was equated exclusively with the rule of the Alliance Party. The opposition parties were implicitly defined as parties of either right or left totalitarianism. Second, the viability of the ruling party depended upon its ability to make an economic payoff; the masses had to be fed, poverty had to be eliminated. Third, and most important for the present discussion, poverty would be eliminated through the espousal of output goals in government development programming. The peasants' pots would be filled if government provided amenities and social overhead capital to the rural areas.

At the same time this editorial comment recognized that government's call for popular support was a two-faceted appeal. On the one hand it was a simple appeal for popular support at the polls to maintain both the Alliance Party and its democratic institutions. On

---

[2] *The Sunday Mail,* 6 December 1959.

the other hand the appeal implied a recognition that popular involvement, or a new set of attitudes and behavior, was required for economic
development. This was essentially a recognition that economic development requires more than output goals in development programming; some form of cultural goals are needed as well.

This editorial comment is particularly significant in its recognition
that modern political pressures in the new state had produced a
development organization with predominantly output goals, but with
important internal pressures to broaden those goals.

In January 1960 a National Rural Development Council was formed,
bringing together all the political power the state could mobilize. The
Prime Minister acted as Chairman and the Deputy Prime Minister
(then Minister of Rural Development) as the Deputy Chairman. The
position of secretary was filled by a European civil servant who has
played a key role in the entire rural development program. The future
of the development program was previewed in the composition and
work of the Council. It contained all cabinet ministers in their dual
capacities as heads of technical and administrative services and as
representatives of the people and thus holders of political power.

The Council's work consisted essentially of defining the immediate
tasks to be accomplished. Plans for the development of the rural areas
had to be created and integrated into the Second Five-Year Plan then
being prepared. Reinforcing the output character of the goals of development was the fact that the details of this Second Five-Year Plan
are concerned almost exclusively with public investment, though
targets for employment, private investment, and aggregate and sectoral
output were also included.[3] The business of rural planning was to be
symbolized in the Red Book, though this name was not applied to the
rural plans until July. The organizational instruments for planning
and executing were to be the state and district rural development
committees. Having accomplished this primary definition of tasks, the
National Rural Development Council languished into inactivity, for
reasons to be discussed below.

The Ministry of Rural Development began its task of over-all planning and coordination by issuing explicit instructions for the formation
of the local committees.[4] This step would allow the Ministry direct
access to the local units despite the nation's federal structure, which
gave the states responsibility for the District Officers and for land

---

[3] These latter, however, were sheer guesses.

[4] The events described here are placed in a simple and somewhat ideal sequence
rather than in their real sequence, though the description remains essentially
faithful to the latter.

matters. The Chief Minister of each state was made chairman of the State Rural Development Committee. The executive secretary was a Ministry officer, the State Development Officer.[5] Thus the Ministry could always approach the lower administrative units through its own officer, who spoke with the formal authority of the Chief Minister of the state. The State Development Officer also provided the formal mechanism by which federal funds were made available to the states for their development projects.

The composition of the State Rural Development Committees reflected the Ministry's attempt to coordinate all government development efforts. All heads of technical departments, such as agriculture, drainage and irrigation, and public works, were on the committee, along with Members of Parliament from the state. District Rural Development Committees were constructed on the same lines, containing district heads of technical departments, State Councillors, and Members of Parliament from the district. The District Officers were designated chairmen of the committees.

To activate these state and district committees, the Ministry also issued detailed instructions, giving the committees two basic tasks. They were to plan for rural development, and they were to go ahead with the implementation of those plans.

Planning was organized around a standardized master plan that came to be known as the *Red Book*. Between March and May 1960 a series of more and more detailed planning instructions were issued to the local committees. At this point the major task of planning lay with the district rural development committees, for it was there that the basic plan was formed. To give force to his directives and instructions, the Minister began an extensive series of visits to state and district committees to explain the plan and the purpose of the new program, and to bring the force of his political and administrative power to bear upon local officers. The Department of Information and the Malayan Film Unit followed these tours closely (as they have since) and gave maximum publicity to the program.

As it finally appeared, the Red Book form was a large loose-leaf binder measuring slightly over two feet square. It instructed the com-

---

[5] This was previously the RIDA state rural development officer. The existing post was simply taken over by the new Ministry when it assumed the coordinating function with which RIDA had previously been charged. It provides a good example of the administrative competence of the new Ministry in using the simplest and most direct method of creating the organizational structure necessary to accomplish its task. Much of the Ministry's effort has been concerned with this type of successful reorganization and mobilization of administrative capacity rather than with the slower and more costly process of creating completely new structures.

mittee to solicit from the rural people all requests for roads, bridges, schools, land, and other improvements. Requests considered practical were to be included in the plan. Requests that were not practical must be rejected and *the applicants were to be informed of the reason for rejection.* Criteria for acceptance and rejection were left to the district committee. In addition, all proposals from existing government departments were to be considered and integrated with the people's requests into a single plan.

All these proposals were to be included in one of twelve sections, each with a map overlay:

I	Basic District Map
II	Land Map
III	Road Map
IV	Rural Water Supplies
V	Minor Irrigation Works
VI	River Clearing Proposals
VII	Schools, Health Centers, and Playing Fields
VIII	Rural Processing and Marketing Facilities
IX	Rural Industries
X	Cooperative Development
XI	Telecommunications Facilities
XII	Rural Electricity Supplies

Each section contained a page of detailed instructions for preparing the map, giving standard symbols and colors to be used, and an overlay on which the existing and proposed facilities were to be located. A foldout map of the district on the inside of the back cover could be placed under these overlays. Proposed facilities or projects were listed in order of priority on a separate form, giving a reference number, name, location, justification (number of people to be served, etc.), and an estimate of cost. This separate list was kept in a plastic bag attached to the lower left-hand corner of the map overlay in each section. The responsibility for preparation of each tracing lay with the appropriate officer, named by the Ministry, who was instructed to sign the map tracings and the lists of projects. In each case the priority of the projects was to be decided upon by the district rural development committee.

A series of appendices gave further instructions to the committee. Appendix A gave details of the committee procedure. Meetings were to be informal, but must be conducted in a businesslike manner. All discussions were to be contained in the minutes, each separate item given a separate numbered paragraph with the numbers running consecutively throughout the year. Minutes need not be formally confirmed at each meeting, but corrections could be made. Each set of minutes was to close with a paragraph stating the time and place of the next meeting, and two copies of the minutes were to be forwarded to the State Rural Development Committee (and thence to the Ministry) within three days after the meeting.

There were also special procedures to be followed during the visits of the Minister, the Chief Minister, or other officials. The District Officer was to brief the visitor on the general stages of the plan, a specific statement of progress on land development, and a clear statement of problems faced. Then the technical heads of departments were to continue with specific reviews of projects under their jurisdiction, again stating problems faced. Each part was to be followed by questions and answers, and a summary note of the briefing was to be sent within three days to the State Development Committee and to the Ministry.

Two appendices (B and C) presented detailed technical specifications for rural roads and a standard form for survey of existing wells. Financial policy was outlined in Appendix D. "In planning the important thing is not to consider whether or not funds will be available." All good projects must be included, with no concern given to the total estimate of costs; projects need simply be listed in order of priority. "In brief, the Policy is that Federal Funds will be made available, provided that State Governments show that they have geared their own Policy, Funds and Efforts towards giving the maximum to the development of the Rural Areas." If it were clear that the state has done its best, the Federal Government would provide all necessary funds. Development was not to be a series of paper battles between State and Federal Governments, "but a co-ordinated and determined effort in which both Federal and States Governments will give of their best in a combined effort, to ensure that in the next few years the utmost is done for the Rural People."

Appendix E instructed the officers of government to tour the district. In the past this had been done individually by the officers; now they were to tour together and as much as possible to solve the problems of development through joint discussion on the ground. When possible the entire committee should tour as a team, to organize meetings of village people to explain the program to them, to get their suggestions, and to explain why certain desired projects must be rejected, "and so clear up misunderstandings in an atmosphere of good will."

Finally the book ended with Appendix F on community development. Here there were no specific instructions, only a general statement that the people must be won over to a full participation in their own development.

The actual procedure used for eliciting proposals from the people varied greatly among the approximately 70 districts in the nation. In some cases the committees organized village meetings and went in force to explain the program and to get suggestions for projects. In other cases the village headmen or the *Penghulus* (heads of *mukims*) were called to a general meeting at the District Office and asked to solicit suggestions from the people. In still other cases the suggestions were drawn up in the District Office by the committee members, with the rationale that the elected representatives on the committee and the District Officer already knew what the people wanted. Meetings began in March, but spread rather slowly in some states. The Red Books were to be completed by mid-July, and this schedule was actually met by most committees. In some cases this necessitated committees working around the clock for the last week.

Red books were prepared in three copies, one each for the district, the state, and the national development committees. At the state level all district proposals were collated and selected for inclusion in a state rural development plan. These were then passed to the Ministry where state proposals were collated and selected for inclusion in the Second Five-Year Plan. Of the total public investment for the Second Five-Year Plan, M$ 2,150 million, Red Book projects accounted for M$ 440,670,000, or about 20 percent.[6]

The Red Book was designed to be used continuously in revising and in implementing plans. This plan broke down at the upper levels of the bureaucracy, but appears to have been partially successful at the lower levels. In the collation and selection of projects at the state and national level the lower units should have been advised of what projects were included in the higher plans. This was not done. Thus the total estimates for all district plans were considerably larger than the total estimates for the state plans, and the total for all state plans were larger than the total for the national plan.[7] Thus in a purely

---

[6] This does not represent the full public investment to the rural sector, however. No breakdown into rural and urban sectors has been made by the Economic Planning Unit, but from the schedule of investment, one might estimate roughly that another M$ 400 to M$ 500 million is directed primarily to the rural sector, making a total of approximately 40 percent of total public investment for the plan.

[7] This information is from interviews; I have not been able to draw up actual totals for the state or district plans. The breakdown in communications here was partially explained by different time horizons at different planning levels. The national level was working on a five-year plan as its most immediate problem, though it also embraced less specific longer ranged economic goals. Thus the total number of proposals from below could be accepted as part of the longer range

technical sense the Red Book as a planning instrument was obsolete as soon as it was completed.

The program of project implementation, however, appears to have given some utility to the Red Book at the district level. The districts have from the beginning had complete control over minor development projects. In the first place, the Ministry provided what was called "quick results money" (generally about M$ 50,000) to a large number of district committees, to be used immediately to implement projects of highest priority in the Red Book. Following this, money from the state and from the Ministry had been granted generally in accordance with Red Book procedures. No additional justifications for projects in the Red Book needed to be included in requests for appropriations from the state governments, unless the estimates had changed radically. In Perak, for example, where this plan worked smoothly from the very beginning, it was possible for the State Development Officer to inform the District Officers in December what their appropriations would be for the following year. Thus the District Committees were able to go ahead with receiving tenders and making contracts for 1961 as early as December 1960. The first appropriations actually came out in January, followed by the final ones in April. In effect, as far as minor development projects were concerned, the Red Book took responsibility out of the hands of the state and placed it in the hands of the district, but allowed for accountability at the state level. Thus, it greatly speeded up the process of allocations for public investment.

To provide a physical setting for the development program, operations rooms were created for the state, district, and national committees. These followed a standard pattern, with large wall maps showing development projects and plans on overlays, with charts, graphs, and pictures showing projects completed and planned, and the state of completion of current projects. The Red Book generally occupies a prominent place on an easel or a stand on a table. The rooms are equipped with conference tables and chairs. They are in rather constant use both for normal committee meetings, which are generally held once a month, and for briefings of visitors.

ORGANIZATION AND WORK

The term "Ministry of Rural Development" actually refers to three organizational spheres. Though the Minister is in a position of direct

---

program, even though only some of the proposals could be included in the five-year plan then being formulated. This information was contained in the informal communications between national and state levels and their subordinate levels, but was not integrated systematically into the planning program.

control over these three spheres, they each have different functions. For the sake of convenience, we shall refer to these as the *Portfolio,* the *Ministry,* and the *Executive* of the Ministry.

The total portfolio of the Ministry of Rural Development contains six major departments: (1) The Ministry of Rural Development, (2) The Commissioner of Lands, (3) The Geological Survey, (4) Mines, (5) Survey, and (6) Game.[8] This represents essentially a number of functions taken over from the Ministry of Natural Resources, which was dissolved in the cabinet reshuffle of 1959. They were placed under the Ministry of Rural Development partly because there was no place else to put them, also partly because they were in some sense relevant to rural development. This is especially true of the Commissioner of Lands and the Survey Department.

The Ministry of Rural Development (1 above) itself contains a central *Executive* and Administrative unit, a unit for *Lands,* and a unit for *Adult Education and Community Development*. Each of these is headed by a deputy secretary. The Ministry has two major functions. The function of coordinating other agencies and stimulating them to increase their output is performed primarily by the *Executive*. The other sections of the Ministry, especially Adult Education, are concerned with doing those things that no one else is doing but are still considered important for development. The Executive is by far the most important and powerful unit in the Ministry.

Although the Minister is in control of all three spheres, he appears to be most active in and most concerned with the Executive. Within the Executive the most powerful post is that of Deputy Secretary for Development.[9] This is not an independent post, but an administrative extension of the Minister himself. Through this post the Minister maintains direct control over the Federal Land Development Authority (FLDA) and the Rural and Industrial Development Authority (RIDA), and is involved in the direction and coordination of the State Rural Development Officers and the District Officers, and of the Ministries and their agencies at the national level.

The formal organization gives the Minister control over State De-

---

[8] In this discussion, we use the form as of 1963. Game was actually not separated from the Ministry of Rural Development (1) until late 1962. With the exception of the term executive, these are the terms used in the estimates. See Federation of Malaya, *Estimates of Federal Revenue and Expenditure for 1963*, Ministry of Rural Development, pp. 239–254.

[9] Until 1963 this post was filled by C. G. Ferguson. In 1963 Ferguson was promoted to a new post called Director of Planning and Implementation. The post of Deputy Secretary was then filled by a Malay.

velopment Officers and District Officers through their respective development committees. State Development Officers are Ministry officials located in the states, functioning as the development executive for the Chief Minister of the state who is the chairman of the State Development Committees. District Officers are formally responsible to the state's Chief Minister, normally through the Chief Secretary of the state. In development matters, however, they are responsible to the State Development Officer as an executive of both the state's Chief Minister and the National Minister of Rural Development. The Ministry of Rural Development has no formal control over the other Ministries in the cabinet. The Ministry does, however, exercise control because the Minister is both Minister of Rural Development and Deputy Prime Minister.

The Executive of the Ministry is a small organization that does not appear destined to further growth. Its past growth can be seen in table VI-1. It functions by consolidating and exercising power over

TABLE VI-1

MINISTRY OF RURAL DEVELOPMENT: EXECUTIVE UNIT GROWTH OF
PERSONNEL FROM 1961–1963

Personnel	1960	1961	1963
Top leadership:			
Minister, assistant, secretary and deputy secretary	7	7	8
Supporting executives:			
State development officers and assistant secretaries	15[a]	16	13
Higher clerical (Division III)	14	28	29
Lower clerical (Division IV)	7	17	17
TOTAL	43	68	67

SOURCE: Federation of Malaya, *Estimates of Federal Revenue and Expenditure* for the years 1962 and 1963.

[a] The ten state development officers were provided by RIDA in 1960, although they were directly under the Executive unit of the Ministry.

existing administrative units, rather than by creating new units formally subordinate to itself. In effect it functions much like a super district officer, shorn even of the formal control over land that the district officer carries. It does almost nothing by itself; it merely coordinates existing agencies and stimulates them to work according to its plan.

Below the Ministry, the state and district Rural Development Committees retain the structure and functions originally laid down in the Red Book. Throughout the entire rural development organization the legacy of the Emergency is evident. The state and district Rural Development Committees take their inspiration from the state and district War Executive Committees. The operations rooms were instruments developed during the Emergency, although at that time they were clothed in more secrecy than are the rural development operations rooms.

This was the organization created to increase government activities in stimulating development. Its major function was not to engage in development activities itself, but to increase the output of existing government organizations, to get them to do more of what they were already doing. The success of this new organization is widely recognized in Malaya, but it is difficult to document it conclusively. The recently prepared review of development under the Second Five-Year Plan[10] shows a significant increase in government activities. Although it is impossible to demonstrate with any precision the part the Ministry of Rural Development has played in this increased activity, it is widely acknowledged by Malayan government officers that the Ministry's role has been a crucial one. Some indication of the importance of that role can be gained from a summary of the development statistics, especially those that show the emphasis upon public investment in the rural areas.

In the first place we can examine allocated and actual development expenditures for all of Development, and for Public Works Development. The latter is instructive because it has been the single largest development activity during the period, and because it is the one ministry most directly involved in the achievement of the output goals of the Ministry of Rural Development. Table VI-2 shows a rapid increase in allocated funds for both total development and public works. Further, the greatest increases in allocations came just as the new Ministry was establishing its control over the larger decision-making process of development planning. Actual expenditures also increased rapidly, but the significant trend of increasing proportions of actual to allocated funds only begins after 1960. The high proportion in 1958 results partly from a cutback in allocations due to the recession. The decrease in 1959 can be attributed to the elections, which drew heavily upon administrative machinery that was both

---

[10] Federation of Malaya, *Interim Review of Development in Malaya under the Second Five-Year Plan*, Kuala Lumpur, 1963, *passim*.

TABLE VI-2

MALAYAN DEVELOPMENT EXPENDITURES 1955–1963
(in million Malayan dollars)

Expenditures	1955	1956	1957	1958	1959	1960	1961	1962	1963[a]
Total									
Allocated	---	---	---	173	203	282	430	569	548
Actual	97	147	168	140	142	141	264	415	460
Actual as percent of allocated				81	70	50	59	73	84
Public works									
Allocated				45	47	90	133	210	
Actual				32	25	39	99	151	
Actual as percent of allocated				71	53	43	74	72	

[a] Estimated.

limited and not highly specialized in electoral procedures.[11] The further proportionate decrease in 1960 is partly the result of rapid increases in allocated funds.

Thus from this table we can infer a two-faceted pattern of establishment of Ministerial Control over development. First, control was established over the decision-making process on resource allocation. The second, and perhaps more intractable, problem lay in establishing control over the implementation of the development program. Success in the latter is indicated by the steadily rising proportion of actual to allocated development funds after 1960. In short, the government was increasing both the allocation of funds to development and the ability of the administration to use the funds that were available.

We can also examine the record of physical achievements associated with formation and operation of the new Ministry.[12] Selected categories are shown in Table VI-3 which shows physical achievements during the First Five-Year Plan period, compared with those for the first half of the Second Five-Year Plan period.[13] The increased output can be taken as a measure of the success in achieving output goals. Even these

[11] All local officers, including District Officers and RIDA officers, were heavily involved in administering the elections of 1959. Further, the elections were spread over three months, as state elections were held separately from federal elections. The justification for splitting state and federal elections was that holding them together would provide too heavy a burden on the administrative machinery, as well as upon the national political organizations.

[12] *Interim Review of Development in Malaya*, p. 24.

[13] *Op. cit.*, pp. 65–76.

TABLE VI-3

SELECTED ITEMS OF PHYSICAL CONSTRUCTION IN
MALAYAN DEVELOPMENT PROGRAMS

Items	Increase 1956–1960 (5 years)	Increase Jan. 1961–June 1963 (2½ years)
Education: Classrooms		
Urban: Primary	1,990	1,061
Secondary and other	485	811
Rural: Primary	6,233	2,803
Secondary and other	65	289
Health:		
Urban: Hospitals	—	—
Clinics	—	—
Rural: Clinics and subcenters	16	105
Midwife clinics	26	396
Dental clinics	57	99
Irrigation: Acres irrigated for double cropping or for new cultivation	61,633	61,476
Electricity:		
Urban households served	52,118	40,176
Rural households served	9,949	6,606
Telephones:		
Urban phone booths	136	140
Rural phone booths	201	373
Road Construction (Miles Constructed)		
Bitumen surface	147	165
Nonbitumen surface	325	1,300

increases understate the success of goal achievement and the impact of the new Ministry, however, because the achievements of the last year of the first plan should be attributed in large part to the work of the Ministry.

Although a breakdown by years is not available for all classes of expenditures, it is available for road construction, an activity on which the new Ministry placed great emphasis.[14] In the entire five-year period of the first plan, 472 miles of new roads were constructed, compared with 1,465 miles in the first two and a half years of the second plan. However, during 1960, the first full year of the new Ministry's operation, 260 miles of new roads were constructed. Thus a more accurate comparison would show that prior to the formation

[14] *Op. cit.*, p. XV. This gives the total miles of new road completed in 1960, not broken down by type of surface.

of the Ministry, 212 miles of new roads were constructed in four years, whereas after the formation of the Ministry 1,625 miles of new roads were constructed in three and a half years. In all areas we see both a great increase in physical construction, and an even more rapid increase in construction in the rural areas. In effect, the new Ministry gained rapid control over those elements of the bureaucracy that were especially concerned with the production of physical amenities and social overhead capital.

CONTROL

An organization structure does not by itself bring control over relevant activities and officers. It provides the avenues through which communication flows and control is exercised, and the formal structure at least partly determines the quantity and quality of the obstacles raised to communication and control. Of as great, or greater, importance, however, is what Selznick calls "the work put into the organization." The way the functionaries act, with what motives, speed, and in what directions, is of real significance in giving life to an organization. We have seen, for example, that RIDA created state and district development committees early in the 1950's. We have also seen that these were almost totally ineffective except in assisting RIDA to process a few applications for its meager resources. The Ministry of Rural Development, on the other hand, has succeeded in building an organization of considerable vitality, especially in its chosen field of stimulating increased public investment in the rural areas. We must now attempt to account for this success.

Part of the difference between the RIDA attempt and the current attempt can be explained simply by the resources available. RIDA had a total of about M$ 5 million per year for all its activities, whereas the Ministry of Rural Development has commitments of at least between M$ 100 and M$ 200 million a year for the current five-year plan for development expenditure alone.[15] These were, however, only commitments of resources, and these were made only because the new Ministry had been able to present a detailed plan for resource expenditure. Commitments alone are not sufficient. Money also has to be spent, and however simple this may seem to an individual, it is a task of tremendous proportions for a complex organization, especially

---

[15] Assuming between the M$ 440 million for Red Book projects and an estimated M$ 900 to M$ 1,000 million for the total sector in the Second Five-Year Plan.

if the legal structure provides for a fair degree of accountability.[16]

It is necessary to emphasize once again the nature of the task as originally conceived by the Minister and his close subordinates in the Executive unit of the Ministry. The Red Book structure clearly shows a strong orientation to what we have called output goals—items of social overhead capital and amenities; items that could be constructed. There was no place for the analysis of human productivity, or of the organization of either production or distribution. The leaders clearly defined their task as one of increasing the output of existing, technically competent, elements of the bureaucracy.

These leaders also had a clear idea of the problems they faced, essentially problems of coordination and stimulation. They also recognized the character of the organization with which they had to work —essentially a colonial bureaucracy. They saw that in the development of this bureaucracy the specialization of functions had progressed faster than their integration. Technically competent agencies had grown up, splitting off from more general agencies. As functions became specialized and located in distinct agencies, those agencies developed a jealous concern for their boundaries and for the protection of their integrity and the exclusive right of access to their constituency or resource. Integration had proceeded less rapidly because the entire bureaucracy was oriented to custody rather than to development. The initiative for development lay in the specialized agencies and the lower level administrative posts of the District Offices. In itself this initiative was of considerably narrow bounds, concerned as it was with the development of one resource (as forest resources) or of a small segment of the population (as a district). The exercise of this initiative was contained and obstructed by the upper levels of the bureaucracy, which controlled total resource allocation. We have already seen that these upper levels were motivated by yearly fiscal policy. Decision-making on resource allocation was centered in the Financial Secretariat where accountability, budget-balancing, and reserve accumulation were clearly superordinate to development.

In addition, the development of the colonial bureaucracy was set in the context of the British alliance with the traditional Malay elite. Princes and lesser nobility became involved in the growing colonial

---

[16] It is only partly true that capital scarcity is a major problem of the underdeveloped countries. Often more financial resources are available than can be absorbed by the weak and limited administrative structures of these countries. Malaya's is only one of the common experiences of the critical importance of the administrative and technical capacity to spend what is available. In most cases the experience is the unhappy one of lack of capacity; Malaya's was the happy experience of increasing capacity to use available resources.

bureaucracy. The Malay College at Kuala Kangsar, open only to Malay nobility until after World War II, was a major avenue of educational mobility through which a select class of Malays moved into the modern government. There were significant variations in this pattern, which we shall analyze below, but on the whole the indigenous sector of the colonial bureaucracy was more an ascriptive than an achievement-based bureaucracy. This, combined with the custodial orientation of the government, gave to the colonial bureaucracy a relaxed and even a languid air. Such an organization required some form of shock if it were to increase its output of improvements and social overhead capital.

The problems of coordination and stimulation faced by the new Ministry were largely internal problems. The external problem, that of acquiring state resources of money and power, was solved because the Ministry rode the crest of the wave of changing goals of government. The indigenous leaders had come to power on the basis of promises of more government concern for the masses: independence in 1955 and more improvements and social overhead capital in 1959. Thus the top decision-makers were well disposed to increase government spending.

The Ministry of Rural Development did have to fight, however, for its specific approach to development. The greater its power in the cabinet and at the vanguard of the development process, the more resources it would be able to command for its program. In the first place, the structure of the party and the cabinet provided paramount power to the new Ministry. Malaya's electoral system gave considerable power to the central party. Nominees for office could contest in any constituency, with no residency qualifications. Thus the party could allocate safe seats to loyal members and precarious seats to the more recalcitrant. In addition, the Alliance Party has good local organization and, through the Chinese wing and favorably disposed foreign companies, financial resources to support loyal candidates. All of this gives the central leadership of the party control over the legislature and the cabinet, thus assuring tight control over decisions on resource allocation.

The composition of the cabinet has also contributed to the power of the Ministry of Rural Development and its specific approach to development. The single most important ministry for the achievement of output goals is the Ministry of Works. This Ministry is in the hands of the only Indian member of the cabinet, Dato Sambanthan. Politically Sambanthan's position is highly tenuous. It can be said that he exists only at the sufferance of the other two ethnic wings of the

Alliance, primarily to maintain the pan-ethnic image of the Alliance.[17] This gives Tun Razak, as Deputy Prime Minister and Minister of Rural Development, extensive control over the one ministry most crucial to the success of his program.

In the second place, the Ministry of Rural Development increased its already considerable political power through the popularity of its program. It has always been far ahead of other ministries in presenting its image to the public. From the very beginning, the Minister demanded that the program be visible; there must not only be results, but the results must be visible. The program has always received a great deal of publicity, and a large proportion of the press releases of the Department of Information have been devoted to rural development.[18] The Malayan Film Unit follows all the Minister's tours and has produced a series of documentary films on rural development, which are shown in public movie houses throughout the country. The operations rooms have also been designed to show not only the officials but also the general public what is being done under the new program. Civic groups, school children, and groups of local leaders are continually given briefings on the program.

Some of this was intended when the program began, but it soon became apparent that the new program had considerable publicity value of its own. The Red Book provides a good illustration of this development. We have seen that it was first mooted as a master lower level development plan in February and March of 1960, but did not attain the name "Red Book" until July. The color was accidental, but it quickly became a popular symbol for the new surge of development in the country. The Indian newspaper, *Tamil Nesan,* held a Red Book essay contest, and Tun Razak promised that ideas expressed in the winning essays would be taken into consideration in planning. University students produced a Blue Book to assist in development, and various business associations followed with their own book plans. All of this made rural development a popular program, with which the person of Tun Razak was closely associated, and brought to the program additional political power.

[17] This refers to Sambanthan's position, not his person. Personally he is an indefatigable campaigner, speaks excellent Malay, and has brought considerable support to the party. In addition, he has the reputation of being incorruptible, an important trait for such a corruption-prone position. Together with the image of pan-ethnicity he brings, this may give Sambanthan moral and persuasive power in the cabinet, but it does not give him real political power. There is no single constituency in the entire Federation in which the Indian vote is really critical.

[18] In the first half of 1962, there were about 50 separate Department of Information press releases on rural development per month out of a total of about 200 releases per month.

Establishing control over the process of state resource allocation was only a part of the new Ministry's pattern of successful action. It was even more important to activate the bureaucracy, to coordinate its specialized agencies, and to stimulate them to increase their output. Although it is impossible to confirm this proposition, it seems probable that the Ministry would have lost much of its power in the higher echelon arena if it had not been able to use the resources it was demanding and to force the bureaucracy to act effectively.

The internal problems associated with increasing the output of the existing bureaucracy were essentially those of coordination and stimulation. The specialization of the colonial period had cut the bureaucracy in two directions: hierarchically into national, state, and district levels, and functionally into specialized agencies. For example, road-building required coordinated route planning between national, state, and district levels; coordinated financial and equipment allocation, most of which came from the higher to the lower echelons; and the coordination of specialized functions at all levels. Survey planned routes, District and State land offices arranged for land acquisition. Geological Survey and Mines advised on mineral resources, Forest advised on timber resources and watersheds, and Drainage and Irrigation had to be consulted with respect to their projects. School construction required the same type of multiagency coordination, including as well Education with its projections of future classroom requirements and its standards of plant construction. In all cases, before work could actually begin, a highly complex communications process had to be set in motion. The determinants of the rate of communications flow lay partly in the formal structure of the network—the channels that each agency used to communicate with other agencies—and partly in the degree of compliance of the lower level functionaries.

The internal problems the new Ministry faced can best be understood by analyzing the four mechanisms—technical, bureaucratic, legal, and social[19]—by which lower level functionaries insulated themselves against the encroachments of the emerging central power. Engineers best illustrate those capable of using technical kinds of insulation against the demands of the central power. An engineer could not be asked to approve and sign a crude drawing of a proposed road or a

---

[19] The *ad hoc* quality of these categories or spheres makes them of limited analytical utility for comparative research. However, since this is just one case study, unilluminated by comparative materials, it was considered best to keep the categories as close as possible to the processes being described. It is hoped that these categories will give way to more analytical ones in a proposed study of development organizations in six counties.

crude estimate of its cost. All his professional training, all of his previous bureaucratic experience had instilled in him the values of accuracy and thoroughness, especially in planning; and accuracy and thoroughness required time. In addition, his specialized skills had always given him the exclusive right to make judgments on questions of accuracy and thoroughness. This was, in fact, why the bureaucrats and politicians had hired him in the first place. Thus, if anything, he should be telling the new Ministry what it could and could not do, not the other way around.

The power of procedural rules in the bureaucracy gave administrators at all levels some insulation against the power of the new Ministry. Permanent secretaries of national ministries, state secretaries and their staffs, and even district officers had been fully trained in the rules of procedure. Correspondence had to be prepared properly and sent through proper channels. Delays were inevitable and were accepted as such, or were not defined as delays; "it simply takes time to get an answer, one has many pressing matters." The sheer volume of correspondence and the time required for its proper handling could always be legitimately used to explain why work had not been completed.

Legal forms of insulation derived largely from Malaya's federal structure. Land is constitutionally defined as a state subject, and its acquisition and its cost are matters over which the state governments have exclusive legal control. The state civil servants of the old Unfederated Malay States—Johore, Kelantan, Trengganu, Perlis, and Kedah—are under the exclusive jurisdiction of the respective states. Only the Chief Minister and the Chief Secretary can transfer, promote, or discipline them. They cannot be transferred out of the state without their own consent. Further, the states have the right to accept or reject federal officers posted to the state. The new Ministry could exercise legal control over the Malayan Civil Service, but not over the Civil Services of the old Unfederated States.

Social insulating mechanisms were primarily located in the District Offices and became visible in the contrasting positions of the Malayan civil servants in the old Federated Malay States—Selangor, Pahang, Perak, and Negri Sembilan, and for our purposes Malacca and Penang —and the state civil servants in the old Unfederated States. The basis of social insulation lay in the relation between occupational position and social status.

In the State Civil Services the District Officers were part of what can be called the states' landed gentry-bureaucratic elite. There were considerable family ties throughout the bureaucracy. Brothers and sisters of officers had married other officers or their sisters. A wide range of relatives—aunts, uncles, cousins—were in other government positions. Officers visited one another often and maintained closer ties with their narrow occupational community than they did with the variegated local communities in which they lived. Close friends and associates were in the same occupation and also tended to be fellow Malays. This pattern kept the occupational-gentry community conscious of its cohesion and its separateness. Further, when asked if they would join the Malayan Civil Service if they were given the opportunity, most answered in the negative. They had no desire to subject themselves to out-of-state transfers and they did not wish to compete with the better educated officers of the Malayan Civil Service.

Malayan Civil Service District Officers were in a different position. In addition to being better educated they were more geographically and socially mobile. They did not always serve in their home states, and almost all had served in a state other than their own at some time. Many came from families of nongovernment occupations, and some had low-class peasant origins. They had achieved their positions through educational and examination performance. Their close friends were widely scattered throughout the country and in a wide range of government and private occupations. They maintained close associations with government and private persons, often non-Malays, in their local communities.

In effect the relation between occupational position and social status was reversed in the two groups of officers. The high occupational positions of the state officers derived from the high social status of their families. The high occupational position of the federal officers, on the other hand, gave them a high social status. State bureaucracies were more ascriptive; the federal bureaucracy was more achievement-based. When to this is added the legal insulation of the state officers, the contrast between state and federal officer systems appears pronounced. In the case of the federal officers, the central government had legal power over a specialized position that determined both class and status, occupational position. In the case of the state officers, the central government had no legal power over a diffuse position that reflected class, but was itself determined by ascribed status. The compliance structure of the federal bureaucracy was predominantly utilitarian and the central government had complete access to that structure, whereas that of the State Civil Services was only weakly utilitarian, and the central government had no legal access to that structure.

These differences in compliance and access were reflected immediately in the new development program. The federal District Officers offered little resistance and few problems to the new Ministry. They have always been the most rapid in transmitting instructions and in translating them into action. The state offices took longer to form the rural development committees, and in some cases did not begin work on the Red Books until a few weeks before they were due. For example, the first meetings of the State Rural Development Committees in Pahang and Negri Sembilan were in March and April, with all of the district committees following in quick succession. In Johore the state committee did not meet until August, though some of the district committees met and were functioning before this. In Kedah the state committee met for the first time at the end of May, but it was June and July before most of the district committees were functioning.

In breaking through these forms of insulation, the Minister of Rural Development used his wide range of powers in the state. As one of the four major chiefs of the state of Pahang, he commanded the deference of Malays, who still regard their traditional nobility as legitimate claimants upon loyalty. As Deputy Prime Minister he was second in command of the ruling Alliance party, the super-bureaucratic decision-making body. In this position he was also first among equals in the cabinet, which directly controlled the bureaucracy. These traditional, political, and bureaucratic bases of power gave the Minister firm control over the allocation of the state's material, and to a certain extent symbolic, resources.

At the time the Ministry was being formed, these resources were by no means meager. The government held considerable reserves and had an excellent source of continuing revenues. Further, these financial resources had become highly available in the change of the broad goals of government.

In addition, the Malayanization of the bureaucracy was moving ahead at a rapid pace, giving the Minister opportunities to advance rapidly the men who performed according to his wishes. Tilman shows that 1,687 expatriate officers made up 61 percent of the entire senior bureaucracy in 1957.[20] By the beginning of 1960, about 1,000 expatriates had left Malaya and their places had been filled largely by Malayan Chinese and Malays. In the next two years, when the rural development program was getting under way, an additional 250 expatriates left, and over 200 new places were added to the bureaucracy. Thus, in the two years from independence to the beginning of rural development, the government and the bureaucracy had gained considerable experience in rapid promotion to very high levels for in-

---

[20] R. O. Tilman, *Bureaucratic Transition in Malaya*, Durham, 1964, p. 70.

digenous people. Then during the first two years of the rural development program, approximately 500 additional such promotions were made. Many of these promotions were made in the context of that program and provided the Minister with a very effective control mechanism.

Although power and available resources were necessary to the goal achievement of the Ministry of Rural Development, they were not sufficient. Of greater importance was the type of work the Ministry put into the bureaucracy. In activating the Rural Development Program, the Minister defined and allocated tasks, authority and responsibility, created specific modes of communication, and established criteria for the evaluation of performance. In the context of this specific goal-directed activity, the Minister broke through the resistance to the new program and shaped a new character for the entire bureaucracy.

The task was an extremely delicate one, largely because the goals of the development program were output goals. That is, in order to increase the rate of production of the bureaucracy, the Minister had to change its character without destroying its competence. The record of bureaucratic corruption and decay common to most new states only serves to indicate how difficult was the task faced by Malaya's Ministry of Rural Development.

In the first year of the program, the Minister exercised his power in a number of specific contests with the bureaucracy and its functionaries. These contests, some of which are described below, became the dramatic folk tales of the program, and were told over and over to the author in interviews with senior government officers.

An especially delicate task was breaking through the insulation of the engineers and professionals whose technical competence was needed. In a series of personal and bureaucratic exchanges early in 1960, the Minister imposed his will and goals upon the engineers, but at the same time left them free to judge technical requirements and provided them with the resources needed to meet his standards. When the Red Books were being prepared, some of the engineers refused to sign the required map tracings and project estimates. The engineers argued that these had been prepared too hastily and they would not accept responsibility for what they knew to be potentially inaccurate. The Ministry responded with a sharp note: estimates were recognized by the government to be inexact; local officers would not be held to these estimates if further study revealed different costs; and failure to accept these conditions and to sign the maps and estimates could only be taken as attempts to subvert the development program. The recalcitrant officers signed.

On one field inspection trip, Tun Razak was approached by Malay village leaders for a road to their mosque. He approved their request on the spot, but was contradicted publicly by an engineer (a European) who argued that resources were insufficient. The Minister immediately and publicly ordered the transfer of the engineer, who was subsequently Malayanized out of the bureaucracy.

Accompanying these sanctions was considerable positive technical inducement. The Ministry was able to make large long-term financial commitments to the engineers, enabling them to build up their stocks of plant and equipment. The engineers argue that this has been of considerable importance in making the task of public construction more efficient.[21] In addition, the engineers have been left in full control of the actual technical aspects of construction. The folk tales of the engineers are dated almost exclusively in 1960. Interviews with engineers in 1961 through 1963 indicate an effective and apparently mutually satisfying cooperation between that group and the Ministry of Rural Development. The cooperation is also evident in the meetings of development committees at all levels.

The social and legal insulation of the State Civil Servants was broken in a similar series of clashes in which the Ministry of Rural Development established its power in both utilitarian and social forms of control. In what was perhaps the most dramatic clash, the Minister called on a District Office in one of the old Unfederated States in July 1960 and found that no work had been done on the compilation of the Red Book. The negligence of the District Officer appears to have resulted largely from a continuation of old relaxed behavior, rather than from any intention to resist the development program, but this was precisely the type of bureaucratic apathy the Ministry has often identified as its major problem. The Minister publicly and forcefully reprimanded the District Officer and removed him from responsibility for the Red Book. He gave responsibility directly to the entire District Rural Development Committee, acting under the direction of the Assistant District Officer and demanded that the Red Book be completed within two weeks—with no excuses.[22] The committee worked continuously on the assignment and had the Red Book completed in just over a week. In relating this experience, other officers in the country report that Tun Razak also used his power over the State Alliance organization to block the recalcitrant officer's promotion to the State

---

[21] The importance of this type of commitment was first called to my attention by the State Engineer in Sarawak in an interview in February 1962.

[22] Reported in the *Straits Times* of 26 July and 9 August 1960.

Secretariat. Whether or not this is true,[23] other officers believe it to be true, and that is sufficient to ensure that they will comply with the Minister's wishes.

In this case, as in others involving state officers, there was the use of intricately intertwined utilitarian and social forms of control to break through the legal and social insulations of those officers. The legal insulation was essentially an obstacle to the Ministry's use of material rewards to control state functionaries. To obtain access to the control over the material rewards the Minister used his political power, imposing upon the legal decision-makers of the state. Since the legal decision-makers were also part of the Minister's popularly elected government, they were vulnerable to his political arguments. His case to them was simple and direct; it was made privately to them on a number of occasions and was constantly reinforced in the public discussion of politics and elections carried by the press. The Minister argued that the government would stand or fall as a result of this development program. If state leaders wanted to continue to be elected, they must ensure that their bureaucratic functionaries give full support to the development program.

The social insulation of the state officers was broken by the face-to-face contacts in which the Minister applied his material rewards. While an officer's status and self-conception could be protected by his occupational community, it could not withstand the public onslaught of the highly prestigious Deputy Prime Minister of the newly independent nation, especially since he was also a member of the traditional ruling class. The status of the local officer might be protected if the contacts were distant, private, and formal, but when they were face-to-face contacts, in the presence of colleagues and subordinates of the officer, the latter was almost totally vulnerable. If this were not sufficient to give the Minister strong symbolic weapons, he had another source of symbolic power. He was an elected leader of a newly independent democratic nation. The development program he had created and the demands he was making upon the lower level functionaries were not for his personal gain, nor for the gain of the local officers. They were for the benefit of all the people, the citizens, the voters and their families. Thus the effective local officer was contributing greatly to the benefit of his nation and his people, the only real divine source of authority in the modern nation-dominated world.

Aside from these dramatic clashes in which the aims and the powers of the new Ministry were made visible to the entire bureaucracy, there

---

[23] I was unable to confirm the report.

was a less dramatic aspect of the process by which the new character of the bureaucracy was formed. This was the steady day-by-day work of the Ministry as it planned for and implemented the rural development program.

The language of the Red Book instructions provided the bureaucracy with its first formal statement of the aims of the new Ministry. Here results were elevated above procedures as the aim of the program. In the first directive, signed by the Prime Minister, and the supporting letter by the Minister of Rural Development emphasis was explicitly placed upon results. Tun Razak closed his letter with large bold-faced type proclaiming "Results Are What We Want." In the section "Principles in Committee" is the argument that talk is only a means to an end. Discussion itself will not produce results. Decisions must be translated into action. Under instructions for the preparation of the plan: "Officers responsible for planning will avoid exchanges of correspondence. They will in all cases proceed by personal discussion and joint consultation." On production of the lists of projects: "Reasons in support of each project will be given in brief, clear and forceful language." On the use of the completed books: "Necessary correspondence will be kept to a minimum and written briefly and to the point. Unnecessary correspondence will not be written at all." We have already seen that financial policy called for cooperative implementation rather than paper battles between state and federal governments.

Maximum support for the value of results, or output, was provided by instructions that were both highly explicit and extremely vague. In mechanical or technical matters instructions were explicit. Maps were to be prepared with standard symbols and formats. Meetings were to be held in a given manner, minutes recorded and sent according to a fixed schedule to the state and federal offices. In many tasks this explicitness of instructions standardized procedures and thus made evaluation by the Ministry simpler. It also facilitated implementation, because it gave local officers definite and clearly defined tasks to perform. The letter of the law was clear and officers were expected to follow it.

The spirit of the law was protected more by the vagueness of instructions than by their explicitness. In less tangible matters, the ends laid down by the Ministry—results—provided the only clear criteria for evaluating performance, but the instructions nonetheless aimed at eroding the procedural orientation of the old bureaucracy. "Unnecessary correspondence" could be defined as that correspondence that did not produce results. For example, a District Officer might write many letters making way for land appropriation for a certain project, but if agreements were not reached with the land owners, his correspondence could be defined as unnecessary.

The work of implementation of the development program took place largely in the meetings of the District and State Rural Development Committees, and meetings between the Minister and other cabinet level agencies. In these meetings a new pattern of communications was established, and in these meetings the Ministry made direct contact with, and established its control over, the bureaucracy. The meetings brought together all local officers concerned with the development program, along with local elected representatives. Full state and district meetings were held monthly, with smaller executive meetings at least weekly. At the full meetings the progress and problems of the program were presented. With all responsible technical officers present decisions could be made rapidly on the allocation of resources and the programming of work.

The elected representatives provided direct and rapid communications with the people. This was especially useful in facilitating land acquisition, where projects were located on privately held land. Formal land acquisition procedures in Malaya are detailed, specific, and generally lengthy, providing protection for individual and state interests. As the development program became organized at the local level, and as the people saw the increased emphasis on public investment, informal preliminary acquisition techniques were developed. In many cases informal agreements were reached and construction begun while the formal process was still going on. As much as six months could be saved by the use of such informal agreements.

The Ministry activated these meetings by the use of a specific control technique, the briefing. Throughout 1960, 1961, and 1962, the Minister toured extensively, attempting to visit each of Malaya's seventy district offices twice a year. In a typical briefing at the district office, the Minister would appear with his immediate staff, generally for a half- or one-day tour of the district. The tour would begin with a meeting in the district operations room, with all technical and elected representatives of the district present. The District Officer would open the briefing with a summary of development products, plans, and problems. He would then be followed by relevant technical officers, who would present a more detailed analysis of specific projects.

It was in the analysis of problems in the briefings that the drama of control emerged. If projects were behind schedule, the Minister would relentlessly pursue the cause. If it lay in dilatoriness of local officers, which was impossible to conceal since all officers were present, the Minister would administer reprimands and commands in the meeting. If the cause of delay lay outside the control of the local offices, the Minister would attempt to locate its source and make a personal phone call during the meeting to effect the necessary decision.

The briefing would be followed by field inspection of projects under construction, often with the Minister performing some public, quasi-political act in the process. Local elected representatives were always present and used the Minister to strengthen their own local position. In his turn the Minister used the tours to strengthen local party organizations and to remind the people of the source of this new emphasis on development for their welfare.

Briefings were held at district, state, and federal levels. Those at the state level were similar to those at district level described above. At the federal level, briefings normally concentrated on one or two ministries rather than on all of them. They were held in the national operations room, which contained up-to-date project maps for each ministry. Presentations were normally made by the Ministers themselves, followed by their permanent secretaries and relevant technical officers. In all cases the Minister of Rural Development demanded that his officers be constantly informed about the state of their programs. Especially where construction was involved, representatives of the Public Works Department would also attend the briefing. As at the district and state levels, the representation of all relevant offices at the briefing enabled the Minister accurately to locate the source of delay in projects. As Ministry officers reported, "There could be no buck-passing in the briefings."

For the most part briefings were held on schedule, with the offices given a week or more to prepare for them. The Minister also required that his officers be ready to give extemporaneous briefings at any time he requested. Often in returning from field trips the Minister would stop in unannounced at a district office to receive an informal briefing on the program. The Ministry used this control technique deliberately and delicately. It was explained by the Minister as follows.

We have to keep them on their toes, so we want them to know that we will stop in anytime. That way they know they have to keep informed about the progress of their programs at all times.
[In answer to the question how often this type of briefing was used:] We have to be careful not to overdo it. It's enough if they know we will drop in unannounced, and we do it once in a while. If we did it too much, we would interfere with their work and shake them up too much. You have to let them get on with the job, too.[24]

_____

[24] Interview with Tun Abdul Razak, October 1962.

This referred essentially to district and state offices. At the federal level, the Ministry of Rural Development was somewhat more severe. It maintained close telephone relations with state and district officers, who were encouraged to phone the Ministry about any problems they could not solve. The Ministry carried local development problems directly to the federal offices in a constant attempt to locate sources of delay and to speed the process of public investment. Ministry of Rural Development officers kept informed of meetings of other Ministries and agencies and would often attend these meetings unannounced to hear of other problems and plans and to communicate its own problems and plans.

The briefing technique was initiated by the Minister of Rural Development, but it soon became a standard mechanism of control used by political and bureaucratic leaders throughout the country. Chief Ministers of the states often carried out their own development tours, receiving briefings from the district officers. Federal ministers have done the same, meeting with their local functionaries throughout the country. Federal and State Departments of Information follow most development tours and briefings carefully and keep the press supplied with a steady stream of press releases on development activities.

The operations rooms provide a distinct setting for the briefings as well as the meetings of the development committees. On the one hand these rooms serve to emphasize the importance and distinctiveness of the new program, both to the officers and to the general public. This gives the Minister a distinct set of symbols to manipulate, increasing his social control over the bureaucracy. In addition, the operations rooms make visible the progress of both individual projects and the entire development of the district, or nation. This has facilitated central control over the development activities of the bureaucracy, because it provides objective criteria for the evaluation of performance.

The private reactions of development officers throughout the country indicate that the operations room and briefing techniques are quite effective in increasing the rate of public investment in Malaya.[25] The Ministerial visits are feared. No matter how well prepared they feel, the District Officers normally look with trepidation upon a forthcoming visit. At the same time, in describing their attitudes toward briefings and inspections, the local officers do not fear the arbitrariness

---

[25] What follows is based on over 100 interviews and informal discussions with State Development Officers, District Officers, and officers of many technical services, in which they were asked generally to describe the briefings and their relations with the Ministry. I also attended a number of briefings for the Minister and other state officials.

or capriciousness of the Minister. They feel that they have a clear idea of what is required of them and that the tasks are not impossible, though they certainly require hard work. They realize they have to produce results, they have to move the bureaucracy, and sometimes the people, to do what is required. They also see that if they get out of their offices and tour their districts they can keep well informed of the progress and problems of projects. They also know that there will be considerable rewards for them if they show industry and ingenuity in solving problems and moving ahead on projects. In describing the way other officers were reprimanded and punished by the Minister, they acknowledge that the major cause of such punishment is negligence or lack of industry on the part of the affected officer.

Furthermore, when these field officers described the current development program and their previous experience in the bureaucracy, they clearly indicated a change in the bureaucratic atmosphere. With the force of a powerful Ministry at the top, they could get things done themselves and see others around them accomplishing things. They also saw that the development was not due to the Ministry alone, but was also affected by their own increased ability to evaluate what was being done, what needed to be done, and how to get it done. The distinct impression formed from interviews with these officers was that they felt themselves to be on top of their organizations, not inundated by them. It was also apparent that one of the single, most important, factors producing this feeling of control over the organization was the sheer amount of physical developmental activity being accomplished by the bureaucracy.

Success in achieving output goals was obtained as the Ministry of Rural Development activated the bureaucracy and increased greatly the tempo of its work. This was accomplished by a series of organizational innovations whose power was increased by the application of the political strength that was inherent in the Ministry.

At the district level and for minor projects, the Ministry increased amenity production in four ways: (1) It facilitated the allocation of funds from state and federal governments first by standardizing the request procedures, and second, by giving the requests the moral and political power of voter demand. (2) It facilitated spending by decentralizing control over development expenditures. In creating technically competent district committees and giving them the power to plan projects, to call for tenders, make contracts, and control the progress of work, the Ministry in effect greatly increased the manpower available to spend the authorized development funds. (3) In addition, the

Ministry increased the rate of bureaucratic communication at the lower levels by creating local committees and giving the District Officer coordinating power, and by transforming communications from a predominantly paper process to a predominantly oral process. (4) At the state and federal levels the Ministry increased the efficiency of the technical departments partly by providing them with the long-term financial commitments they needed for the rapid buildup of plant and equipment.

At all levels the operations room and briefing technique provided the Ministry with criteria for measuring performance. These allowed the Ministry to locate points of resistance to production and to use its great traditional, bureaucratic, and political power to overcome this resistance and thus to speed up the production of social overhead capital.

In the entire program these organizational innovations were infused with a sense of force and a sense of urgency, brought about largely by the political power of the Minister. This was a reflection of both the strong governmental commitment to development, and of the commitment to specific output goals.

The actual control the Ministry could exercise through its organizational innovations was heightened by the political power of the Minister, which gave him the ability to overcome legal, bureaucratic, and social obstacles to his manipulation of material rewards. In addition, the small size of the country and the ease with which the Minister could personally inspect the working elements of the bureaucracy allowed him to reinforce his control mechanisms with face-to-face contacts. Social controls reinforced utilitarian control, ensuring that the functionaries of the bureaucracy worked with commitment as well as with skill in pursuit of the goals of the new organization.

In addition, the vacant positions at the top of the bureaucracy that resulted from Malayanization gave the Minister powerful material and symbolic rewards without disrupting the system within which those rewards were structured. This protected one of the important marginal material rewards, security. It also meant that the Minister did not have to destroy key elements and create a reservoir of personal animosity.

Thus, these organizational innovations provided the technical capacity to make accurate evaluations of performance; the political power of the Minister and the vacancies created by Malayanization gave him almost complete freedom to allocate punishments and rewards rationally; and the application of social control through face-to-face contact reinforced the commitment of the functionaries and gave the Ministry an extra margin of control.

VII

THE MINISTRY OF RURAL DEVELOPMENT AND ITS AUTONOMOUS AUTHORITIES: FLDA AND RIDA

When the Ministry of Rural Development was established, it assumed responsibility for the Federal Land Development Authority (FLDA) and the Rural and Industrial Development Authority (RIDA). We saw earlier that by this time both organizations had become committed to output goals, though their specific programs of action differed. FLDA was concerned primarily with opening land, RIDA with producing amenities and granting loans. In the process of mobilizing the bureaucracy for rural development, the Ministry left the function of land development in the FLDA and gave that organization the political support it needed to increase its rate of activity. At the same time, however, the Ministry removed the improvement-providing functions from RIDA, leaving that organization with little more than its loan program. Without that function, which we have argued was central to the new Ministry's output goals, RIDA lost importance for the Ministry and could be largely ignored. The limited attempts to change RIDA's character and remaining functions illustrate both the pressures on the Ministry to broaden its goals, and the obstacles to this goal broadening.

Before proceeding to an analysis of this process, it will be useful to consider the problem of organizational autonomy and the politics of development as manifested in the experiences of these two organizations.

ORGANIZATIONAL AUTONOMY AND THE POLITICS OF DEVELOPMENT

FLDA and RIDA were created as autonomous authorities by British expatriate civil servants before Malayan independence. Both authorities were designed to provide organizations with freedom from day-to-day control by government. As authorities they could borrow money independently of the treasury and could thus acquire financial independence. This would also give them freedom from political pressures operating through budget manipulation, and would provide for continuity in the face of possible changes in ruling parties. In addition, as authorities they could appoint and control staff independently of the personnel rules of the established bureaucracy.

FLDA and RIDA were not isolated cases of expatriate preference for autonomous authorities. There was also an attempt before independence to transform the Malayan radio service into an autonomous authority similar to the BBC. All these moves have met with the same fate. The old colonial government rejected the authority form for radio from the outset. RIDA and FLDA soon lost—if they ever really achieved—the functional autonomy for which their structures provided. As soon as the new government turned its attention to development, it subordinated both FLDA and RIDA to the new Ministry created to stimulate development. The legal autonomy of these authorities could thus be exercised only at the sufferance and for the convenience of the new Ministry.

This pattern of authority formation for organizational autonomy prior to independence and the subversion of autonomy after independence is in itself an interesting sociological phenomenon that deserves closer study. Here we can only analyze in a cursory fashion what appear to be the major determinants of the process.[1] Three considerations appear to be most important.

1. In the first place, the creators of the authority were attempting to accomplish new tasks that were not specifically provided for in any existing government agency. By creating a new and autonomous authority, they were attempting to cut red tape, to get around the bureaucratic obstacles and delays that could stand in the way of changing

---

[1] The following is derived from interviews with civil servants, some of whom were instrumental in establishing the two authorities in question.

functions in the bureaucracy. To innovators in the old bureaucracy it appeared easier to accomplish new tasks by creating a new organization than by redirecting existing organizations.

The attempt to cut red tape by creating a new organization was misdirected for two reasons. First, the use of new organizations assumed that an additional supply of competent staff would be available. This assumption could not be made easily in most nonindustrial countries, and Malaya was not an exception in this case. Without a reservoir of qualified people to draw upon, the new organizations turned to government and received officers on loan from other agencies. With these officers the new organizations could not use their freedom from established personnel policies. The most the organization could offer would be the possibility of upgrading. Thus, in so far as the accomplishment of new tasks depended upon a new staff organized and controlled in a new manner, the new organizations were prevented from achieving their goals.

In the second place, the civil servants elected to create new organizations rather than to redirect existing ones primarily because they lacked the power necessary to achieve this redirection. This is perhaps the most important consideration in this process, and it derives from the different views of politics and development taken by the expatriate civil servants and the new indigenous leaders.

2. It is important to note that these autonomous authorities were created by the expatriate civil servants, a class that has hardly been sympathetic to the growth of political or ministerial control over the bureaucracy.[2] Thus the authority was created to give development organizations freedom from what generally has been considered the unhealthy play of politics in the new state.

3. The third consideration is allied to this. It lies in an approach that opposes economic development and politics, a view not at all uncommon among students of economic development. This approach argues that by definition, economic development requires some restrictions on consumption. If the political process is open and democratic, government is vulnerable to the demands of the masses and finds it difficult to restrict consumption and thus to provide the capital formation required for development. In addition, this point of view distinguishes between economic judgments and political judgments in

---

[2] Interviewing in North Borneo shortly after the Federation of Malaysia was mooted, I found the expatriate civil servants extremely hostile to emerging political developments. Their most common reaction was to note that until a few months previously, North Borneo had been a paradise, undisturbed by any hint of political activity.

determining the type, location, and timing of specific development programs. It opposes, for example, the location of roads in economically useful areas in preference to the location of roads in favored constituencies. This entire approach is based on the view of the economist as a rational calculator of costs and returns and of the politician as the winner of votes through the manipulation of the state's resources.

On both these counts the emerging indigenous leaders held views totally different from those of the British authority-creators. Where the expatriates disliked the emergence of political control over the bureaucracy, gaining such control was precisely the aim of the indigenous leaders. More important, however, where the expatriate civil servants tended to distinguish economic development from politics, the indigenous leaders saw in political power the only means by which they could achieve economic development.

Further, the indigenous leaders appeared to see far more clearly than the authority-creators the implications of government dominance and of weakness in the private sector. They recognized that if something were to be done about development, government would have to do it. The corollary of this was the observation that if government considered an area of activity important it could mobilize extensive resources to bear upon that area, and if government did not consider the area important, it was quite likely that little or nothing would be done in that area.

As an autonomous authority, RIDA had neither the power nor the resources to coordinate the functions of other agencies in amenity provision. Consequently it had to take over this function by itself, but at the same time it did not have sufficient strength to perform the function well. When the indigenous government turned its attention to development, it found improvement too important a function to leave in the hands of such an impotent organization. In addition, with its great political power the new Ministry was able to force other elements of the bureaucracy to increase their output of the physical infrastructure far beyond what RIDA could ever have done alone.

Similarly, FLDA lacked the political power to overcome obstacles placed in the way of land development by state prerogatives. As we shall see, only when FLDA and its function moved to the center of political power was it able to overcome these obstacles and to increase its rate of work.

Thus by attempting to provide development organizations with independence from the political process, the authority-creators cut those organizations off from the sources of power that alone could give them the strength to accomplish their tasks. Only when these functions became politically important were the responsible organizations given sufficient power to perform them. That this involved the subordination of the authorities and the subversion of their legal autonomy was irrelevant, partly because they had never been in a position to exercise that autonomy, and partly because under the new arrangement work could be done.

THE FEDERAL LAND DEVELOPMENT
AUTHORITY (FLDA)

One of the first pressures the new Ministry of Rural Development encountered was a great popular demand for land. During the Japanese occupation and the Emergency, land transfer had almost come to a complete halt. The drafters of the Red Books found backlogs of thousands of land applications in almost every district. Even acknowledging that as many as half of these applications might have been speculative or false,[3] the objective demand for land was great.

Three different types of programs for allocating land were worked out either just before or along with the formation of the new Ministry. Fringe allocation would set aside areas of state land adjacent to existing villages and give out parcels of three to five acres to villagers whose land holdings were of an uneconomic size. In addition the states themselves could go ahead with Group Settlement projects. These were essentially small versions of FLDA projects financed and directed completely by the states. In both these plans the actual work on the ground was done by the district officer, aided by his district rural development committee. The Ministry attempted to increase the rate of transfer under these plans by simply calling for their inclusion in the Red Book and putting pressure on the district committees to do the work faster.

Finally, there was the FLDA with its very large projects financed out of Federal Loans. Since the Ministry had direct control over FLDA, it simply instructed that organization to increase its rate of land development. FLDA was given the task of opening twelve new projects, for about 4,800 settler families each year of the second five-year plan period, 1961–1965. This would mean that FLDA would have to do as much each year of the plan period as it had done in its entire four years of life up to mid-1960. Table VII-1 illustrates the change in FLDA's rate of activity under these pressures.

It is obvious from this table that the instructions from the Ministry

---

[3] Applicants sometimes filed a number of applications under names of wives and children, or falsely claimed to have no land.

had some effect. At present there is every reason to expect that FLDA will achieve its goal of twelve projects for about 4,800 settler families each year of the plan period. The large gap between the eventual number of families to be accommodated and those actually on all projects is a result of the period of preparation required before the settlers can be moved onto the projects. A more accurate measure of work done is provided by the actual acres under development at one time. This figure is generally not available, partly because of the difficulty of ar-

TABLE VII-1

FLDA ACTIVITIES 1957–1963

Activities	1957	1958	1959	1960	1961	1962	1963
Projects started							
yearly	1	5	5	4	10	11	13
cumulative	—	6	11	15	25	36	49
Eventual acres (000)							
yearly	4	28	10	7	50	51	61
cumulative[a]	—	32	39	46	90	137	198
Eventual settler families							
yearly	400	2,800	1,296	780	4,240	5,000[b]	2,970[b]
cumulative[a]		3,200	4,496	4,662	8,302	13,000[b]	15,970
Actual settler families on							
schemes, cumulative	n.a.	400	1,370	2,530	3,367	3,648	5,844
Total staff	n.a.	33	58	131	293	465	687
Estimated total cost at completion (M$ million)	n.a.	n.a.	22.6	24.3	n.a.	112.6	n.a.
Average total cost per eventual acre, M$	n.a.	n.a.	570	530	n.a.	820	n.a.

SOURCE: FLDA annual reports.

[a] Actual cumulative totals as given in the reports are shown here. They differ from yearly totals because the latter are adjusted each year.

[b] Approximate.

The FLDA year is from 1 July to 30 June. Years here are mid-year dates, except that 1963 is as of 31 August 1963.

riving at an acceptable definition, when there are many different tasks that have to be completed even before land clearing begins. However, in August and September 1963, of the roughly 200,000 acres planned for development, 123,000 were to be in rubber or oil palm and 85,000 of these acres had already been planted. Of the 34,000 planned for fruit trees and other small crops, only about 2,000 had been planted. The approximately 11,000 acres for village areas had practically all been cleared, and an additional 32,000 acres of swamp and hill land had to be left as unarable. The roughly 5,800 settler families already on projects were to be joined by an additional 2,100 scheduled to move in before the end of the year.

By any measure, then, FLDA greatly increased its rate of work under pressures from the Ministry. This was not accomplished by FLDA alone, however. The Ministry gave lavish attention to the Authority, assisting it to increase its output. We can distinguish three types of support the Ministry gave to FLDA.

1. First, the Ministry made more money and staff available to the organization immediately—perhaps the easiest task for the Ministry. At its inception, FLDA had been given the promise of a grant of M$ 10 million from the Malayan government. This was loan capital and was to be conserved. In addition, in 1958 FLDA concluded a loan agreement with the Colonial (now Commonwealth) Development Corporation for M$ 511 million. This total amount was essentially committed by FLDA with projects planned and in progress by the end of 1960. In the second five-year plan FLDA was allotted M$ 175 million of federal funds for land development.

All of this was loan capital and had to be conserved. Ultimately the settlers would have to bear the total cost of development. It was planned that when their rubber or oil palm became mature the settlers would repay the cost of development, together with interest, to the Authority. In 1960 and 1961 the Ministry asked the Authority to prepare an estimate of headquarters and administrative costs to examine the possibility of government bearing these costs by a direct subvention. By mid-1962 this policy change had been effected. By bearing the organizational costs of the authority, the Ministry was actually lowering the cost to the settlers, to include only the direct cost of land development. It had become obvious that if FLDA were to increase its rate of land development, more of the work would have to be done by contractors, more planning and direction would be required at headquarters, and the total cash costs per acre of developed land would rise considerably; we can see from table VII-1 that they actually did.

At the same time, the Ministry helped FLDA to increase its staff. The original Working Party that planned for FLDA considered that the organization could be run by a part-time chairman, especially since it was to be only a loans board. The first chairman, D. E. M. Fiennes, left at the end of 1958 and the present chairman, Taib bin Haji Andak, was appointed as a full-time chairman. In 1960–1961 a Ministerial review committee recommended that a deputy chairman and a planting director be appointed; this was done almost immediately. The post of deputy was taken over by a Malayanized Malayan Civil Service district officer, J. P. M. Clifford. The rapid increase in total staff can also be seen from table VII-1.

2. In the second place, the Ministry began a subtle attack on state prerogatives in land matters, carried on ultimately through the National Land Council. This was perhaps the most crucial part of the processes that changed the character of the FLDA.

Land is a state matter, but it is more than a mere constitutional formula to give some recognition to the Federal character of Malaya. Traditionally land has been the property of the sultan of the state. The constitution actually vests all unallocated land in the ruler, though in effect the land is not held as the ruler's private property. The revenues from land form a part of state revenues, not a part of the personal revenues of the rulers. That is, the constitution places land in the hands of the state government, in which the sultan (or governor in Malacca and Penang) is only a constitutional monarch.

As state property, land is generally one of the largest single internal sources of state revenue.[4] Finally, with the inexorable division of labor and specialization of functions, the state has gradually lost control over a wide range of activities whose direction has become centralized in Kuala Lumpur. Land is therefore one of the last remaining functions left to the state administration. Given these forces, it is understandable that the states should hold to their control over land with some jealousy.

In addition to designating land as a state matter, the Constitution also recognized the necessity for some uniformity in land matters in the Federation. This was to be provided for by a National Land Council. The NLC is made up of one representative from each state and eleven members appointed by the central government, including the chairman. The NLC is in effect the cabinet plus the Chief Ministers of the states. The Chairman has an original, but not a deciding, vote in policy matters. This is an important protection for the states, since legally any policy decision taken by the Council, by a simple majority, is binding on all states.

Up to mid-1963 the Council had reached decisions and published papers on sixteen issues. Eleven decisions were reached in 1958, the first year of real operation of the Council. The issues involved show the preliminary character of the Council's work in that year.[5] The

---

[4] Although it can be a significant amount in some states, it is not a large portion of total state income; the allocations from the Federal government amount to half or more of the total income.

[5] A list of the papers with a résumé of their topics is included as an appendix to this chapter.

first paper was procedural, whereas others laid down broad policies for land administration, general use, mining use, cultivation of slopes, reservation of mining land for Malays, and land for secondary industry. Only one paper, No. 4/1958, directly concerned land development: land development should be planned and its rate increased.

Two papers, Nos. 12 and 13, issued in 1960, were directly concerned with development policies and with FLDA. They first divided the functions between state and federal organizations. Fringe alienation and group settlement projects would be handled by the states, and would be concerned chiefly with land near built-up areas. The federal government would make available to the states M$ 49,560,000 over the next ten years to subsidize state land programs. This would relieve FLDA of the necessity of granting loans to these bodies. The State Land Development Boards were to be dissolved and made subcommittees of the State Rural Development Committees. *FLDA was to abandon its loan functions and to be concerned with the direct development of land.* A later amendment was even more revolutionary. FLDA was to take over all group settlement schemes from the states, which would continue to be responsible only for fringe allocation.

One paper, No. 14, produced in 1961, merely agreed that the Federal government would only pay nominal premiums for land acquired for development projects, since these would be to the advantage of the state. In 1962, paper No. 15 set out a plan for controlled allocation in which government would merely lay out lots of ten acres in tracts of 2,000 acres or more and allow people to develop them within five years at their own expense. The last paper also laid down conditions of foreign participation in iron mining.

The revolutionary papers Nos. 12 and 13 were associated with a committee established in 1960 to review the role of FLDA in the national development program.[6] The committee argued that FLDA in its present form could not cope with the task of land development. The relation between that form and the political process was explicitly recognized by the committee. It must be quoted here at length, because it illustrates clearly the argument made above concerning the function of an Authority and the problem of autonomy and development.

------

[6] Federation of Malaya, *Report of the Special Committee to Review the Role of the Federal Land Development Authority Within the National Rural Development Programme*, undated, about June 1961, mimeographed. The committee actually began its meetings only in early 1961. The NLC papers dividing the functions between state and federal governments were produced before the committee met; addenda and amendments of the NLC paper changing the role of FLDA and giving it control over the Group Settlement Schemes were, however, products of the committee's recommendations.

16. We understand that one of the original intentions in setting up the FLDA, with its present Ordinance, was to establish an Authority which would be able to "get on and ahead" with Land Development, independent of Government, in the hope that results would be obtained more quickly.

17. In fact, in practice, the very reverse is happening; by virtue of the Authority's independence, and also because in almost every sphere of its activities, it has to turn to Government Departments for assistance, the present independent method of working has become cumbersome, resulted in confusion, duplication of effort, and loss of efficiency.

18. In practice, the Authority has gone on, in its own independent way until it strikes snags, opposition, or lack of cooperation from States or Government Departments, and then only, when unable to overcome these difficulties, has it been forced to turn to the Ministry of Rural Development for assistance.

19. The main function of the Ministry of Rural Development has been, since its establishment, one of co-ordinating all other Ministries, Departments and State Governments in their functions within the National Rural Development Programme and yet, ironically enough, it has been unable to do this in respect of the FLDA, which, although no more than a department within the Ministry, nevertheless, by virtue of its independent status, is outside the controlling influence of such co-ordination.[7]

The committee argued further that priorities for development could only be directed from one source, and this must be the Ministry. The legal autonomy of the Authority, making it necessary that the Minister consult it before issuing a directive to it, was untenable. Finally, if FLDA were to overcome its difficulties and increase its rate of land development, it would have to be closely set within the Ministry where it could get the power to perform its tasks.

The committee made a number of further recommendations, some of which were included in the NLC paper, such as the FLDA takeover of group settlement schemes. It also recommended that FLDA be staffed by a deputy chairman and a planting director as well as a chairman, since the pressure of work was mounting.

Other changes in the organization of FLDA followed from this committee's work. The most important of these was the removal of the cumbersome individual corporation for each land project. When the state land boards were to be dissolved, FLDA considered establishing a separate corporation for each project, on the lines followed in the Bilut Valley Scheme. This would have produced a top-heavy structure, since the chairman and much of the headquarters staff would have had to attend meetings of all corporations, which would soon have numbered more than 50.

---

[7] *Ibid.*, p. 6.

The individual corporations had been a necessary but preliminary adjustment to the problem of financing. So long as FLDA was to be only a loans board, it would have to set up individual corporations that would borrow money from the Authority for Land Development. When the "loans board" character of FLDA was officially changed, the organization could abandon the idea of local corporations and manage the projects directly. FLDA did, however, set up a series of seven regional offices, each with a regional secretary for administration and settler welfare, and a visiting manager for the technical aspects of the tasks.

Although the Ministry has used the National Land Council to centralize control over land development functions, it has done so subtly and with great caution. This simply reflects the Minister's understanding of the appeal of land to the states. The momentous decisions in regard to land development in papers 12 and 13 have not been rigidly enforced, even though the federal government has the constitutional powers to do so. All states, with the exception of the opposition Pan Malayan Islamic Party controlled state of Kelantan, have accepted the NLC policy decision. Kelantan still refuses to turn over control of its schemes to FLDA. The central government maintains a passive attitude toward this resistance. If the state fails to agree, this simply means no extension of FLDA activities in the state, and the Minister tries to make certain that the people of Kelantan recognize that it is their own state government's refusal that accounts for the state's lack of development projects.

Other states have offered resistance, but have finally been persuaded to accept the NLC policy decision. As might be expected, the resistance was greatest in Kedah and Johore. The list of land projects under consideration for 1962–1965 suggests that Johore's agreement may have been achieved only at the price of more land development for that state. Of the thirty-six plans under development by mid-1962, thirteen were in Johore, and of the fifty-one under consideration for 1962–1965, twenty-three were in Johore. The originally more cooperative state of Pahang had only four of the thirty-six projects in mid-1962, and only eight of the fifty-one under consideration for the entire plan period. This does not take into account, however, the great 200,000 acre Jerantut Triangle scheme proposed for Pahang.

Although to the present the Ministry has proceeded with great caution in the NLC, it is also laying the groundwork for a far more sweeping centralization of land control. At present a new land code for the entire Federation is under consideration. It has been drafted and will probably be presented to parliament in 1964. This code unifies all land procedures, especially in Penang and Malacca, which are still under British-type land laws.[8] In addition, it spells out in detail all the executive powers of the Chairman of the National Land Council, derived from the constitution. When it becomes law, it will greatly increase the direct executive powers of the Chairman, a position now held by the Minister of Rural Development.

3. The third mechanism of change involves the internal control structure of FLDA itself. We have already seen in chapter V that its inability to apply utilitarian forms of control inhibited the achievement of its goals.

FLDA set about changing its compliance structure in a number of ways. We have noted the extended use of contractors to clear land, the ultimate in a utilitarian relationship between organization and workers. In addition, FLDA has changed its form of payment to the settlers. The original plan was to give the settlers a subsistence allowance for their first two years on the project. It varied from M$ 50 to M$ 75 according to the number of dependents. It soon became obvious, however, that if the settlers were to be kept on the projects, they would need more than two years of assistance. It was gradually extended on an *ad hoc* basis decided upon at each project. In June 1962 the Authority attempted to standardize subsistence payments. Out of the discussions around this topic, however, a new form of payment was suggested and adopted. Settlers would be paid on the basis of days actually worked. Their payment would still be considered a subsistence allowance rather than wages, so that workmen's compensation regulations would not apply. Only the method of payment would be altered. Henceforth "The Settler will now have to earn his daily allowance against a measured piece of work. The subsistence allowance cannot be claimed by him as a matter of right any more, irrespective of the number of working days put in." [9]

At the same time a trend toward increasing payments emerged. The rates finally established for the new method of payment would allow M$ 2.90 per day for male settlers. In addition the settler's wife could earn M$ 2.40 per day; his children between 14 and 18 could earn M$ 1.80 per day, and those under 14 (for a four hour day) could earn M$ 1.00 a day. In effect, the possible settler income has in many cases doubled.

---

[8] Actually two laws have been prepared, one for the fully unified land code and one for the purpose of converting Penang and Malacca to the Federation land system.

[9] Federation of Malaya, Federal Land Development Authority, H. O. Circular No. 95, 21 September 1962.

Where the problem of settler control touches the prerogatives of the states, FLDA has also moved to acquire more power. Settler selection was originally completely in the hands of the states. Now FLDA has the final decision on appointments. The states will stipulate how many out-of-state residents and how many non-Malays will be admitted, and present an initial list to the Authority. The Authority takes part in various stages of selection, however, and has the final prerogative in the process. Still, FLDA is left without the final sanction, that of eviction. In this the states must be consulted and the states alone can take the necessary action. If nothing else, they always have the ability to delay action. Together with the Ministry, and working through the National Land Council, FLDA plans to have its officers designated Collectors of Land Revenue by the states. This will give FLDA the right of eviction, placing the use of the ultimate sanction in its own hands.

It is important to see that these moves toward greater settler control have largely originated within the FLDA itself. They are essentially the result of a lack of fit between goals and compliance. The original goal of FLDA was strongly cultural—to create new communities of farmers. In this case its dominantly normative compliance structure, based primarily on the persuasive and leadership abilities of the project manager, were functionally in line with the goals. However, under pressure from the central government, the goals of FLDA became primarily output goals—to open land. Given these goals, the normative compliance structure produced considerable strain. Since FLDA is a subsidiary organization, we should expect that its goals, dictated to it by the parent organization, would take precedence over its compliance structure and any strain between the two would result in changing compliance rather than changing goals. This is in fact what happened.

FLDA now has the appearance of a relatively effective organization. Though its total costs per ultimate acre have risen, the actual contractor costs per acre developed have remained fairly constant and are approximately the same as those paid by commercial estates. Both pay about M$ 300 per acre to have land cleared and planted.[10] FLDA

---

[10] This comparison is difficult to make with any precision, since the cost depends upon the amount of work done and contracts vary considerably in their specifications. When the planting director, a man of long experience as a commercial planter in Malaya, came to work for FLDA in 1962, he prepared an estimate of average estate costs and then matched these with FLDA average actual costs. The totals from this comparison showed estate costs of M$ 270 per acre and FLDA cost of M$ 300 per acre. For 1961–1963, FLDA average cost per acre has been M$ 303, M$

responds to the pressure exerted by the Ministry to minimize bureaucratic delays. The Chairman, his deputy, and planting director spend a great deal of time in the field, making executive decisions in discussions with local managers. Special committees have been established within FLDA, coopting officers from other government agencies whose action is required for land development.

Objectively, FLDA does not appear especially plagued with ethnic considerations. The senior staff is ethnically heterogeneous, containing Malays, Chinese, Indians, Europeans, and others. Although Malay settlers are in the great majority, all ethnic groups are represented. Table VII-2 shows the ethnic distribution of settlers at different stages.

TABLE VII-2

ETHNIC DISTRIBUTION OF FLDA SETTLERS

Ethnic component	On schemes January 1963	Selected for 1963	Total	1957 total rural population[a]
	N = 4561	N = 2249	N = 6810	N = 3,611,000
Malays, percent	90	77	86	70
Chinese, percent	8	19	11	18
Indians, others, percent	2	4	3	12

SOURCE: FLDA Headquarters.

[a] Living in places less than 1,000 inhabitants. 1957 census, Vol. 14.

This table shows that the considerable overrepresentation of Malays in the early stages is giving way to a more equal treatment of the ethnic groups as FLDA assumes greater control over the entire process. This must be seen against rather strong pressures to give preference to Malays. Many of the areas selected for development lie in Malay reservations, where land can be allocated only to Malays. Despite this, FLDA itself has exerted great pressures for equal treatment.

Finally, there has been little ambiguity in FLDA's goals. They have been the almost pure output goals of opening land for settlement,

---

309, and M$ 302, not standardized for changing contract specifications. Other estimates of average estate costs vary around M$ 280 per acre. The major differences between FLDA and the estates lie in the total area developed and in the organization of the labor force. Estates normally do not attempt to develop more than about 200 to 300 acres in one year. FLDA is developing almost 5,000 acres per year. Estates have a resident labor force and resident management, allowing some of the work of development to be done without recourse to outside contractors. Both of these differences act in the direction of raising FLDA costs above those of the estates.

goals very much in harmony with the basic orientation of the Ministry. Thus in this view, FLDA's general appearance of effectiveness appears as a result of fundamental organizational forces. It must be acknowledged that FLDA's leadership is highly regarded for the competence and energy of its individual members. Only our theoretical orientation places emphasis upon the organizational forces that allow competent leadership to be recruited in the first place, and give that leadership freedom to exercise its competence once selected.

We need only note in closing this part of our analysis that FLDA's commitment to the output goals of land development has led to the neglect of the cultural or mixed output-cultural goals of creating communities of farmers. Essentially FLDA is making rubber tappers and oil-palm cultivators out of its settlers. As an organization it gives almost no attention to the broader problem of training the settlers in agricultural methods in order to produce diversified farmers. FLDA has itself no organizational element for settler training. Along with the Rubber Research Institute's Smallholders' Advisory Service, it merely gives some training in the techniques of rubber cultivation. We have already noted the different levels of accomplishment in planting different categories of FLDA land. Whereas 70 percent of the land designated for oil palm and rubber had been planted by September 1963, only about 5 percent of the land designated for the settler's small crops had been planted. For its part FLDA has decided to concentrate upon establishing the large-scale commercial crops first. It has left to the extension services of the Agriculture and Veterinary Departments the broader task of turning the settlers into diversified farmers. Although the FLDA staff admits privately that these services are grossly deficient in quantity and quality to meet the needs of the settlers, its preoccupation with its output goals has precluded its own direct activity in the broader areas.

THE RURAL AND INDUSTRIAL DEVELOPMENT AUTHORITY (RIDA)

We have already observed that by 1959 RIDA had become firmly committed to pure output goals, with its loan program and improvement program as the major instruments of activity. We saw, too, that the new Ministry removed from RIDA the responsibility for the provision of amenities, thus depriving RIDA of one of its two major activities. This was effected by a directive from the Minister of Rural Development to RIDA in January 1960. This actually said nothing about the provision of rural improvements, but directed RIDA to concentrate its efforts and resources exclusively on marketing, rural credit, rural industries, research, and training.

In May 1960 the chairman of RIDA issued a memorandum setting forth RIDA policy for complying with the Ministry's directive in regard to rural industries. The chairman argued that RIDA must stimulate rural industries in order to increase the income of the rural people. RIDA must play a strong role in this program because capital and entrepreneurial ability were still in short supply among Malays. In addition, the services necessary to industrial development were still primarily concentrated in the towns, where few Malays lived. Therefore RIDA would undertake to establish a number of industries by itself. These could be located in rural areas to provide jobs and training for rural Malays, they could be staffed by foreign experts, and then finally transferred to rural Malays organized into companies or preferably into cooperatives. Since these industries would be located and directed to promote industrialization among the Malays, they could not originally be evaluated by simple commercial or economic criteria, and it might be as much as ten years before some could be expected to stand on their own feet.

These instructions were apparently insufficient to achieve the Minister's end, however, for he established a committee in November 1960 to review and to make recommendations on the reorganization of RIDA. The general tenor of the committee's recommendations were to direct RIDA specifically away from amenity provision and to give the Ministry greater direct control over the organization. The committee recommended that RIDA be concerned with rural industries, credit, and training, "leaving pure Rural Development in the hands of the Ministry of Rural Development." [11] Pure rural development meant essentially the provision of social overhead capital and improvements to the rural areas.

In addition, the committee made a number of other recommendations. RIDA legislation needed to be changed and necessary alterations were provided by the parliamentary draftsman for the committee. The membership of the Authority should be changed to remove state members and to include more technical specialists. RIDA should not be concerned with planning, a function that should be performed by the Economic Planning Unit in order to integrate planning for the rural areas with planning for the entire economy. A rural credit division of

[11] *Report of the Special Committee to Consider and Make Recommendations for the Re-organization of the Rural and Industrial Development Authority,* mimeographed, Kuala Lumpur, 1961, p. 4. The committee noted that this recommendation had already been carried out.

RIDA should be established and should take the form of a corporation. In the matter of industries RIDA should first train rural industrial officers, then proceed with specific projects only after careful
technical investigation.

Two basic programs of action can be seen in these three documents.
In the first place, the Ministry wanted to dislodge RIDA from its
involvement in the production of physical infrastructure. This was
largely to eliminate the duplication of functions that was both costly
and unnecessary, since the Ministry held real power over other agencies
of government. In the second place, the Ministry wanted RIDA to
concentrate on activities that would directly raise the per capita
product, and thus the income of the rural Malays. This was one of the
earliest attempts of the Ministry, through its subsidiary organization,
to broaden its goals from purely output to mixed output-cultural goals.

From the very beginning, however, it was apparent that RIDA and
the Ministry had different ideas about how this was to be accomplished,
or about the type of output-cultural goals to be adopted. Though
neither organization appeared really cognizant of the issues or the
alternatives involved, they appeared to differ in their basic orientation
to the problem. The Ministry was concerned with developing good
credit facilities and efficient industries, whereas RIDA was concerned
with developing industries for Malays. One important result of this
effort as far as RIDA was concerned would be to cut out middlemen,
and to protect Malays from competition with non-Malays. That is, the
Ministry's orientation was to goals that would provide institutional
change, and RIDA's orientation was to goals that would be restrictive.

To what extent were these programs of action carried out? The
dislocation of RIDA from amenity production was implemented immediately. In 1960 RIDA transferred to the Public Works Department
more than M$ 200,000 worth of plant and equipment.[12] In addition,
the state RIDA officers became State Rural Development Officers
directly under the Ministry, and RIDA redesignated its own posts as
State Rural Industries Officers. After winding up a few projects in the
early part of 1960, RIDA ceased to work in this area.

The only major change in the character of RIDA's work after 1960

---

[12] Typically, RIDA accounts are not clear or consistent on this issue. In the 1960
financial report statement 2, Administration and Schemes Income and Expenditure,
shows that equipment valued at M$ 222,139.45 was handed over to the Public Works
Department. Individual statements of fixed asset, however, show that in the administration and schemes fund, M$ 183,335.35 worth of equipment was transferred, and
in the projects fund, at least M$ 44,000 worth of equipment was transferred. I have
been unable to obtain a satisfactory account of this discrepancy.

appears to be an increase in its loan program. Table VII-3 shows both this increase and the change in the character of the program.

TABLE VII-3

RIDA LOANS ISSUED EACH YEAR 1958–1962

	Number of Loans				
	1958	1959	1960	1961	1962
Total number	379	412	612	1054	1204
Commerce, percent	41	39	44	28	36
Industry, percent	11	8	4	7	6
Transport, percent	7	6	5	5	14
Agriculture, percent	19	25	19	18	20
Fisheries, percent	8	10	3	2	2
Animal husbandry, percent	13	10	23	34	9
Other, percent	1	4	2	6	13
Average Amount of Loans: M$					
Total amount loaned (M$ 000)	717	726	962	1,784	4,433
Average amount per loan (M$)	1,900	1,750	1,550	1,700	3,700
Commerce (M$)	1,700	970	1,600	1,500	2,200
Industry (M$)	1,700	2,700	2,000	2,900	3,800
Transport (M$)	5,000	4,300	5,700	6,700	8,000
Agriculture (M$)	1,100	1,400	1,700	1,300	1,700
Fishery (M$)	2,100	3,300	700	1,000	1,700
Animal husbandry (M$)	1,200	800	700	300	700
Other (M$)	1,300	4,000	3,500	6,000	9,200

SOURCE: Prepared by RIDA Headquarters.

It is apparent from this table that the removal of the construction function allowed RIDA to increase its loan program, especially when we note that the staff of RIDA did not increase appreciably in the same period. Both the number of loans and the amount of money loaned increased sharply with the removal of the construction function. In addition, a survey of loans carried out in 1963 found that the State officers and their assistants in the districts spend approximately 70 percent of their time on loans work.

Since loans have dominated RIDA's work since 1960, it might be expected that the attempts to broaden the goals of RIDA would be reflected in the loan program. RIDA's activity does not fulfill this expectation, however. The character of the loan program has changed slightly, but not as a result of the attempt to change RIDA's goals.

With one exception, there have been no instructions from the Ministry affecting the loan program, and even within RIDA itself, there has been almost no concern with integrating the loan program into a broader program designed to pursue new goals.

The failure to see the loan program as part of its total resources in goal achievement is most evident in the case of industrial loans. The absolute number of industrial loans did increase from 1960, but at a rate less than that for the total number of loans. The average size of industrial loans also increased, but this appears to have been the result of a changing environment rather than a change of RIDA policy.[13] RIDA did not decide to concentrate on larger loans, though this had been recommended by Fiennes as early as 1955. It was simply that Malays were beginning to use RIDA loans for larger and larger concerns, such as for petrol stations. In addition, commercial loans, which might have been used to stimulate enterprises associated with industries, showed a decrease in their proportion of total loans between 1960 and 1961.

This could have been anticipated from the 1960 RIDA memorandum on industrial development. The RIDA chairman considered the proper course of action to be the creation of RIDA-operated industries. He accepted uncritically the assumption that Malays are lacking in capital and entrepreneurial skill and decided that industries would have to be built for the Malays. Therefore, he did not see the use of loan capital to stimulate entrepreneurial development as a viable alternative.

This was, however, the area in which the Ministry and RIDA apparently held different views. It was also one of the few areas in which the Ministry gave RIDA instructions on a specific policy. In 1961 the Ministry asked RIDA to help Malays enter the contracting trade to take advantage of the increased rate of construction that was the major goal of the Rural Development Program. The Ministry suggested that Malays might form themselves into cooperatives or companies to do the contracting for minor projects that were under the direct control of the district rural development committees. The Ministry conceded that Malays might not have the capital and the skills to enable them to work in this area, but it wanted RIDA to do whatever possible to assist in this matter.

As a result RIDA began to experiment with a program of loans to contractors. In the table above, these are classed as "other" loans. There was a sharp increase both in the number of these loans and in their average size. By the end of 1962, 230 of these loans to contractors had been granted for a total of M$ 2,268,000, or an average of about

---

[13] From an interview with a RIDA Loans Officer.

M$ 10,000 per loan. Of these 175 were for construction, and averaged about M$ 7,500. The 55 loans for land clearing, quarry work, and rubber planting averaged M$ 17,000.

The distinctive feature of this loan program has been the use of a different type of security. For the most part no fixed security is used. The contractor merely transfers to RIDA the right to collect payments from the government agency giving the contract. After making deductions for loan repayments, RIDA then turns the balance over to the contractor. In addition, these loans are peculiar in that they have no specified terminal date. Nonetheless, of the 230 loans granted up to the end of 1962, only twelve appeared to be in "a difficult position" when the loan survey was done in mid-1963. These twelve loans totaled M$ 641,700, of which only M$ 324,600 had been repaid, though this does not indicate that the remainder has been lost.

The contractor loans must be seen as an imaginative attempt on the part of RIDA to achieve the broad goal given to the organization: to raise the economic position of the Malays in the rural areas. It appears to be one of the few successful ventures of RIDA, especially in working out new techniques to stimulate the economic growth of the Malays. It is important to note that in this one activity in which RIDA showed innovating ability, the original stimulus came from the Ministry and was in support of the Ministry's dominant goal, the construction of social overhead capital in the rural areas.

In the total peasant sector, there was both stability and change in the loan program. Loans to agriculture and fisheries remained quite constant throughout the five years. The absolute number of loans grew at the same rate as the total program, making up about one fifth of the number of loans in the three years under the new Ministry. In this case, however, the last year has seen an increase in the average size of the loans. Again RIDA is merely reacting to its environment. The loan program has created a demand for larger loans and RIDA has simply acquiesced to this demand. There was considerable fluctuation in the loans to animal husbandry, however. There was a great increase in the number of loans in 1960 and 1961, then a drastic reduction in 1962. With the great increase, there was also a decrease in the average size of the loans. In large part this reflects only the vacuum left by the removal from RIDA of responsibility for improvements. RIDA used its newfound freedom in the only way it knew, by greatly increasing the number of those loans that were easiest to process. RIDA could always obtain applicants for small loans for chickens or goats. These could be secured by land or by personal guarantors, especially if the loans were for very small amounts.

This flexibility was accorded to RIDA partly because its loans program has never had to be self-supporting. Administrative or other overhead costs could be met from the administration and projects fund, financed by the yearly grant from the central government. The actual principal of the loans had to be conserved, of course, but simple repayments could accomplish this, and even the low interest charged could give the appearance of success because the total amount available would continue to grow.

In the 1963 loan survey it was estimated that the total cost of the loan program in administrative staff for 1962 was M$ 520,000, or an average cost of slightly more than M$ 400 for each of the 1200 loans granted that year. Other estimates by RIDA staff have been as high as M$ 800 per loan. It has also been noted by RIDA staff that the staff time required to process a loan is not a function of the size of the loan, so that the average cost is rather close to the real cost for each loan. Regardless of what estimate is accepted, it is obvious that if the loan program had to be self-supporting, RIDA would not have this flexibility to use its manpower resources simply by increasing the number of small loans.

The review committee of 1960 suggested that the departments of agriculture and cooperatives take over responsibility for such things as rural marketing and agricultural stimulation in general. This was not acted upon, however, and therefore is not reflected in the loans program. In the loan survey of 1963 the surveying committee suggested once again that agricultural and marketing loans be the exclusive concern of the agricultural and cooperatives departments. Early in 1963 (after Azis bin Ishak had left the cabinet), talks began between RIDA and the Ministry of Agriculture and Cooperatives to separate functions and remove responsibility for these activities from RIDA. It is likely that this will be reflected in the pattern of RIDA activities after 1963. The effect will be further to concentrate RIDA's activities on industrial and commercial activities.

In the last year in this series, there was also a considerable increase in loans in transport. This again reflects merely RIDA's adjustment to its environment rather than its own policy change. Malays have been given preference in taxi licenses, and RIDA is offering loans to enable Malays to enter this type of business. The preference is actually of longer standing, but it had only been recently suggested to RIDA that more assistance might be given to potential Malay taxi-owners.

In other respects, RIDA's new industries program has not been an overwhelming success. The number of rubber-processing factories has been increased, a number of new industrial ventures have been entered, and RIDA established a small industries services institute with a modern retail shop to display Malay handicraft articles, including RIDA's own products.

The accounts for the ventures are not available after 1960, but interview materials strongly suggest that the over-all program has not achieved even limited success. The rubber-processing factories continue to cost more than they earn. The industrial ventures have been no different in quality from those of previous RIDA experience, and the experience of the small industries service institute has not yet given any hope for success. The problems are generally the same as those noted for the last decade. RIDA lacks the technical and administrative competence and the ideological stance needed to make economic decisions. The most immediate cause of failure in the industrial ventures is lack of proper technological and economic survey and planning. The ideological stance behind this is both a mild anticapitalist and stronger anti-Chinese commitment, and a desire to shield Malays from competition in the market place, because it is feared they cannot effectively compete with the Chinese.

RIDA has been especially subject to ethnic problems. There has been considerable ambiguity over the ethnic commitment of RIDA. The public stance of the organization has been rural rather than Malay. From Dato Onn to the latest chairman, policy statements have been issued stating that RIDA is not for Malays only, that it is for the rural people. At the same time the work of the organization and the views of its staff and other government officers make it impossible to see the organization as anything other than an organization of, by, and for Malays. RIDA attempts to explain this publicly by the high proportion of the rural population that is Malay. However, Malays constitute about 70 percent of the population living in places of less than 1,000 inhabitants, yet the 1963 loan survey showed that over 95 percent of the loans went to Malays, less than 5 percent being for non-Malays. In addition, 18 percent of the loans and 27 percent of their total value went to people in places larger than 10,000 in population. In effect, though RIDA has attempted to establish an image of itself as a rural oriented organization, it has used ethnic criteria to evaluate its operations. RIDA will engage in almost any activity that appears to be for Malays; it will be reluctant to enter into activities that involve non-Malays. From the point of view of increasing per capita product, this can only be called irrational.

There has also been considerable ambiguity about the goals of RIDA, an ambiguity that stems in part from ethnic forces. With every attempt to redirect RIDA, as in the last act of the British High Commissioner in 1957 and the first act of the Minister of Rural Development in 1960, there has been a reaffirmation of the original statement of purpose of the organization: "It shall be the duty of the Authority to stimulate, facilitate and undertake economic and social development in the Federation and more particularly in the rural areas thereof." [14]

In interpreting this statement of purpose, both superordinate powers have tried to move RIDA to a commitment to mixed output-cultural goals rather than to pure output goals. Neither set of pressures seems to have had any marked effect on RIDA. In part this is due to the failure to exercise superordinate power. The move of the High Commissioner in 1957 could not have been effective because it was almost the last move of that superordinate power. The pressure from the Ministry has been ineffective, largely because RIDA has not been important to the Ministry's own goals. Perhaps a more important source of the failure, however, lies in the ethnic irrationality inherent in RIDA, which affects RIDA internally as well as the relation between RIDA and the Ministry.

RIDA's ethnic commitments have largely prevented it from developing any competence to evaluate its own activities, or to act upon whatever evaluation it is able to make. Although RIDA has at times had a special research unit, which was sometimes staffed by trained economists, it has on the whole shown little interest in an objective evaluation of its own activities. Whenever confronted with such evaluations from an outside agency, RIDA has insisted that its activities are experimental and aimed at the development of a backward sector and therefore cannot be evaluated by criteria of costs and returns.[15]

The backward sectors in which this applied were primarily those of Malay producers. The relation between RIDA's perception of Malay backwardness and the inapplicability of objective criteria for evaluating programs was made explicit in the industrialization memorandum of the chairman in 1960. At the same time, RIDA's ethnic irrationalities have prevented the organization from acting upon any available objective evaluations. We have already seen how this worked in the issue of the size of loans. RIDA remained committed to small loans because of the anticapitalist sentiments of its leadership, sentiments

---

[14] From the Ordinance; quoted here from Policy Directive of 23 January 1960.

[15] In almost every annual report, RIDA accounts have been questioned by the Auditor General. For example, in fruit canning operations, RIDA had no account of the full costs of the operation, and did not include the stocks of canned fruit in its accounts. When questioned about this, RIDA replied that the costs were treated as experimental, and the sale of the fruit considered only a subsidy to the experiment. This was apparently considered by RIDA sufficient to explain its failure to ascertain the cost of the operation.

that we argue have been strongly supported by anti-Chinese sentiments.

Capitalist, Chinese, middleman, and exploiter have been largely synonymous terms to RIDA. We have also seen that the small size of loans precluded the espousal of any but purely output goals. In other areas, the process has been almost identical. Without the organizational and ideological ability to evaluate either the effects of its programs or the economic structure to be changed, RIDA has been able to do little more than concentrate on the output of goods and services.

In addition to RIDA's embodiment of a pro-Malay and anti-Chinese sentiment, its lack of confidence in Malays has tended to prevent goal change. Pervasive among Malayan government officers is the fear that Malays cannot compete successfully in the modern world, especially with the Chinese. In addition, there is a strong reluctance to admit this fear publicly, or even to draw attention to the problem, because of the strains it produces in Malaya's emerging national plural society. This has helped to make RIDA reluctant to attempt economic evaluations of its own programs, and it has made the Ministry reluctant to force a goal change on the organization. The changes in the RIDA ordinance recommended by the 1960 review committee have not yet been made primarily because the Ministry is reluctant to take RIDA to the floor of parliament. Though the government has sufficient command of votes to effect any legislation it desires, it appears to fear that a public debate on RIDA would introduce too many divisive forces in the nation as a whole and too much criticism of government itself. "Communalism" is still too potent a divisive force, too powerful a source of irrationality, even to be discussed.[16]

The relations between the new Ministry and its two subsidiary Authorities illustrate both the firm commitment of the Ministry to output goals and the weakness of sources of initiative other than the central power, which we have argued is one of the outstanding characteristics of economically underdeveloped areas. In its two authorities, the new Ministry inherited two sets of tools that it could use to achieve its ends. In its land program the FLDA was closely attuned to the achievement of the Ministry's goals and therefore received strong and effective support from the Ministry. Its original goals were

---

[16] This is evident more generally in Malayan public political discussion. The image projected by government is one of success in achieving a harmonious mixture of races in Malaya, and most attempts to raise the question of differences is met with the charge of "communalism." This is still one of the most derogatory epithets that can be applied to a Malayan politician.

somewhat out of line with those of the Ministry, but these had changed considerably by the time the Ministry was formed and the Ministry itself helped to bury the old goals and reinforce the new. The compliance structure had not changed, however, but was brought into line with the goals when the lack of fit between goals and compliance threatened goal achievement. In this subsidiary organization, the goals were firm because they were fixed by the superordinate organization; it was the compliance structure that had to be changed.

Although the commitment to amenities production in RIDA was qualitatively in line with the dominant goals of the new Ministry, RIDA's ability to achieve these goals was far below what the Ministry demanded. The Ministry removed this function from RIDA, locating it exclusively in the previously developed, technically competent agencies of the bureaucracy. Since the new Ministry had strong political power over those agencies, this change greatly increased the ability of the Ministry to achieve the level of production it desired. However, the change left something of a vacuum in RIDA, which the Ministry attempted to fill by broadening RIDA's goals, and thereby its own, to include mixed output-cultural goals. This proved futile, largely because the Ministry itself is only weakly committed to these broader goals and therefore gave little direction or assistance to RIDA. Without this direction, assistance, and insistence from the Ministry, RIDA itself was incapable of accomplishing the change, largely because of the inherent irrationalities derived from its ethnic commitment.[17] The circle of RIDA failure and lack of ministerial control becomes a vicious one when we observe that the ethnic bias of RIDA makes it difficult for the Ministry to control the organization. This is because such control would necessitate activities that might be potentially detrimental to, or at least not fully supportive of, Malay protection. Given the delicate balance achieved in Malay's political accommodation, the organizational failure of RIDA might be accepted as small enough cost for the maintenance of that accommodation.

APPENDIX: PRÉCIS OF NATIONAL LAND COUNCIL PAPERS

1/1958: *Procedure:* Allowing members to initiate issues and setting out procedure for their discussion and resolution.

---

[17] This interpretation is supported by the observation that in the one area in which RIDA showed some inventiveness and activities in the direction of broader goals, the case of contractor loans, the original stimulus came from the Ministry, for activities that were essentially in support of the Ministry's dominant concern with amenity production.

2/1958: *Basis of Land Policy and Administration:* Policy is based on the fact that land is the source of all wealth; as such it must be both developed and conserved. The administration is to develop and conserve the land. Land use is to be aimed at increasing total yield, increasing and improving resources, and putting the land to the best possible use. Conflicting claims for land use are to be judged according to all-around and long-term best returns.

3/1958: *Report of the Commission on Land Administration:* The report is accepted and it is decided to reorganize the land administration in all states. There will be a federal commission of lands and a commissioner in each state. The state governments shall decide what lands are to be allocated, select these areas and lay them out, publicize the alienation, offer lots to applicants, and permit peripheral allocation outside these areas only if the applicants have blood or land ties with the areas.

4/1958: *Land Development:* Land development is to be planned, especially to allow for economic size, to protect against fragmentation, and to provide for proper use. The National Land Council will coordinate federal and state development, with the Ministry of Natural Resources especially responsible for the work. Staff shortages mean that the administration should concentrate on the positive rather than the negative or restrictive aspects of administration. Legislation should be drafted for mass land settlement.

Appendix A: More emphasis is to be placed on planned land development. Estates are to be complementary to small holdings and both are to be planned. Development of cooperative marketing facilities is to be integrated with land development. There is to be more fringe alienation. Applications are to be closed and no more temporary operating licenses are to be granted. Delays must be cut. Land administration is to foster good husbandry.

Appendix B: Lays out a sequence for executing the program of land development, designating the steps to be taken and the specific departments responsible for each step.

5/1958: *Divisions of State and Federal Property:* Reserved areas for state and federal governments are to be established and published.

6/1958: *Development of Land for Secondary Industries:* The growing urban population requires that more jobs be created. Therefore land development is to assist industrial development.

Land is to be made available with attractive conditions for industrial development and this is to be done equally all over the country. The Ministry of Commerce and Industry will be specifically responsible for this.

7/1958: Not available.

8/1958: *Land Use: Cultivation of Slopes:* Gives detailed rules for the cultivation of slopes of different degrees. Rubber tea and oil palm can be planted on the steepest slopes cultivated; there is to be no cultivation on slopes greater than 18½ degrees.

9/1958: *Land Use: Mining:* Mining policy is to be part of general land policy. The policy should provide for the interests of industries. When in conflict with government the latter will prevail. Where there is no conflict, the requirements of industries will be met.

10/1958: *Land Use: Mining in Malay Reservations and Malay Participation in the Mining Industry:* The Federal government is to maintain a mineral investigation drilling unit to search for minerals on Malay reservation. Where Malays are not trained to make use of these leases, the government may appoint engineers to do the prospecting, with 50 percent Malay employees in certain job categories, and 75 percent Malay employees over-all. These leases are not transferable; the actual work of clearing and mining is to be done by individuals, firms, or cooperatives, not by government. The government is to train engineers and technical personnel, not accountants and clerical personnel for the mining industry. All mining leases outside as well as inside Malay reservation are to include 50 percent Malay employees in the special job categories and 75 percent Malay employees over all.

11/1958: *Land Use: Mining: Special Cases:* In protective forests, mining is to have the lowest priority. In commercial forests mining is to have highest priority. In water catchment areas an absolute conflict of interest goes to water; no conflict goes to whatever use is established first.

12 and 13/1960: *Group Settlement Policy:* Accepts the ideas of group settlement and fringe allocation programs. FLDA will work best in more remote areas. Group settlement best near populated areas.

Addendum: The Federal government is to make available M$ 49,560,000 over the next ten years to subsidize state schemes, precluding FLDA giving loans to state boards. The State Land Development Boards are to be discontinued and to become subcommittees of district rural development committees, with advisory rather than executive functions. FLDA is to abandon its purely loan function and to undertake land development directly. Land is to be for the landless, not for the expansion of existing farms.

Amendments: The division between FLDA and Group schemes in remote and populous areas is not to be implemented. FLDA is to take over the State Group Settlement Schemes. Visiting agents are to be employed by FLDA. States are to continue to be responsible for fringe allocation schemes.

14/1961: *Terms and Conditions of Alienation of State Land to the Federal Government:* Since Federal development projects increase the wealth of the entire country, the states will charge only nominal premiums for land transferred to the Federal government.

15/1962: *Controlled Allocation:* 2,000 acre blocks of land are to be surveyed into ten acre lots after proper suitability surveys. These are to be allocated for development, which must take place within five years. No transfers, leases, mortgages, or charges are to be allowed for a period of fifteen years from date of allocation. This is to be for people with less than six acres of land, and for retiring laborers and government employees with pensions of less than M$ 350 per month.

16/1962: *Foreign Participation in the Iron Ore Mining Industry in the Federation of Malaya:* Japanese and other firms are not to hold more than one third of the share capital in any iron mining company in Malaya.

VIII

MOVES TO THE BROAD FRONT: GOAL CHANGES IN A SUBSIDIARY ORGANIZATION

Although the Ministry of Rural Development has remained almost exclusively committed to output goals, it has been under constant pressures to broaden its goals, especially to include more cultural goals. The pressures are both external and internal to the Ministry, deriving from the Party and the Cabinet, and from the Ministry's own adjustment to its environment, which was itself changing as a result of the Ministry's work. Here we shall examine the two major moves of the Ministry in the direction of cultural goals and show how these have been partly subverted by the organizational structure of the Ministry.

The basic impulse to broaden goals lay in government's generalized desire to gain the support of the people, a desire that had both economic and political meaning. The economic meaning lay in the desire to abolish poverty, to increase standards of living, and to create a wealthy nation. National wealth was seen as the sum of individual wealth. If individuals produced more and gained more income, the nation would be more wealthy.[1] Thus in order for the development program to be successful it must gain popular support in the sense of stimulating people to produce more.

The political meaning lay, naturally, in the desire to gain voter

---

[1] The fallacy of composition reflected here has not bothered the government, partly because its public thinking on economic issues has not been very sophisticated. That is, government has been more impressed with the positive value of production than with the more problematic character of the market as a determinant of wealth.

support for the governing party. We have already seen that government leaders tended to perceive a close relation between economic and political development. The struggle against Communism involved an attack on poverty. The creation of a viable national state in Malaya's plural society required both an equalization of wealth along ethnic lines and sufficient total economic advance to give all groups a firm stake in the existing system. Finally, a stable and wealthy state required high levels of literacy and a dissolution of the barriers that kept large numbers of people in small isolated communities outside the life of the total national community. This line of argument was fairly explicit and provided a rationale and an impetus for engaging in programs with essentially cultural goals.

That is, the Ministry saw two major tasks facing it. One involved forcing the old bureaucracy to increase its output of improvements, especially but not exclusively to the rural areas. The other involved making the old society an active, involved, productive national society.

The former task implied the espousal of almost pure output goals, and we have seen that the new Ministry achieved considerable success in carrying out these goals. The latter task was approached through two specific programs directly under the responsibility and control of the Ministry of Rural Development. The creation of *kampong* rural development committees was aimed primarily at increasing rural output, and the adult education program was aimed primarily at breaking rural psychological isolation and providing greater skills for production and greater support for government.

PHASE II, *KAMPONG* RURAL DEVELOPMENT COMMITTEES

After about a year of activity the Ministry began to conceive of its work in two phases. The first phase had been launched with the Red Book operation early in 1960; phase II was initiated on September 4, 1961, with the opening of the new national operations rooms. In launching the second phase the Minister explained at a press conference that it was only right that the first act of an elected government should be to show the people that the government is theirs and is concerned with their welfare. Further, given the isolated condition of much of the rural population, government must extend its activities widely in order to bring the image of an effective government close to all people. Regardless of how far away from the capital people lived, they must be made to feel that their wishes were never far from the heart of their government. The task of mobilizing the entire bureaucracy to this end had been carried through successfully in the first phase of rural development.[2] Though this would continue, and even increase in tempo, it was now time for the government to call on the people to take a more active part in their own uplift.

In phase I the government demonstrated what it was willing to do for the people. In phase II government was asking the people to come forward to help themselves.[3]

Phase II was launched administratively by Rural Development Directive Number 3.[4] The stated aim of this directive was "To mobilize the Spirit and Energy of the Rural people for their own betterment and for the progress of the nation." The scope of the aim included cultivating existing land to the fullest extent, learning and applying the best methods of husbandry, creating cooperatives and developing rural industries, learning ways to guard good health and hygiene, and using adult education facilities to eradicate illiteracy and improve knowledge. The directive went through the state committees to the district committees, which were to create *kampong* committees, to consist of the *kampong* headman and not more than ten others who were to be selected and nominated by the district committee and approved or formally appointed by the Chief Minister of the state.

The *kampong* committees were to plan programs for local development. They were provided with a standardized Red Book and a four foot square bulletin board to be hung in the community hall or in some public place. The board listed development ideas included in the scope of the directive. There was a place for a map of the *kampong,* on which development plans could be located. In addition there was a set of graphs to record the amount of land developed and planned for development in major crops, and designated spaces for establishing goals and recording progress in self-help (*getong royong*) projects, rural industries, cooperative development, and adult education. Through the bulletin board an attempt was made to duplicate the operations room technique and to provide the rural people both with a new group oriented to development, and with a set of measures for establishing clear-cut goals and evaluating achievement of those goals.

---

[2] In this first phase government explicitly rejected the mechanism of self-help in infrastructure construction, especially that had been identified with RIDA programs. It argued that government should build the roads because government had the ability and the machinery to do the job most efficiently.

[3] Still, a natural division of labor was to be maintained. Government would build the roads and the people would cultivate their own land and develop their own industries.

[4] In their published forms all rural development directives have been undated.

The actual creation of the *kampong* committees proceeded in a somewhat erratic fashion. District and state committees were left to their own devices in programming the creation of committees. Some District Officers went ahead immediately to form a committee in each *kampong*, others started with pilot committees in each *mukim* or just one for the district. Other District Officers waited for further instructions. Gradually, however, all districts entered the program and at the time of writing (February 1964) *kampong* committees have been created in every *mukim*, if not in every *kampong*.

One potentially major problem arose in the formation of the committees. It would not do, of course, to allow these new local organizations to become tools of the opposition parties. It was understood by the District Officers that activists from the opposition parties, and perhaps even weak supporters, were to be avoided in selecting the committee members. This proved to be a relatively simple matter, however; District Officers concentrated on selecting "progressive" leaders in the *kampongs*. This included people with ideas, people who were willing to work, and people who were concerned with local development. Activists from the opposition could easily be excluded on the grounds that they were more interested in oppositional politics than in local development. In any event, party politics do not appear as divisive on the local level as on the national level, and the selection of committee members did not often present a critical issue for the district committees.[5]

This program was in many respects similar to the Community Development programs that had been begun and allowed to atrophy or were explicitly rejected in 1953 and 1958. As in previous programs, Phase II attempted to organize the rural people, to mobilize their energies toward increased production. More important, however, were the ways in which the new program differed from its rejected predecessors.

First, the new program was more directed. The aim was not to discover the felt needs of the rural people, but to induce them to work on what government felt (probably rightly) to be their known needs. Rural people were asked to increase their labor on the available land resources that were lying idle. Second, the new program was more structured in that local groups were given standardized packages of goals and evaluative criteria.

Finally, the new program was more integrated into the bureaucracy

---

[5] This is based especially on interviews with district officers in Kedah, Pahang, Negri Sembilan, and Johore, all of whom were interviewed in the three months following the beginning of Phase II.

than were its predecessors. There would be no special units and no specialized functionaries for the new program. Even the new *kampong* committees were simply extensions of district committees to coordinate normal activities of the bureaucracy. Nor was there any attempt to exclude from the program the government's capacity to produce amenities, to provide pork barrel projects. In Phase II success depended upon closer coordination of local with government activities rather than upon government's absence of activity.

All of this helped to make the new program acceptable in a plural society precisely at those points where the old programs had been unacceptable. Government could continue to demonstrate its concern for the voters, and no invidious distinctions were made between Chinese and Malays. This was accomplished partly because rural development had originally (though not explicitly) been oriented to the Malay sector, and partly because the program explicitly emphasized the positive rather than the negative aspects of the development problem.

A clear example of this latter was provided during the press conference at which the Minister launched Phase II. A reporter from a leading local newspaper asked the Minister if the emphasis given to the cultivation of all *kampong* lands implied that some lands were lying idle, and if so, was there any estimate of the amount of land involved. The Minister rejected this implication, but then evaded the question by simply restating the government's desire that the people should use all the opportunities government was providing to increase their standards of living. After the conference the reporter remarked privately, "[a government officer] has told me he estimates that as much as 30 percent of alienated arable land is now unused simply because people do not want to take the trouble to work it. But they always evade the question this way in public. And you can't try to pin them down, because they think you're trying to get at them." If moves were to be made to broaden the goals in a cultural direction, they must be carefully designed not to arouse divisive ethnic sentiments.

In creating the new groups to provide rural society with new pressures and criteria for evaluation, the Ministry did not attempt to develop a specialized competence for over-all evaluation. In line with its previous policies of decentralization, the Ministry essentially left the task of day-to-day control in the hands of the state and district committees which were to visit the local groups as a team and help them to plan and control their own development. For its part the Ministry would continue to use only its briefing and inspection techniques to provide its own evaluation of the program.

Evaluation by briefing and inspection places emphasis upon dramatic and visible types of activity. The Ministry appears to have a vision of what it would like to see in the rural areas, and there can be little doubt that the signs desired are closely related to economic development. That is, the Ministry would like to see people working actively on their land, branching out into a number of new (and successful) crops, marketing their own produce, engaging in other forms of income-earning activities, and taking an active (and supportive) role in local politics. Further, it wants to see people working together on common projects, developing a sense of community.

The Ministry's evaluative techniques show this type of activity when it exists. Unfortunately, this activity is generally not highly visible or dramatic unless explicit attention is drawn to it by those more familiar with the immediate scene. Where local officers have projects that suit the Ministry's model, they make it a point to include these in the briefings. In general, group development projects are more visible and dramatic than individual projects, and are always given special mention.

Many cases fit the Ministry's model of right behavior, helping to reinforce its commitment to this type of program. However, the necessarily unsystematic nature of the evaluative techniques and the emphasis these give to dramatic projects have brought two different kinds of pressures from the Ministry. In the first place the committees themselves are under pressure to engage in *gotong royong* (self-help) projects. For example, on 21 October 1961 the Assistant Minister of Rural Development approved on the spot M$ 5,000 for surfacing a road built by the collective effort of the people of a Negri Sembilan *kampong*. In his speech to the people he emphasized the important role *gotong royong* was to play in the Phase II programs.

On visits throughout the country both Ministry and state officials gave the same kind of rewards for this type of activity. Money could be granted directly for roads, bridges, community halls, mosques, and prayer houses where the people showed a willingness and capacity to help themselves. In the press statements and motion pictures of rural development continued emphasis has been given to this type of collective construction activity. In this manner the Ministry is giving support to the more pure output goals of the local committees.

In the second place, the Ministry has had difficulties in operating with the almost contradictory images of Rural Development inherent in the two phases. This was illustrated during a ministerial inspection trip to Perlis in October 1963. The Minister remarked in a small group that about half of the *kampong* committees seemed to be doing well, but others seemed to think that their only task was to devise new requests for government projects. That is, they continued to operate with the image of Phase I. This implied that one criterion of a good local committee is quiescence, refraining from making requests for Ministerial aid. At the same time, a major feature of the visiting-briefing technique is that the Minister be able to establish control by dispensing rewards and punishments at the scene of action. We have already seen that this was an effective tool for reshaping the old bureaucracy, but its use in the Phase II program was somewhat subversive of the aims of that program. Although rewards were given for useful work, they were seldom given without a request; and they could also be given on the basis of promised as well as accomplished activity.

Thus in the image the Ministry provided for the local committee there was incentive for the committee to make a request for aid from the government. This was reinforced by the Ministry's own desire to give power to the committee's leaders, to make them influential in community affairs. Granting a request made by the committee members demonstrated the solidarity of the Ministry with the local leaders and enhanced their position in the *kampong*. Failing to grant such a request could weaken the local leadership, especially where opposition members were present to exploit the Ministry's lack of public support for the local leadership.

Thus, the techniques of evaluation and control available to the Ministry essentially subverted the cultural goals of its Phase II program. These techniques placed a premium upon collective construction projects and upon making requests for government aid. However, the extent of actual subversion among the local committees is not known, precisely because the Ministry itself has no means of measuring the effectiveness of its program. Although it has attempted to give to the local units clear-cut criteria for establishing goals and measuring achievement, it has not integrated these criteria into its own compliance structure. Thus it has no means of evaluating the general achievements of the program or even the extent to which the criteria are being used by the local bodies.

ADULT EDUCATION

During the 1950's adult education was in the hands of a voluntary association, the Federation of Malaya Adult Education Association, which had local autonomous bodies in each state. This over-all organization was primarily concerned with literacy training and gave instruction in English, Malay, Chinese, and Tamil. The Ministry of Education supported adult education by a grant to the voluntary association. In 1959, for example, the government grant was M$ 290,000 or about 77 percent of the total cost, M$ 374,554, to the association for the year.[6]

With independence came a drive to further the use of the constitutionally defined national language, Malay. Between 1957 and 1959 desultory beginnings were made in the Ministry of Education to increase instruction in the national language. Since the Ministry was already supporting adult education through a grant to the voluntary association, it was only logical that it begin to consider adult education as a mechanism for furthering instruction in the national language. It considered establishing a section for adult education within the Ministry and made an abortive move to stop the grant to the voluntary association. The stand of the Ministry at this time was that it could give assistance for teaching the national language, but not for adult education in the broader sense. Essentially it maintained that it could give assistance for the eradication of illiteracy in the national language only. The grant was partially restored, but the voluntary association was essentially forced to end this activity by the first part of 1962. In its last year of operation it had slightly more than 700 classes, more than half of which were in the national language and about one fifth of which were in English.

In 1960 a committee was formed to decide upon the proper government policy for adult education. The chairman of the committee was Haji Abdul Khalid, then Assistant Minister of Rural Development. The recommendations of the committee have not been made public, but various indications of them have been discussed occasionally. The result of the committee's action, however, was that the responsibility for adult education in the rural areas was lodged in the Ministry of Rural Development. The Ministry of Education assumed responsibility for adult education in the urban areas.

Although the initial government interest in adult education lay in its significance for the national language, the impact of the Ministry of Rural Development soon infused the program with its own orientation. This began even before the Ministry was formally given the responsibility for adult education. From the appointment of the Assistant Minister of Rural Development to the position of chairman of Government's review committee, it appears that the Ministry's interest in

---

[6] The balance was met from state association funds, collected largely as fees for classes. The actual cost is deflated because teachers in the voluntary association were unpaid.

adult education considerably antedated the formal delegation of responsibility, which was made only after the committee gave its report.

In June 1960 the committee issued a press release on its then largely completed work.[7] The recommendations of the committee could not be made public, but the Prime Minister announced his interest in the subject and wanted the report to go to cabinet immediately. In the press release, the chairman of the committee also gave some indication of its thinking on the issue. He argued that the aim of adult education would be to make all people literate in the national language by 31 August 1967. "The National Language could then be firmly established as the medium for the communication of ideas and as a vehicle for promoting the social, cultural, economic and political advancement of a strong, united, democratic nation." [8]

The broad modernizing function of both the national language and of adult education was further elucidated in the contention that

The Committee's recommendations are based on the firm conviction held by all its members that through a strong and active adult education movement, it would be possible to cultivate a national outlook and consciousness, promote national unity, instill a sense of loyalty and patriotism, foster democratic principles, and abolish poverty and social backwardness, thus firmly establishing Peace, Justice, and Prosperity in this country.

This theme was reiterated constantly in official speeches before adult education supervisor and teacher training courses in the months that followed. On one issue, however, the public statements have remained silent. Why was the responsibility for adult education given to the Ministry of Rural Development rather than allowing it to remain in the Ministry of Education? The specific interest of the Ministry of Rural Development in adult education has never been discussed. In part this may be because the interest is obvious and there has been some reluctance to belabor the obvious. Rural Development must aim at arousing the rural society to increase its standards of living. Adult education was simply one logical means to that end. This reflected, however, important goal-broadening forces within the Ministry itself. In political-economic issues, the Ministry could move easily toward the espousal of cultural goals.

With this orientation the Ministry moved into the field of adult education when it formally assumed responsibility for the program

---

[7] Department of Information 6/20/207.

[8] The Constitution stipulates that Malay shall be the national language, but that English may also be used in an official capacity for a period of ten years after independence, or more if desired.

late in 1960. With characteristic effectiveness the Ministry proceeded to translate its aims into practical programs. A separate section was created within the Ministry and plans were laid for a national organizational structure that would bring classes to all *kampongs*. State organizers were recruited and trained. These in turn recruited district supervisors, usually about three per district, who were trained in centralized classes. Next, local teachers were selected and given short courses in the aims and methods of the program. Finally students were recruited. Rural people were advised that they could apply for a class through their *kampong* headman, the *penghulu* of the *mukim*, or through the District Officer directly. Applications were processed and collated at the district level and the district supervisors, together with the District Officer or his assistant, laid out tentative class schedules and requirements and forwarded these to the state organizers. Shortly thereafter teachers and students were assigned to specific classes and the classes were begun.

The formal program called for three levels of classes: elementary, intermediate, and advanced. In addition there were to be two broad types of classes. For the rural Malays, who already knew their own language, instruction was given in literacy, using the Rumi script. These have been known as the Rumi language classes, *Kelas Bahasa Rumi*. For non-Malays, instruction was given in reading, writing, and speaking the national language; these have been known as national language classes or *Kelas Bahasa Kebangsaan*.

The classes were launched with some trepidation because the Ministry was uncertain about the popular response, though it had directed the Department of Information to give much advance publicity to the program. The Ministry hopefully set an original target of 4,000 classes for the year of 1961, all to be elementary classes. By the end of the year, however, slightly more than 6,000 classes were in operation with a total enrollment of 168,000 adults. The next year the total was over 7,500 classes with more than 200,000 adults enrolled, and as of August 1963 there were more than 11,000 classes with an enrollment of over 300,000. The specific items of this growth can be seen in table VIII-1. By any measures this growth has been phenomenal.

The state organizers are in established positions covered by the Public Services Commission, though at present most of the organizers are on loan from other services to the Ministry. District supervisors were recruited outside the bureaucracy's personnel structure. They receive no official salary, only an honorarium of M$ 200 per month plus M$ 100 per month for expenses. Although a systematic study has not been made of the district supervisors, a relatively large number of

TABLE VIII-1

GROWTH OF ADULT EDUCATION IN MALAYA 1961-1963

	1961	1962			1963			
	Total[a]	Elementary	Intermediate	Total	Elementary	Intermediate	Advanced	Total
Classes								
Kelas Bahasa Rumi[b]	4,679	2,883	3,256	6,139	3,446	2,501	2,911	8,878
Kelas Bahasa Kebangsaan[c]	1,484	654	959	1,613	1,021	521	773	2,315
Total	6,163	3,537	4,215	7,752	4,487	3,022	3,684	11,193
Enrollment[d]								
Malays	124,825	n.a.	n.a.	165,426	n.a.	n.a.	n.a.	239,812
Chinese	34,146	n.a.	n.a.	33,236	n.a.	n.a.	n.a.	45,184
Indians	7,121	n.a.	n.a.	10,041	n.a.	n.a.	n.a.	17,465
Others[e]	1,388	n.a.	n.a.	2,691	n.a.	n.a.	n.a.	4,363
Total	167,480			211,421				306,824
Percent Females								
Malays	52	n.a.	n.a.	59	n.a.	n.a.	n.a.	60
Chinese	41	n.a.	n.a.	45	n.a.	n.a.	n.a.	44
Indians	14	n.a.	n.a.	13	n.a.	n.a.	n.a.	16
Others	22	n.a.	n.a.	25	n.a.	n.a.	n.a.	29
Total	48	n.a.	n.a.	54	n.a.	n.a.	n.a.	55
Expenditures (M$ millions)								
Total	1,760.2	n.a.	n.a.	6,277.7[f]	n.a.	n.a.	n.a.	9,877.8[f]
Teachers', Supervisors' Salaries	1,134.4	n.a.	n.a.	4,827.3[f]	n.a.	n.a.	n.a.	6,966.6

[a] In 1961 all classes were elementary classes.
[b] Rumi classes, for Malays.
[c] National language classes, for non-Malays.
[d] Actual attendance is unknown, but is probably only about 60 to 70 percent of enrollment.
[e] Includes aborigines.
[f] Estimates.

interviews provides a consistent picture of the process of recruitment.[9]

Few of those chosen had the necessary qualifications for administrative posts comparable in salary with those they obtained in adult education. They were chosen largely for their organizational abilities, demonstrated primarily in local political party organization. Opposition parties have charged that district supervisors and teachers have been chosen on the basis of political considerations, positions going only to supporters of the Alliance Party. This has been officially denied, but it could only be considered extraordinary, and politically foolish, if it were not true. Undoubtedly some patronage has been involved in the selection, though the Ministry reports that it was necessary to get rid of quite a few in the early days, and the general emphasis upon results makes it appear that this form of patronage has not been simply an allocation of sinecures. In fact, if anything, the district supervisors have demonstrated a capacity and a motivation that seriously undermine the rationale of the bureaucracy's insistence upon formal qualifications for positions, especially since emphasis is placed upon the ability properly to use the Queen's English. Though many of the supervisors can speak English, few could pass formal examinations in the subject.

Teachers used in the program are for the most part rural teachers with low qualifications. In 1963 4,000 of the total 6,921 teachers had primary Malay school qualifications only. About one fourth were women, and the great majority were teaching in the *kampongs* in which they lived. Teachers were paid M$ 4 per hour and each class met for three one-hour sessions each week. A teacher was allowed to teach no more than two classes. Thus the 7,000 teachers could earn between M$ 50 and M$ 100 per month, which could be as much as half of their normal teaching salary. Again, it would be unusual if the Ministry did not tend to select teachers supportive of government or at the very least to avoid hiring active opponents.

Students in the classes have been primarily Malays, with all other ethnic groups underrepresented. Among the Malays women have always been in the majority, and their preponderance over men is even increasing slightly.

Subjects taught are different for the Malays and non-Malays. Malays receive instruction in language with the romanized script and in arithmetic. More recently, religious instruction has been included in all states except Kelantan. Like land, religion is a state subject and protracted negotiations between the Ministry and the states were re-

---

[9] During 1961, 1962, and 1963, unstructured interviews and informal talks were held by the author with over 50 district supervisors.

quired to reach agreement on the religious curriculum. Following the agreements the Ministry prepared the curriculum and trained local religious teachers, but the teachers themselves were selected and paid by the states. For obvious reasons the opposition-controlled state of Kelantan refused to take part in this program. In fact, its opposition to the entire adult education program was so strong that it attempted to establish its own classes, to run concurrently with the Ministry's classes. Kelantan's administrative and financial capacity was, however, no match for that of the Ministry and its competitive program has largely atrophied.

For the non-Malays, instruction has been limited to the national language, which is already spoken by many in its crude market form. More recently plans have been made to include civics, and curriculum and teachers are now being prepared for this course. Finally, the most recent plans include the proposed teaching of home economics subjects, for which a national organizer was recruited in November 1963. Immediate plans are that instruction will be given by volunteers of the Women's Institute of Malaysia. Although the Women's Institute has refused to accept payment for its instructors, the Ministry considers it likely that in the not too distant future it will pay the home economics instructors.[10]

To supplement the work of the Ministry, the Language and Literature Institute has developed its own teaching method for the national language, a method that has superseded the Lubach method used by the earlier voluntary adult education organization. In addition, the Institute produces a monthly magazine in about 100,000 copies to be circulated through the classes. Simply worded articles on health, child development, religion, civics, and some technical materials related to rural development are published in this magazine.

Evaluation of the adult education program is carried on with the same visiting-briefing techniques used in other parts of the Ministry. No attempt is made to achieve a systematic and objective assessment of the effects of the program. The adult education division itself does its own testing in order to issue certificates and to advance students, but the testing is purely in the matter of literacy, and the criteria for evaluation are somewhat flexible.

In the place of systematic evaluation there has emerged a folklore

---

[10] The decision not to accept payment has apparently been made by the top leaders of the Women's Institute, whose financial security allows them to seek protection for the organization from ministerial control in this manner. The women who will do the training, however, will generally be drawn from lower income groups and will probably arrive at a different calculation of gains and losses that will put pressure on the organization to accept payment.

indicating those positive effects of instruction in which the Ministry and its officials are most interested. At the Ministerial level three stories illustrate the kind of positive effects the Ministry desires. One concerns an elderly woman who learned to read and write in the adult education classes and thereafter could qualify to stand for local election as a government candidate. The case became dramatic when her opponent questioned her qualification to stand for the election, alleging that she was illiterate and had been trained only in the adult education classes. In a test given by the District Officer, the woman performed better than her rival and her name was allowed to stand on the rolls. In Negri Sembilan customary law requires that a man must receive his wife's written permission in order to take a second wife. The case is told of a man who presented a permission form to his wife for her signature, telling her that it was nothing important. Having been to adult education classes, she was able to read the form and refused to sign it. Finally, cases are reviewed where adult education classes increased local reading of agricultural pamphlets and increased the normal school attendance of children, whose parents are now able to help them and take a greater direct interest in their education. At the level of the district supervisors, the folklore includes cases of women and men who are now able to guard against being cheated by the Chinese middlemen because they now know something about figures themselves.

Beyond this folklore the Ministry essentially knows little or nothing about the impact of the adult education program on the rural population. There is, of course, some justification for believing that such education will broaden individual horizons and will have a positive effect on the rural economic and political structure, but there has been no attempt to put this belief to a rigorous test. In fact, the very structure of the program itself insulates it against pressures for objective evaluation. The program is highly specific and thus tends to generate its own criteria for evaluation: number of classes, enrollment, and examination passes. These criteria have the further advantage of being clear-cut and easy to assemble. Thus they are easily substituted for measures that relate to the broader cultural aims of adult education.

At the same time the evaluative techniques used by the Ministry, together with the small and transient character of the adult education division within the Ministry, offer considerable flexibility and a sensitivity to the demands of students and local officers. To the Ministry adult education is a new program, in which it has little specific competence and few preconceived ideas. The emphasis on the national language makes the Ministry see its adult education function as a transient one. When all or most of the people have been taught the national language, it is now argued, the Ministry's responsibility in this field will cease and it can be taken over again by the Ministry of Education. Finally the basic orientation of these cultural programs makes their popularity the most important criterion of success. Thus the adult education directors are made sensitive to popular demands and are willing to shift the program in directions that will increase popularity. This partly explains the inclusion of both religion and home economics in the curriculum. Thus the internal dynamics of the program move in many directions: from use of pure physical criteria of classes, enrollment, and passes, through the broadening of the curriculum to include a wide range of subjects designed to change the rural social system.

THE EVALUATION OF PERFORMANCE

In both attempts to broaden its goals, the Ministry has relied on the same evaluative techniques used in connection with its output goals. Although these techniques were well suited to the measurement of achievement in such things as road-building, they were incapable of providing an accurate evaluation of changing standards of production or living, primarily because the units of measurement for output goals were unambiguous and the processes involved well understood. Miles of roads constructed, bridges or buildings built were all unambiguous measures, and they could easily be obtained. State totals were simply aggregates of district totals, and national totals were aggregates of state totals. In addition, the total process of construction—from original investigation through financial allocation and construction—was well understood and highly standardized. This made it easy to locate obstructions and bottlenecks and to order their removal. Many obstructions were simply small delays that seem inevitable in a complex bureaucratic communications process. The operations rooms and briefing techniques were admirably suited to remove these obstructions, to speed up the process of construction. It must be recognized, however, that the power to remove obstacles swiftly was based on a reliance upon unambiguous and easily obtained units of measurement. Where these did not exist, the application of power could be highly dysfunctional, and these techniques could not easily be applied.

The raising of living standards or changing of social structure presented special difficulties in evaluation. Units of measurement were neither unambiguous nor easy to obtain. Partly because of this, and partly because of the almost total lack of empirical microeconomic studies of the rural sector in Malaya, little was known about the determinants of rural standards of living. This meant that its normal evaluative mechanisms gave the Ministry almost no measurement of the achievement of its broader goals—the cultural or mixed output-cultural goals involved in increasing rural standards of living. In effect, though not in public statements, this has channeled the goal-broadening movements into what is popularly called a political direction.

This politicization of development was reinforced by three other sets of forces. One was the strong proclivity throughout the modern period to identify political and economic development. Another was the ability to measure political support quite unambiguously and objectively in the electoral process. The third lay in the character of the parent organization, the cabinet, or the central decision-making body of the government and the party. This body existed essentially by political suffrage, and therefore had an ultimate interest in maintaining political mass support.

The moves in a political direction have reinforced a tendency recognized as a universal tendency of complex organizations—the desire to gain exclusive right of access to the organization's constituency. This has been dominant in the goal-broadening activities of the Ministry of Rural Development.

We earlier noted the attempt of the Ministry to take over the control of cooperatives from the Ministry of Agriculture. In the immediate political arena, this was a struggle between Tun Razak and Aziz bin Ishak to gain control of the instruments symbolizing leadership of the rural people. Organizationally, this was a struggle over the units of access to the rural people, the constituency of both Ministries. It would not be accurate to say that because the Ministry failed to gain control of cooperatives, it moved into adult education and *kampong* rural development committees. It is accurate, however, to observe that the access rights gained through local committees and adult education were functional equivalents of control over cooperatives.

In harmony with the character developed in the pursuit of output goals, the Ministry could have placed responsibility for adult education in the Ministry of Education, and the responsibility for local committees in the Ministry of Agriculture, along with cooperatives, farmers' associations, and agricultural extension work. Had this been done the Ministry would have operated in a manner identical to that used to increase the output of roads and bridges. It would have brought pressure to bear on other Ministries to increase the rate of activities in which they were already at least partly engaged.

The failure to act according to this character, the assumption of direct responsibility for these two functions, must be seen as a move to attain exclusive right of access to a constituency. Organizationally, the motivation lies in the Ministry's attempt to protect, and to further, the integrity of its own character by imposing its own view of the development process on the rural people.

All of this had the effect of making Rural Development something of a political tool. In gaining protected if not exclusive right of access to the rural population, the Ministry was also gaining access to the voter, to the ultimate source of life of the parent organization. In this process the organization of the Ministry served it well. The Ministry's role in increasing the output of the existing bureaucracy could easily be dramatized and made visible in the visiting and briefing techniques. More important, the formation of district rural development committees gave the Ministry the ability to bypass state governments controlled by the opposition parties. This was nowhere better illustrated than in the relation between the Ministry and the States of Trengganu and Kelantan, where the Pan Malayan Islamic Party won control in the 1959 elections.

In his inspection tours in 1961 Tun Razak took the opportunity offered by his district committees to make development grants directly to the districts, especially in Trengganu and Kelantan. In other states, he could allow development grants to come through normal channels, from the Ministry and the Cabinet to the state government. Only occasionally did he use independent financial grants at the district level to emphasize his leadership of the rural development program.

In July 1961 Tun Razak made a much publicized tour of Trengganu. One of his first visits was to Kemaman, a district in which the Alliance Party was in control. Here he granted over M$ 400,000 for roads, bridges, and schools, including M$ 38,000 for four mosques.[11] In Besut, another Alliance stronghold in Trengganu, the Minister granted M$ 387,000 for development, including M$ 15,000 for mosques and M$ 25,000 for community halls. The same pattern was followed in Kelantan, where the Minister dispensed M$ 500,000 in his visits to the eight districts. In addition to roads, jetties, and other projects, the grants were for forty community halls. At the same time, he refused a State request for M$ 1 million for a fifteen-mile road, arguing that he was displeased with the existing projects and thought the money would be wasted.

Shortly after this July trip, the Trengganu government was faced with a series of crises. The ruling Pan Malayan Islamic Party in the

---

[11] This and the following examples were taken from the daily press releases of the Department of Information.

state had never displayed much administrative competence and was rent by personal conflicts of people essentially attempting to gain greater personal power. For example, the party was unable to fill the post of Deputy Chief Minister of the state, because agreement could not be reached on who should obtain this plum. Criticisms of the government failures to push forward in development began to mount. In October the party's slim majority of thirteen of the twenty-four seats in the State Assembly dissolved as six members defected to the Alliance, giving the Alliance the slim majority of thirteen out of the twenty-four seats. A vote of no confidence was achieved, the Pan Malayan Islamic Party government resigned and requested that the sultan call for new elections. It seemed quite likely that elections would simply bring the PMIP back to power, for their hold on the rural voters was felt to be undiminished by the defection of party leaders. Instead of calling for fresh elections, the sultan (after a short hesitation) asked that a new Government be formed by the new majority party, the Alliance.

With this change in government, party efforts were increased at a rapid rate. The PMIP governments in both Trengganu and Kelantan had steadfastly refused to accept the central government's land policy and had gone ahead, though with no real progress, with their own land development projects independently of the Federal Land Development Authority. In Trengganu the change of government brought a change of land policy and the FLDA moved in rapidly to establish new projects. The one existing Trengganu project at Chalok was turned over to FLDA, and five new ones were begun in the next year.

The state itself set about organizing its own complementary development program, highly integrated with that of the Federal Government. In March 1962 Tun Razak made another visit to Trengganu, together with the chairman of the FLDA. At this time the new Chief Minister and Tun Razak announced a large M$ 5.5 million development budget for 1962, which included a M$ 2.5 million budget for schools.[12] Much of the remainder of this new expenditure was for a road program that had been planned before the 1959 elections. The original plan was for a large road project for the entire east coast, including eventually a major highway from Singapore to Kota Bahru, along the entire east coast, to be financed largely by a loan from the U.S. Loan Development Fund. During the 1959 elections the PMIP had campaigned against the use of foreign loans, arguing that the government was selling the country to foreign powers. When the PMIP won control of the state, the Central Government was given the rationale for trans-

---

[12] The State development budget increased from M$ 5.5 million in 1961, to M$ 12.0 million in 1962 and an estimate of M$ 14.5 million in 1963.

ferring the entire LDF funds to a road project in Tun Razak's home state of Pahang. Now that Trengganu had been regained by the Alliance Party, the original road program could be set in motion again.

With Alliance control over the state, it was also possible for the Ministry to allow the new state government to take credit for minor development projects. In slightly more than two months after gaining control the new Alliance Chief Minister had visited all parts of the state and granted M$ 43,000 for minor works in "on-the-spot" inspection tours. Now it was the Chief Minister who was visiting local committees, lamenting the inactivity of the past government, and striving to make up for time wasted by exerting pressures on all elements of the bureaucracy to increase production.

This policy was not exclusively oriented to the rural areas, as it was in the more urbanized west coast states. For example, a government press release in June 1962 pointed out that in the district of Kuala Trengganu (containing the state capital of Kuala Trengganu, with about 30,000 of the district's total population of 124,000), M$ 270,000 had been allocated for minor development projects for that year. An analysis of the projects gives some indication of the types of expenditures the Government, or Party, thought would best achieve its aims (table VIII-2).

TABLE VIII-2

MINOR DEVELOPMENT PROJECTS, KUALA TRENGGANU DISTRICT, 1962

Projects	Malayan dollars	Percent
17 Mosques	81,000	32
11 Community halls	66,000	24
1 Playing field	3,000	1
6 Weekly markets	81,000	30
52 Village wells	20,000	8
Village roads	8,100	3
Phone booths and miscellaneous	3,100	1
Total	270,000	99

SOURCE: Department of Information Press Release 6/62/221 (Statren), 21 June 1962.

This was in part also a reward for the town voters in Kuala Trengganu. Earlier in the year Dato Onn, one of the most articulate opponents of the Alliance Government, died, vacating a Federal Parliament Seat from Kuala Trengganu North. By-elections for this seat were scheduled for 19 March, just a few days after Tun Razak and the new Chief Minister announced their massive new development program for the state. The Alliance increased its power in the state by winning this seat, and the minor development projects can in part be interpreted as just rewards given to loyal voters.

Thus in the arena of electoral politics the Ministry of Rural Development found some clear-cut criteria for evaluating the achievement of its output goals. This meant, however, that to the extent the goals were cultural, they would be goals of creating a society supporting government rather than goals of a society increasing its per capita output. In order to move in the latter direction, the Ministry would have had to be able to demonstrate success in increasing rural incomes, and a positive correlation between income and supportive voting (that is, voting for the party in power). There was neither the organizational competence nor the raw data to do either. In all of this the Ministry might have looked to the Economic Planning Unit for support, especially in economic research. Unfortunately, the EPU has been primarily concerned only with preparing and controlling development expenditures and making requests for technical assistance. The Planning Unit's inability was largely due to staffing. The original design for a planning unit included a rather large research staff, but this never materialized.[13] The major implication for the Ministry is that the EPU has no real competence to reinforce the goal-broadening forces within the Ministry.

This is not to argue that the programs of the Ministry of Rural Development have not and cannot increase rural human productivity and rural income. Quite the contrary. Impressionistic evidence of the Malayan scene indicates a general increase in the level of living in the rural areas. Common sense evaluation can be applied to the rural development program, and the small size of the country enables a normal impressionistic evaluation to be rather complete. Among Ministry officials there is a high degree of intuitive feel, based on past experience, for the needs of the rural sector, and many of the development programs are based on this kind of experienced pragmatism. It is easy to see that isolated villages need roads and schools, that sun-parched or flood-damaged fields need irrigation and water control. It is also easy to accept the relationship between this kind of construction and long-term increases in human productivity.

---

[13] Here we return to an earlier problem of the control over development planning. This function moved out of the Treasury and into the Prime Minister's office, but not without delaying action by the Treasury. In what can only be called an organizational attempt to retain power in planning, the Treasury cut the original staff estimates for the EPU almost in half, and at the same time brought in a foreign planning expert and began to build up its own planning capacity.

It must be acknowledged, however, that this experienced pragmatism works far better for the visible and more easily understood problems of road-building than for the more subtle and illusive problems of changing the economic structure. Further, although the gross observation of association between infrastructure development and human productivity may be accurate, there can well be sectoral or periodic variations that may even negate the gross relationship. Irrigated fields can normally produce more than comparable nonirrigated fields, but there is no assurance that the provision of irrigation waters will directly and immediately raise yields and farm incomes. Other factors—labor, capital, seed—and other organizational elements—market and communications structure and land tenure—also impinge upon the productive process. Unless these are favorably arranged it is not certain that irrigation alone will increase yields, and it could even conceivably decrease yields and income.

In its briefing and operations room techniques, the Ministry of Rural Development had excellent means of evaluating performance in pursuit of its output goals. The Ministry did not, however, have the organizational capacity to evaluate performance in pursuit of other types of goals. It can even be argued that the evaluating competence it did have precluded the development of other types of competence, precisely because its existing competence was highly developed. In their insistence upon results, upon "getting on with the job," Ministry officials have displayed impatience with the argument that more systematic studies had to be performed before a clear course of action could be decided upon.

When, in response to external and internal pressures, the Ministry began to move to a change of goals, the deficiency of its evaluating techniques became crucial. The original orientation to pure output goals derived from the large and complex set of new national forces to which the cabinet (or the top national decision-makers) was most sensitive as an organization. In order to change this orientation, the Ministry would have had to demonstrate to the Cabinet, its parent organization, a competence in other goals as relevant as the output of amenities and social overhead capital. Unable to do this in the area of the economic structure, the Ministry essentially remained captured by the narrow character of the parent organization and operated in the realm of the political structure. Although it cannot be said that the Ministry resisted this orientation, the real alternative and its subversion should be noted. Goal-broadening pressures both within and outside the Ministry did offer the alternative of direct concern with human productivity in the rural areas. Tentative moves in this direction were subverted, largely by the lack of competence to evaluate performance in this direction, and to relate that performance to both the long- and short-term goals of the parent organization, the Cabinet.

IX

NEW STATES, ECONOMIC DEVELOPMENT, AND COMPLEX ORGANIZATIONS: CONCLUSION

RÉSUMÉ

Before examining the implications of the Malayan experience for the broader problem of new states, economic development, and complex organizations, it will be useful to present a brief résumé of the argument developed in the preceding chapters.

We noted first that Malaya is best seen as a social system in the midst of radical change. The old colonial system with its relatively well-balanced components—the dependent polity, the export economy, and the ethnic plural society—was thrown into considerable dis-well-balanced components—the dependent state, the export economy, and the ethnic plural society are incompatible with the new independent polity, especially since that polity is characterized by institutions of parliamentary democracy, making government vulnerable to mass demands. Malaya's Rural Development Program is one of the major mechanisms in the modern period functioning to bring the economy and the society into equilibrium with the new independent state.

The first manifestation of strain in the emerging system, and attempts to relieve the strain, are found in the change of the broad goals of government: a change from custodial goals to developmental goals. This was the direct effect of the shift in the center of power from London to Kuala Lumpur, and the passing of control from the hands of British bureaucrats to Malayan politicians. On the one hand the change meant a diminished concern for fiscal stability and an increased concern for an expanding economy. This reflected both the world-wide importance given to the value of economic development, and the different aspirations and standards of the good life brought to the Malayan government by new indigenous leaders. On the other hand, the change in broad goals reflected the political pressures upon an indigenous government vulnerable to mass demands. Thus the change also included an increased emphasis upon social services, and upon rural as opposed to strictly urban or industrial development. It is most important to note that the change was a change in both public and operative goals. The new leaders *proclaimed* an attachment to different goals, and they actively *worked* for the achievement of those goals.

The congruence of public and operative goals, an uncommon phenomenon in the new states of the world, was partly due to Malaya's favorable position in the world market. The country has had no marketing problems, and probably will not for some time to come. It has been in the fortunate position of being able to sell all of its major produce—rubber and tin—at prices that have on the whole been highly favorable. The market advantage, however, is an exogenous one, over which Malaya has had no real control. Of greater importance in this study is the observation that the congruence of public and operative goals has also resulted from the new organizations created to stimulate economic development within the country.

These new organizations, created to give life to the emerging commitment to development, manifest two partially separate and partially related dimensions. One concerns goals, the other control.

GOALS

Between 1951 and 1959 three separate organizations were created to stimulate economic development: the Rural and Industrial Development Authority (RIDA), the Federal Land Development Authority (FLDA), and two embryonic community development organizations. The total organizational pattern was characterized by early experimentation with different goal patterns and gradual change to exclusive output goals. The culmination of this commitment to output goals came with the creation of the Ministry of Rural Development in 1959. Efforts to stimulate development took on the character of producing the social overhead capital of a modern state. Road-building, or physical construction, has come to symbolize Malaya's attempt to stimulate economic development.

The almost exclusive espousal of output goals in development organ-

izations was not simply a historical accident. It is understandable
primarily from a consideration of the political forces reflected in
government organizations. Output goals provided the least amount of
strain in, and the greatest amount of support for, the emerging social
system. They offered something for all the important groups in the
system, and they trod on the toes of none. To the Malays output goals
offered the physical manifestations of a government that was theirs
and that was concerned for them. These goals also offered a larger
share of the physical amenities—the roads, utilities, and especially
schools—whose disproportionate abundance in the towns had come to
signify government neglect of the rural areas and of the Malays. For
the Chinese businessmen and laborers output goals offered contracts,
purchases, and employment. For the electorally impotent, but still
influential, foreign business houses, output goals offered an increased
demand for imported capital goods and some technical skills. Only the
estate Indians were omitted from the table at which this wealth was
distributed, but their dispersion and their small numbers—in short,
their political impotence—made this omission of little importance.

   While output goals offered something for all major groups in the
system, other goal choices offered little more than strain and tension.
The cultural goals embodied in Community Development programs
were a sustained insult to the Malays. It was only they, the programs
argued, who needed to change their values, to learn to work hard, to
save and to invest. Malays were told to emulate the Chinese, whose
industry and achievement orientation were responsible for their rapid
rise from poverty to wealth. No approach could be better designed to
alienate followers and lose voters.

   The mixed order-cultural goals that aimed at changing the economic
structure through proscribing the activities of the money-lender and
middleman were similarly unacceptable because they involved a direct
attack on the interests of the Chinese. Middlemen could not be legis-
lated out of existence because the middlemen were largely Chinese.
Whether or not their functions could have been performed by others
was not the issue, though in any rational attempt to change the
economic structure it would have been. Attempts to proscribe the
middlemen foundered on political grounds—the necessity of protecting
the interests of an important group in an embryonic democratic state
that was changing from an ethnic to a national social pattern.

   The adoption of mixed output-cultural goals, probably those most
suited to the successful stimulation of economic development, was precluded by Malaya's lack of technical competence to analyze the old

economy and society, and to plan effectively for the broad changes involved in increasing per capita output.

It is important to our argument that alternative goal patterns were available and had been tried. Thus the emergence of output goals as dominant can be seen as a natural adjustment of development organizations to basic forces in their environments. We saw goal alternatives in the cases of RIDA, FLDA, and Community Development. All of these preceded the formation of the Ministry of Rural Development. Late in 1962, after the Ministry had been in operation and had demonstrated considerable competence in the achievement of output goals, there was a dramatic and public recapitulation of the alternatives and choices seen earlier.

During 1961 and 1962 the first Minister of Agriculture, Aziz bin Ishak, had promised the (largely Malay) rice growers in Perak and Province Wellesley that he would transform private rice mills, largely owned by Chinese, into cooperatives. He attempted to induce the states, which control milling licenses, to give cooperatives exclusive buying and milling rights. The issue received little public attention, but occasioned a fierce battle in the executive committee of the Alliance Party. Informants report that the MCA was ready to leave the Party over the issue, knowing its already tenuous leadership of the Chinese community was at stake.

The MCA did win its case. The Prime Minister revoked Aziz' moves with the observation that they were unconstitutional.[1] Aziz was shortly afterward forced out of the cabinet and thenceforth lost political influence.

The issue illustrates both sides of the process of goal selection: rejection of one type and acceptance of another. Here was on the one hand a goal alternative that was highly divisive given the delicate demographic balance out of which accommodating politics grew. On the other hand, it is important to note that this issue also involved a personal struggle between Aziz and Razak, essentially over who was to be the next Prime Minister. Both are strong-willed men, and the cabinet was too small to contain both of them. It is more pertinent

---

[1] Article 153 of the Constitution provides economic protection for both Malays and Chinese. Malay economic positions are to be furthered explicitly, by the reservation of a portion of certain licenses (e.g., in transport) for them. At the same time, government is forbidden to revoke any license, to refuse to grant renewal, or to refuse to grant a license in the case of activities carried on before licenses were required wherever "this might reasonably be expected in the ordinary course of events." This is an implicit protection for Chinese, whose licenses are a pervasive indicator of economic activity.

to our analysis, however, to point out that the two men represented widely different goal choices for development organizations. The cabinet, especially because it was an Alliance cabinet, was too small for the complete espousal of the different goals. The leadership of Razak and the expulsion of Aziz thus represented the process of goal selection we have already noted in the longer histories of the organizations concerned with development.

CONTROL

The history of control in Malaya's new development organizations divides naturally into two phases, marked by the formation of the Ministry of Rural Development in 1959. Prior to 1959 *authorities* were created, largely by the retreating British bureaucrats, aimed at giving the development organizations autonomy from political control and from colonial bureaucratic control. This was done in the belief that political control would introduce irrationality, and that colonial bureaucratic control would preclude speed and flexibility in organized stimulation of development.

Though the retreating bureaucrats were partly right on both counts, their efforts were largely defeated because they were not in a position to understand both the emerging political forces and the organizational requirements for success in a new state. Organizations as important to the new society as the new development organizations had to reflect political balance between the major ethnic groups. Further, in a society lacking multiple organizational centers of initiative and power, only government could provide the strength and the control mechanisms necessary for successful stimulation of development.

The new indigenous leaders saw what the retreating bureaucrats could not see. The creation of the Ministry of Rural Development marked the major effort of the new indigenous leaders to take control of the administration they had inherited with independence and to use it to do the work of development as they saw it. The autonomy of the authorities, which had in any case been more dysfunctional than functional, was violated, and the new leaders were brought within the power structure of the major government effort to stimulate development.

In the case of the Federal Land Development Authority, whose functions of land settlement were vitally important to the new government, the violation of autonomy brought the organization the power it needed to achieve its goals. The power of the Ministry of Rural Development allowed FLDA to cut through the dysfunctional federal structure, which slowed land development by placing its responsibility in the hands of the organizationally and financially less adequate state governments.

In the case of the Rural and Industrial Development Authority, the violation of autonomy all but destroyed the organization in order to accomplish the ends of social overhead construction. Between 1951 and 1959 RIDA had become in large part an amenity-providing and social overhead constructing organization. However, its very autonomy, its lack of power over the states and the other agencies of the bureaucracy reduced its activities in this field to pitifully small proportions. The function of construction was removed from RIDA in 1959–1960 and returned to the agencies technically competent to perform the task successfully. For the new government overhead construction was too important a task to be left in so weak an organization. Further, after the formation of the Ministry of Rural Development, construction could be entrusted to the technically competent agencies because the Ministry had sufficient power over them to ensure that the tasks would be done as deemed necessary by the new political leaders.

With the removal of this important function from RIDA, that organization became largely unimportant to the new government. Even more, it became a potential source of strain, because its other activities, especially in rural credit and rural industries, might threaten the political balance of ethnic interests. Thus since 1959 RIDA has been allowed to languish, and its own inherent irrationality, resulting from its ethnic orientation, has prevented it from moving under its own independent direction.

In addition to establishing control over its authorities, the new Ministry was faced with the more difficult task of establishing control over the entire bureaucracy, including an increase in the bureaucracy's speed of movement. Against the intrusion of the new Ministry and of the new central government, the bureaucracy had a variety of insulating mechanisms: legal, technical, bureaucratic, and social. The insulating mechanisms were essentially obstacles to the application of Ministerial rewards and punishments. These obstacles had to be broken if the new Ministry were to impose its will upon the entire administration. The insulating mechanisms were broken by the creation of certain formal structures, and by the application of the Minister's paramount political power in less formal patterns of control.

The Red Book and the district, state, and federal Rural Development Committees provided formal mechanisms to increase the rate of social overhead construction. This was accomplished largely by increasing financial allocation, expenditure, and the rate of communication, key elements in public investment programs. Allocation was facilitated by the standardization of the request procedures provided by the Red Book. Expenditure was facilitated by the decentralization of spenders, which among other things simply increased their number. Communication and coordination were facilitated by insistence upon oral rather than written communication and by the use of the development committee, which brought together the functionaries of the technical departments that had to be coordinated in order to achieve expenditure of funds on development projects.

The paramount political power of the Minister was applied largely through the mechanism of the briefing. As a standardized description of all development projects in the company of all relevant technical functionaries, the briefing gave the Minister the opportunity to evaluate performance of the total team and of its specific members. This allowed him to use his political powers to reward performance in support of the new goals and to punish—and punish severely—performance that obstructed goal achievement. The briefing allowed the process of control to be rational, and the political power of the Minister allowed him to cut through the insulating mechanisms of the administration.

These two dimensions of control, rationality and power, were inextricably intertwined. In fact, their congruence allowed the Ministry to gain firm control of the administration. Rational evaluation without the power to apply sanctions is ineffective in gaining the compliance of functionaries. On the other hand, irrational or arbitrary application of power is demoralizing and destroys the advantages gained through decentralization by making lower level functionaries fearful of assuming initiative. Although Malayan administrative and technical officers were apprehensive at Ministerial visits and briefings, theirs was not a fear of arbitrary Ministerial sanctions. The officers were generally aware that they could avoid punishments and win rewards by producing the results that the Minister wanted, and they had been left in little doubt as to what the Minister wanted.

Along with the strong commitment to output goals, the Ministry was under pressures to broaden its goals, especially in the direction of cultural goals. These pressures stemmed largely from the Ministry's (and the government's) recognition that modernization or increased human productivity required more than physical construction. There was more than an intuitive grasp of the idea that human factors are just as important as, if not more important than, physical factors in determining levels of production. Malay's leaders realized that modernization and increased productivity required a change in values and attitudes, as well as a change in the level of public investment.

In response to goal-broadening pressures, the Ministry of Rural Development engaged in two specific programs designed to produce attitudes and values attuned to the modern state. One involved a re-definition of the Rural Development Program to include two distinct phases. The first phase was defined as that in which the Government would demonstrate its ability to serve the people by providing the improvements and the social overhead capital that they wanted and needed.

The second phase, which began in September of 1961, was defined as the self-help phase, the phase in which the people would demonstrate their willingness and ability to work for their own uplift. The symbol of this program was *gotong royong*, a traditional form of peasant Malay cooperation in such activities as house construction, field preparation and harvesting, and limited infrastructure developments. In its formal structure the Phase II program involved the formation of *kampong* or village rural development committees and the erection of Red Book-type bulletin boards that would provide standardized definitions of tasks and criteria for evaluating task performance.

The second program was an adult education program, aimed largely at eradicating illiteracy among rural Malay adults and breaking their intellectual isolation from the modern world, and at making the non-Malay rural adults literate in Malay and instilling in them a greater consciousness of their responsibilities to the modern Malayan state. The program advanced rapidly in all states, establishing a direct line organization from the Ministry through state organizers, district supervisors, and local teachers to many thousands of rural adults who attended adult education classes.

Both programs have been subject to a double-barreled kind of goal subversion, though this does not mean that the programs have failed —or succeeded. Both programs suffered from a narrowing of goals back to the original output goals of the Ministry. In its Phase II program, the Ministry continued to use the same criteria of evaluation and the same mechanisms of control it had utilized in Phase I, its predominantly output goal phase, largely because it lacked the ability to evaluate value change. The use of the older evaluative and control mechanisms—bestowing rewards and punishments on the basis of physical output—meant that the Phase II program became largely a program in which collective village labor was used to produce more of the overhead capital whose production dominated Phase I. In the adult education program, lack of criteria for evaluating or controlling value change made the Ministry concerned primarily with the numbers of classes and students, with the physical output of an education program.

The second type of subversion experienced by both programs was also related to the Ministry's inability to evaluate and thus to control value change. The Ministry did settle upon the one available set of clear-cut criteria: those provided by election results. In this case the lack of suitable evaluative competence reinforced the prior infusion of politics into the rural development program, and the entire program became a political tool. In states where the ruling party was not in control, the Minister used his district rural development committees to bypass and to undermine the state governments. In states where the ruling party was in control, the rural development program was used in pork-barrel fashion to support local party leaders. On the one hand this reinforced the output goal commitment of the Phase I program, as local leaders were supported by Ministerial allocation of funds for local construction projects, especially for mosques, schools, and community halls. In the adult education program rewards and support were given to local leaders on the basis of their ability to organize the rural population in classes, and the content of the pedagogical materials took on a decided political bias.

The latter was not in any sense dysfunctional for general development, because a major problem was that of breaking the power of the local Islamic functionaries, the *imams,* who symbolized the physical and intellectual isolation of the rural peoples and represented a reaction against modernization. Breaking the power of the local *imam,* shifting the center of religious gravity from the closed village to the more rational and more modern centers in Kuala Lumpur, and the Islamic College at Klang, would serve to undermine the power of the antimodern, orthodox religious Pan Malayan Islamic Party. Thus the politicization of the Adult Education Program undermined antimodernization forces and reinforced the forces of modernization.

The use of the rural development program against the Pan Malayan Islamic Party has produced another set of goal-broadening forces in the Ministry and the central government, the effects of which cannot yet be assessed. The weakening of the antimodern wing in Malayan politics pushes the entire political orientation more in the direction of modernization. The major political opponents are now felt to be the parties of the left, with their appeals based in the promise of a changed social and economic structure. Given the government's lack of ideological commitment, its pragmatism, and its desire to stay in power, the Ministry appears to be tending to decrease the appeal of the parties of the left by increasing its own concern for change in the social and economic structure. Programs dictated by this new concern must move toward an espousal of cultural or mixed output-cultural goals, including increased concern for the creation of the modern economic and social institutions normally associated with increases in human productivity. Phase III of the rural development program, announced in February 1964, will focus upon the problems of rural marketing. However, given its current limitations in evaluation and control, the Ministry may experience strong internal pressures toward pure output goals, even in this more direct attempt to change the rural economy.

IMPLICATIONS OF THE MALAYAN EXPERIENCE

GOALS AND GOAL CHANGE

Inevitably, independence in the new states means the assumption of direct political control over the governmental bureaucracy. That is, the assumption of control by functionaries above the bureaucracy, and whose base of power lies outside the bureaucracy, in the electorate. One major significance of this lies in the change that it denotes: rather than emerging in the process of nation building, the bureaucracy antedates the nation in the new states. Thus the assumption of power occurs over an already extensive and complex organization. The prior organization, a colonial bureaucracy, was characterized by an extensive insulation of functionaries from political control. That insulation derived from the distance between the metropolitan center of political activity and the colonial bureaucracy, from the minor part the colonies generally played in metropolitan politics, and from the legal and organizational insulation developed even in metropolitan bureaucracies against political interference.

In the demise of colonialism the governmental apparatus has been a major focus of nationalist activity. The demand for freedom or independence has not been a demand for anarchy or for a return to precolonial tribal rule, but a demand to take over the instruments of rule established by the colonial powers. Thus whereas the colonial bureaucracy was characterized by political independence, the bureaucracy of the new state, to the extent that the new leaders are successful, will be characterized by direct indigenous political control. This means that the bureaucracy of the new states must reflect both the aims of the state as articulated by its political leaders, and local interests or demands.

Empirically, one of the most powerful demands of the new states, whether truly popular or merely representing the aspirations of the new elite, is for economic development. Thus one of the common experiences associated with increasing indigenous control over the bureaucracy has been the redirection of government effort toward economic development. A common form taken by this redirection has been the creation of new organizations specifically charged with planning and implementing development programs. A major problem of the new state is to use these new complex organizations efficiently.

The economic development desired by both the new states and their political leaders involves them in a fierce dilemma. On the one hand such development implies nothing less than a major change of the old society. It means modernization in the broadest sense of the word. It means new institutions, new values, new structures of human organization and control. Many of these changes cannot come about without active repudiation of the old society. Individual achievement must take precedence over collective ascription of status. Limited purpose groups must take precedence over groups whose purposes are diffuse and whose interests impinge on all aspects of an individual's life. Individual behavior must be judged objectively in accordance with specific aims. The homogeneity and exclusiveness of old groups must give way to a plurality of diverse attachments whose aims are not only limited, but may also be in conflict with one another. The new society brings wealth and prestige in the world community, while the old society is associated with colonial dependence and social and economic backwardness. To a large extent the old society must be repudiated to achieve modernization.

At the same time, it has been largely on the basis of the groupings of the old society that the mass following necessary to win independence was gained. The general appeal of modernization can mobilize only the small corps of educated or urban elites. To mobilize the great mass of the peasantry, appeals must be made to people as members of the old society. In Malaya this took the form of ethnic politics, a form that dominates party development even well into the post-independence period. There are elements of the modernization appeal in ethnic politics, however, for the new leaders must promise a change from the colonial society—a future, more wealthy country with a more equal distribution of that wealth, especially to the peasant sector. Thus on the one hand the new leaders must hold out the promise of the new society, and at the same time appear to be a part of and to protect the value of the old society.

In this context it is important to note that government, the new corps of leaders, is not a homogeneous entity. It is a highly heterogeneous group whose members often tend to become carriers of group interests, conflicting values associated with modernization, and diverse values entrenched in the government agencies.

The new development organizations are *subsidiary* organizations created by the government and given specific goals to help achieve government's broadly stated goals. Just as the assumption of political control over the bureaucracy forces it to reflect the balance of interests and the accommodation of the pro- and antimodernization dilemma, so the new subsidiary organizations must reflect this balance and accommodation. Not only is the parent of the new development organization heterogeneous and often torn with internal conflicts, its own goals must necessarily be vague and general. Often, too, the *specific* goals it establishes for its subsidiary organizations will be vague and general, though important for the dynamics of the subsidiary organization.

Unlike autochthonous and countervailing organizations, the goals of subsidiary organizations are resistant to change because they are established by a superordinate body. Thus, *ceteris paribus*, a strain resulting from an inharmonious goal-compliance pattern will normally be resolved, if at all, by a change in the compliance structure rather than by a change in goals. We saw this process at work in the experience of the Federal Land Development Authority, whose effectiveness was enhanced by a change from essentially normative to utilitarian forms of control, especially over the persons doing the work of land development.

The actual formulation of goals, and the possibility of goal change within the subsidiary organization, however, depend upon a number of factors. In the first place, obviously a subsidiary organization will have greater freedom to shape and change its goals if the parent formulates the original goals in only general terms.

The Rural and Industrial Development Authority was originally given a general order to be concerned with the economic development of the rural areas. Subsequently the subsidiary organization selected its own goal specialization—the concentration on output goals—and the substantive content of that specialization—providing small-scale amenities and small loans. Even after 1959 when RIDA was shorn of its amenity-providing functions, it was still left with the vague instructions to stimulate the development of rural industries.

The Federal Land Development Authority was originally given a more specific set of goals—land development—although this originally contained both output and cultural approaches to the problem. With the creation of the Ministry of Rural Development and the formation of the second five-year plan, FLDA was given the more specific task of accommodating 24,000 settlers on new land. This left little room for goal formulation—only a focus on the output goals of clearing land and building houses. Thus within FLDA, not within RIDA, the inharmonious compliance structure was changed to bring it in line with the organization's goals.

In the second place, the degree to which the subsidiary organization's goals reflect the balance of interest in the parent will determine its freedom in matters of goal formulation. Subsidiary organizations may be created to satisfy a minor interest or power within the parent group. In this case the subsidiary may be given considerable freedom to formulate its goals and to change them, with only broad limits set by the more powerful elements in the parent. Formal freedom is achieved, but it may be of limited value because it results essentially from a lack of strong commitment in the parent. Thus whatever may be the public goals of the subsidiary, its operative goals will be limited to those it has the competence and physical ability to achieve.

Neither the colonial government nor the new indigenous government was strongly committed to the Rural and Industrial Development Authority, though one reaches this conclusion from an analysis of resources allocated to RIDA, not from public statements about its importance. This gave RIDA considerable formal freedom to experiment with goals and to fashion its own specific set of goals. At the same time, however, RIDA was almost completely powerless in the total administration. It especially lacked the power needed to coordinate the activities of other agencies or of state governments. Thus in the field of social overhead capital construction, where such coordinating power was especially necessary, RIDA was forced to focus on goals far less grandiose than those envisaged in public pronouncements.

By the time the Federal Land Development Authority was created, in 1956, the indigenous leaders were beginning to take power over the bureaucracy. The functions to be performed by FLDA were of considerable interest to a major power block in the new government. Goals with wide latitude had been established by the colonial government. For a variety of reasons, however, the old government was not able to give the new organization the power to override state prerogatives in land matters, which the organization needed to achieve rapid land development. FLDA was of considerably less interest to the colonial government than to the new indigenous government, and its real interest to the new government manifested itself only after the formation of the Ministry of Rural Development in 1959. Under the new balance of power and interest in the indigenous government, after the 1959 elections, FLDA came to represent a major interest. It lost its freedom in goal formation, but gained the power necessary to achieve the goals it was given.

This process is evident in the experience of the Ministry of Rural development itself, especially in the area of social overhead construction. The Rural and Industrial Development Authority itself chose this area of activity as one of its major goal orientations. The creation of the new Ministry marked a strong commitment within government to the achievement of this, as well as other, goals. Unlike RIDA, the Ministry was a subsidiary organization created by a major power block in government. This gave it less freedom to choose its own specific goals, for more closely than RIDA's, the Ministry's goals had to reflect the balance of power in the government. For the same reason, however, the new Ministry had almost unlimited power to achieve the goals it was given. It could cut through state and bureaucratic resistance with a power that gave it considerable freedom to select the specific pattern of its goals and the manner in which they would be achieved.

Thus we can conceptualize a continuum of subsidiary organizations from very weak to very powerful. The amount of power is determined by the degree to which the organization reflects the balance of interests in the parent. Weaker organizations may have greater formal freedom to formulate specific orientation and type of goal, but in effect they will be limited by their lack of power. More powerful subsidiary organizations derive their greater power from being closer to the interests of the dominant powers in the parent organization.

This poses serious problems for the use of subsidiary organizations to stimulate economic development. If, for example, goals truly relevant to economic development are proscribed by the particular balance of power in the parent organization, we would have a condition in which the weaker subsidiary organizations espouse relevant goals, but could not work effectively toward their achievement. Strong subsidiary organizations could only work effectively toward the achievement of less relevant goals. Such a hypothetical case points to the limitations in the use of subsidiary complex organizations to stimulate development.

The example is, however, normally far from the reality. A wide number of different tasks are relevant to development. Road- and school-building can be as important as land reform or the regulation of monopoly powers. We may find that some activities relevant to development are proscribed by the parent organization, but certainly not all. Thus while the strong subsidiary organization must generally avoid these proscribed activities, it can concentrate its activities on, and achieve considerable success in, areas that are not proscribed but are still relevant for economic development.

A third determinant of freedom in goal formulation is the evaluating competence of the subsidiary organization. The *goals* of the subsidiary organization are essentially the *means* of the parent. They are established to achieve some broader end of the parent organization. For example, the order goals of the police or military in the old colonial governments were means by which the government sought to achieve economic development in which its own nationals could profit. The cultural goals of any state's educational system are means by which the state socializes its members, orienting them to the broader goals of the government, whether those are order, output, or cultural goals. This means that to the extent the subsidiary organization can evaluate its performance as an *instrument,* it can influence the specific formulation of its goals by demonstrating that its given goals are or are not effective means for the achievement of the broader goals of the parent.

In the case of highly specialized functions, such as education and the maintenance of order, the new subsidiary organization's potential freedom is limited by the long history of the organized performance of these functions. Functionaries in both the parent and the subsidiary organizations are presented with a well-defined set of functions, and with knowledge of how these functions will support the broader goals of the parent. They are also faced with the heavy weight of institutionalization, the infusion of those functions with *value,* which makes the functions ends in themselves, thus partially divorced from a rational mean-ends calculation.

This is far less the case for the new subsidiary organization designed to stimulate economic development. The process of development is not fully understood, and the function of stimulating development in specialized organizations is recent enough to make the inevitable process of institutionalization weak. Thus the very vagueness and novelty of organized stimulation gives the new organization considerable freedom, which in turn makes more crucial the issue of its competence to evaluate its performance.

In the Ministry of Rural Development and in its own subsidiary organizations, FLDA and RIDA, evaluating competence was limited almost exclusively to the evaluation of *construction.* The briefing and inspection techniques, and the formal reporting procedures of the Ministry, were highly efficient mechanisms for evaluating the progress of construction projects. The same can be said for the FLDA, though within the narrower framework of land clearing, planting, and house construction. The competence of RIDA was limited to the same type, but with considerably different substance. Prior to 1959 RIDA, too, was best in a position to judge the amount of construction it had achieved. In its loans program, both before and after 1959, it was competent to evaluate no more than the number and monetary value of loans granted. In all these organizations, therefore, there has been a specialized competence to evaluate the achievement only of output goals.

The limited evaluating competence of these subsidiary organizations has limited their freedom to broaden goals—in the case of the Ministry, even in the face of goal-broadening pressures in the parent. To be more concerned with the mixed output-cultural goals of stimulating rural industry and changing the rural economic structure, RIDA must be able to demonstrate to the Ministry (a) that this can be done without disturbing the balance of ethnic interests reflected in the Ministry; (b) that this can be done by paying greater attention to such things as close technical supervision of loans than to the simple processing of as many loan applications as possible; and (c) that such an achievement, implying a real increase in rural productivity, would be politically more advantageous than the use of the loans program as little more than a dole or patronage instrument. To demonstrate this would require a technical and organizational competence that RIDA does not have and seems constantly to avoid creating.

For FLDA to shift its activities more in the mixed output-cultural direction of producing farmers rather than rubber tappers, the organization would have to demonstrate (a) that such an achievement is possible given greater attention to agricultural extension and experimentation, and to the preparation of catch crop lands; (b) that this can be done along with the rapid settlement of land, though it might require more staff or more coordinated service from the existing agricultural agencies; and most important, (c) that this could be done without disturbing the ethnic sensitivities balanced in the parent, and that it would be economically and politically more advantageous in the long run. At present FLDA lacks the technical competence to make any of these three arguments. It can, and has, made the first two arguments from its own wealth of common sense and experience with the settlers, but it lacks the ability to analyze the determinants of economic success in other than the very crude, inaccurate, and politically disturbing terms of ethnic differences.

Even the politically powerful Ministry is caught in the same web of restrictions. Here the lack of evaluating competence is even more critical than in the two authorities, because the Ministry would have the freedom and power to shift its goal orientation if it could justify this to the parent. It might be argued that the Ministry has no desire to change its goals, but this type of argument only confuses the issue. To inject this human, essentially idiosyncratic, motivation into an analysis of the organization would only lead one to make a judgment about "good guys and bad guys." If a different type of goal pattern is necessary to the effective stimulation of economic development, the analysis of organizational goals in terms of human motivation does little more than enable us to say that the Minister is either ill-informed or evil if he does not desire to change the organization's goals to a more appropriate pattern. Both analytically and in reality, such an argument makes little sense. If the Ministry is strongly committed to the achievement of output goals, this is because these appear to Ministry officials to be the goals that are most suited to the achievement of the broader ends of the parent and that are attainable for the organization. This turns the issue back to one of appearance, perception, and organizational evaluating competence.

That output goals appear to be most suited to the Ministry is a result of the competence of the organization to evaluate its own problem area. That competence is in turn a function of the past training of the Ministry's individual members, and of the organizational structure of the Ministry. The Ministry is staffed essentially by civil servants, by men who know how to move the bureaucracy, how to get it to do the things it is already capable of doing. If, for example, the higher functionaries of the Ministry were agricultural extension workers, or agricultural economists, as in Taiwan's Joint Commission for Rural Reconstruction, it is most probable that their major focus of attention would have been upon the income of the rural people. This would have given the organization, as it did in Taiwan, a strong commitment to mixed output-cultural goals. The structure of the Ministry also gives it a specialized ability to evaluate construction achievements. It has, however, no element that can analyze the determinants of rural productivity or the effects of increased rural incomes.

It is, of course, the experience of most complex organizations, especially of government bureaucracies, that attempts at qualitative evaluation of achievements are generally subverted, and most evaluating competences are focused on quantitative achievements. The very nature of bureaucratization, the depersonalization and the increasing reliance upon rules applied in a standardized fashion, exerts considerable pressure for the use of clear-cut quantitative measures of performance.

This observation partly misses the point. Admittedly it is easier to evaluate road and school construction than to measure changes in rural productivity. Nonetheless, rural productivity can be measured quantitatively. The effects of maldistribution of land and insecurity of tenure upon both productivity and political sentiments can be measured quantitatively. The issue is not totally one of quantitative versus qualitative measures of performance, but one of the competence to measure performance in the achievement of different types of goals.

It appears to be true that evaluation of achievement for both order and output goals is simpler and lends itself more readily to the use of clear-cut measures than does evaluation in achievement of cultural goals. This can be seen in the common evaluating functionaries of the three types of organizations. Order goals use guards, whose specific competence is to measure quiescence, or actual or potential attacks on authority. Output goals use paymasters, whose specific competence lies in measuring standard units of product and the relation between input and the value of the product. For cultural goals, one is pressed to characterize the evaluator or his competence. He may be a judge, teacher, priest, or charismatic leader who is faced with evaluating attitudes, intentions, spirit, or creativity. In the case of economic development, however, the evaluator may be the economist or social scientist whose competence lies in analyzing the structure and function of the economy or society. This points on the one hand to the difficulty involved in evaluating achievement of cultural goals, and on the other hand to the competence the social sciences have brought to this evaluation.

The Ministry of Rural Development clearly reflects the interest and power balance of its parent, the top decision-makers in the Malayan government. It has been given the general task of stimulating the development of the rural areas, and has defined for itself the specific manner in which this is to be done. That is, it has focused almost exclusively upon output goals to achieve this general stimulation. Even under pressures, admittedly mild pressures, to broaden its goals in a cultural direction, it has for the most part maintained its commitment to output goals. The pressures to broaden goals include the serious question of whether in fact the construction of the physical infrastructure is sufficient to achieve the increases in real productivity and real income in the rural areas that both the Ministry and its parent desire as long-range and general ends. It would not be argued that such construction is not necessary, only that it is not sufficient. Rather, it is the argument of this study that in large part, the inability of the Ministry to broaden its goals derives from its organizational inability to analyze the larger problem of rural productivity, the effect of its programs on productivity, and the effects of productivity on the interest and power balance in the government.

POLITICS, POWER, AND DEVELOPMENT

The relation between politics and development is often discussed only in terms of the economic irrationalities imposed upon development programs by political developments. A common example is the construction of uneconomic showpieces to please political leaders. They abound in every new state and need no serious documentation. Every state has its luxury hotels, its superhighways, its temples or mosques, even its pharmaceutical plants, steel plants, and atomic energy plants that are not justified by even the most generous analysis of costs and benefits. Less dramatically, every new state has invested in projects that are less productive than alternative choices: superhighways rather than irrigation, or a mammoth water project rather than several smaller ones that would give wider coverage. This type of issue is commonly raised in any discussion of the relation between politics and economic development.

There is another issue, or another dimension to the discussion, that should be accorded more serious attention, largely because of its greater importance for the entire development effort. This might be called the issue of power: the power to implement development projects once they are decided upon, and the power to select goals that are important both to the maintenance of the state and to the stimulation of development. It is more than curious that this issue has not yet received more serious attention in development discussion, and may reflect unfavorably on the often unfortunate hiatus between academic discussions and the actual operation of a development program.

The most common observations made about formal development programs in Southeast Asia, for example, is that they are found in every country in the region, and in almost no case, with the unique exception of Malaya (and Singapore), have they been implemented. Development plans are apparently relatively easy to draft, for every new state seems to grind them out as rapidly as foreign aid or loans are requested. Development organizations, too, are apparently relatively easy to establish, for like the plans they spring up overnight and often change their shapes and colors in rapid succession in the fertile soil of the new state. Yet only in Malaya has there been a serious attempt to implement the development program, to tie yearly development expenditures to existing financial and administrative resources, and to achieve the physical infrastructure construction envisaged in the plan. Perhaps the most significant aspect of Malaya's success is that it has been achieved not by separation of political power from development, but by an infusion of that power into the development effort.

One of the most crucial, and apparently one of the most overlooked, areas in which power is required by the new development organization lies in its relation to the rest of the administration. The common experience in development planning involves an attempt to change the direction and increase the rate of activity of the specialized existing elements of the administration. The simple increase of funds to existing organizations can produce an increase of activity, but this is neither certain nor is it always likely to produce the kind of activity new governments desire. Speed is not ensured, because seldom can one single department perform the entire range of tasks necessary to expend its funds. To build a school land must be acquired, estimates of students made to determine the proper size, and the actual construction must be done. Such a task will often require the action of at least three separate government departments: land, education, and works. There are very few avenues of public investment that do not involve more than one department.

This immediately raises the problem of the coordination of separate and specialized activities. Generally, if the rate of investment is to be increased, there must be both funds available, and more rapid communication between the departments.

One common cause of the failure to implement development programs in Southeast Asia lies in the lack of bodies that have both the competence and the power to speed the rate of effective communication between, or to coordinate, the specialized agencies of the bureaucracy. Conversely, one major reason for the success of the Malayan public investment program lies in the competence and the power of the Ministry of Rural Development. We have seen how the Ministry used its political power to effect this coordination. We have also seen how the Rural and Industrial Development Authority, previously given the same task of coordination, failed miserably because it did not have the political power to force the technical agencies and the states to work according to its program.

Three other specific conditions account for the success of the Ministry in stimulating Malayan public investment, and these help to illuminate the relation between politics and development. In the first place, the ethnic balance of political power made it imperative that something be done in the rural areas. The rural Malays were over-represented in the legislature and the position of the Malays was protected constitutionally. The tremendous power that this Malay electorate gave to the ruling power in 1955, and the threat to take that power away in 1959, led the new leaders to realize that the new government had to pay more attention to the demands of the rural people. In addition, the generally accepted hiatus between the economic positions of the Chinese and the Malays only reinforced the pressures on government to increase public investment, in the rural areas in particular. That is, the goal of providing amenities and physical infrastructure was politically a highly important goal. This would help ensure that much of the power available to the central government would be focused upon the achievement of this goal.

In the second place Malaya's political party structure ensured that the ruling party would have considerable power at its command to focus upon its important activities. The Malay wing of the Alliance provided an extensive organization with considerable vote-getting power. The Chinese wing of the party provided campaign funds. Most of the nominees of the party were Malays; most of these had no independent means, so depended upon party funds to win elections. In addition, since there are no residency requirements in the Malayan constituencies, the party could put its favorites in secure constituencies and run the less favored members in the more precarious constituencies. These factors gave the central organ of the party considerable power over its members. This focused most decisions on the allocation of development funds at one point and gave to the top leadership, largely to the Deputy Prime Minister, wide powers over the entire bureaucracy.

Finally, in the area of public investment the power of the Minister, and therefore of the Ministry, has continually been enhanced by the cooperation between specialized leaders at the top of the Malayan government. The Prime Minister and his Deputy respectively are specialized expressive and instrumental leaders who have been highly cooperative and noncompetitive throughout the tenure of the rural development program.[2]

None of these advantageous conditions appears to obtain in the other countries of Southeast Asia. None has the same tight control of power at the center as does Malaya, differences between unitary states like Indonesia and the Philippines and a federation like Malaya notwithstanding. Nor does any other country in the region have the same ethnic balance that gives development for the rural areas the same

---

[2] See Herbert Feith, *The Decline of Constitutional Democracy in Indonesia*, Ithaca, 1962, especially chaps. III and IV, for a detailed account of the conflict between expressive and instrumental leadership in Indonesia. This conflict has obviously been an important source of the marked failure of Indonesian development programs, especially where they involved output goals.

urgency it has in Malaya. Finally, other countries have experienced far more competition, and far less cooperation, among top leadership than has Malaya.

These conditions appear to give a cyclical or self-sustaining character to both the successes and the failures of public investment programs. Malaya originally had the political power it needed to arouse the bureaucracy and implement its public investment program. The very act of doing this, of publicizing the program and of demonstrating success, has increased the power of the Ministry and the power of the values involved in rural development. The more power the Ministry has, the more success it can achieve; and the more success it achieves, the more power it obtains. The cycle works in reverse as well. The lack of sufficient concentrations of power and commitments to infrastructure development in other countries has led to miserable failures in public investment, which in turn have sapped strength from the central governments, further preventing them from achieving success.

The cyclical nature of power and success in public investment points to another dimension of politics and development that is omitted in most discussions of the subject. Analyses of the politics of new states generally acknowledge that one of the major problems of the new leaders is that of consolidating power. This does not necessarily mean the acquisition of power to destroy opposition. Such destruction can be achieved without the consolidation of power, and may even preclude consolidation. By consolidation of power is meant the ability to achieve sufficient consensus in the state to allow government to work. This is not a static end product, but a dynamic balance that is ever tested as it is achieved.

The Malayan experience suggests that a development program, especially a public investment program, can function as a tool for consolidating power.[3] Malayan leaders have often remarked that they had to build roads in order to get about to administer to the people. This had an even more urgent meaning in the context of the Emergency and its aftermath. The new leaders understood that if they were actually to hold power, they had to demonstrate to the people, especially to those in remote rural areas, that there was an effective government and that it was concerned for their welfare and security. This understanding of the situation made the leaders demand that the rural development program be visible and dramatic. This understand-

---

[3] I have discussed this process more specifically in "Modernization and Indigenous Control of the Bureaucracy in Malaysia," *Asian Survey*, September, 1965, pp. 467–473.

ing also led to the use of the Red Book and the District Rural Development Committees, instruments to publicize the program by involving local people in its planning and implementation.

The type of decentralization this involved appears to be one of the most difficult activities for the leaders of new states to undertake. It cannot be done by a government that feels precarious and fears that decentralization will reduce its strength. Here again we see the cyclical nature of power and its correlates. The Malayan government felt strong enough to allow districts and states considerable initiative powers in the development program.[4] The resulting decentralization increased the success and the impact of the central government's development program, thus increasing the power of that government.

The infusion of development with politics in Malaya has not been without its dysfunctions. There has been waste in the allocation of resources as money is spent on politically useful but economically unjustifiable roads, mosques, community halls, and other physical items. There has been a heightening of ethnic tensions as the rural development program has come to be defined as a program for the Malays, and has come to symbolize many of the frustrations felt by Chinese and Indians at Malay privileges. On the whole, however, the infusion of development with politics must be seen as functional for the system, containing more advantages than disadvantages. The power broadly consolidated through the program has been a cohesive force in a state rent by great potential division. It has given the state a greater capacity to survive and to function as a state in the modern world. The physical infrastructure created through the program has added to the physical capital of the country, and the rapid population growth will in the long run reduce waste in construction, simply by providing an increasing demand for whatever items of capital exist. Finally, the political achievements to which the program has contributed have already shifted the center of political gravity more to the left, both forcing and allowing the government to broaden its specific development goals. If this broadening continues and the program becomes more concerned with efforts more directly calculated to increase income and productivity, then it will have contributed considerably to the achievement of balanced economic growth in the future.

[4] It should be noted that the security and competence of the British government provided the initial model for decentralization. The Rural Development Program was, after all, laid down on the model of local committees that the British developed for the successful prosecution of the Emergency. We might have expected the opposite process, centralization, had the new and inexperienced government been faced with the initial impact of the Emergency.

Bibliography

Allen, G. C., and Donnithorne, A. G. *Western Enterprise in Indonesia and Malaya*. London: George Allen & Unwin Ltd., 1957, 321 pp.

Aziz, Ungku. *The Subdivision of Estates in Malaya 1951–1960*. Kuala Lumpur: Department of Economics, University of Malaya, 1962. 3 vols.

Bauer, P. T. *A Report on a Visit to the Rubber Growing Smallholdings in Malaya, July–September 1946*. Colonial Research Publications, No. 1. London: H. M. Stationery Office, 1948. 92 pp.

————. *The Rubber Industry: A Study in Competition and Monopoly*. Cambridge: Harvard University Press, 1948. 404 pp.

Benda, Harry J. "Non-Western Intelligentsia as Political Elites," in J. H. Kautsky (ed.), *Political Change in Underdeveloped Countries*. New York: John Wiley, 1962, pp. 235–251.

————. *The Crescent and the Rising Sun*. The Hague: W. van Hoeve Ltd., 1958. 320 pp.

Clark, Margaret. *The Malayan Alliance and Its Accommodation of Communal Pressures, 1952–1962*. Unpublished M. A. Thesis. Kuala Lumpur: University of Malaya, 1964. 235 pp.

Coser, Lewis. *The Functions of Social Conflict*. Glencoe: The Free Press, 1956. 188 pp.

Del Tufo, M. V. *A Report on the 1947 Census of Population*. Kuala Lumpur: Government Printer, 1948.

Ding, Eign Tan Soo Hai. *The Rice Industry in Malaya 1920–1940*. Singapore Studies in Borneo and Malaya. Singapore: Malaya Publishing House, Ltd., 1963. 60 pp.

Etzioni, Amitai. *Comparative Analysis of Complex Organizations*. New York: The Free Press of Glencoe, Inc., 1961. 366 pp.

Federation of Malaya. *Report by the Chief Minister of the Federation of*

Malaya on the Baling Talks. Kuala Lumpur: Government Printer, 1956. 13 pp.

———. *Report of the Committee on Malay Education.* Kuala Lumpur: Government Printer, 1951. 24 pp.

———. *Report on the Conference on Community Development.* Kuala Lumpur: Government Printer, 1958. 41 pp.

———. *Report of the Working Party Set up to Consider the Development of New Areas for Land Settlement in the Federation of Malaya.* Kuala Lumpur: Government Printer, 1956. 30 pp.

———. *Report on the Rural and Industrial Development Authority, 1950–1955,* by D. E. M. Fiennes. Kuala Lumpur: Government Printer, 1957. 52 pp.

———. *Scheme for the Reorganization of the Rural and Industrial Development Authority, Federation of Malaya.* Legislative Council Paper, No. 10 of 1951. Kuala Lumpur: Government Press, 1951. 14 pp.

———. *Directive to the Rural and Industrial Development Authority.* Legislative Council Paper, No. 15 of 1957. Kuala Lumpur: Government Press, 1957. 9 pp.

———. *Report on the Rural and Industrial Development Authority.* Legislative Council Paper for the period ending December 31, 1951, No. 24. Kuala Lumpur: Government Printer, 1952.

———. *Report on the Rural and Industrial Development Authority.* Legislative Council Paper for the period January 1 through June 30, 1952, No. 65. Kuala Lumpur: Government Printer, 1952.

———. *Report on the Rural and Industrial Development Authority.* Legislative Council Paper for the period July 1 through December 31, 1952, No. 35. Kuala Lumpur: Government Printer, 1952.

———. *Report on the Rural and Industrial Development Authority.* Legislative Council Paper for the period January 1 through June 30, 1953, No. 84. Kuala Lumpur: Government Printer, 1953.

———. *Report on the Rural and Industrial Development Authority.* Legislative Council Paper for the period July 1 through December 31, 1953, No. 17. Kuala Lumpur: Government Printer, 1954.

———. *Report of the Special Committee to Consider and Make Recommendations for the Re-organization of the Rural and Industrial Development Authority.* Kuala Lumpur: Ministry of Rural Development, 1961. 13 pp. plus appendices.

———. *The Report of a Mission Invited by the Federation Government to Study the Problem of Education of Chinese in Malaya.* Kuala Lumpur: Government Printer, 1951.

Federation of Malaya, Department of Statistics. *National Accounts of the Federation of Malaya, 1955–1960.* Kuala Lumpur: Government Printer, 1963. 19 pp.

———. *Population Census 1957.* Kuala Lumpur: Department of Statistics, 1960. 14 vols.

————. *Rubber Statistics Handbook, 1961.* Kuala Lumpur, Department of Statistics, 1962. 79 pp.

————. *Survey of Manufacturing Industries.* Kuala Lumpur: Department of Statistics, 1961. 104 pp.

Federation of Malaya, Federal Land Development Authority. *Annual Report for the Period July 1, 1960 to June 31, 1961.* Kuala Lumpur: The Economy Printers Ltd., 1962. 42 pp.

————. *No Need to Be Poor, A Policy Statement,* by D. E. M. Fiennes. Kuala Lumpur: Federal Land Development Authority, 1956. 11 pp.

Federation of Malaya, Ministry of Rural Development. *Report of the Special Committee to Review the Role of the Federal Land Development Authority within the National Rural Development Programme.* Parts I and II. Kuala Lumpur: The Ministry of Rural Development, 1961. 19 pp. plus appendices and 10 pp. plus appendices.

Federation of Malaya, Office of the Member for Economic Affairs, The Treasury. *Progress Report on the Development Plan of the Federation of Malaya 1950–1952.* Kuala Lumpur: Government Printer, 1953.

Federation of Malaya, Prime Minister's Department. *Interim Review of Development in Malaya under the Second Five-Year Plan.* Kuala Lumpur: Government Printer, 1964. 76 pp.

————. *Second Five-Year Plan, 1961–1965.* Kuala Lumpur: Government Printer, 1961. 67 pp.

Federation of Malaya, Rural and Industrial Development Authority. *Annual Report, 1954.* Kuala Lumpur: Rural and Industrial Development Authority, 1955.

————. *Annual Report, 1955.* Kuala Lumpur: Rural and Industrial Development Authority, 1956.

————. *Annual Report, 1956.* Kuala Lumpur: Rural and Industrial Development Authority, 1957.

————. *Annual Report, 1957.* Kuala Lumpur: Rural and Industrial Development Authority, 1958.

————. *Annual Report, 1958.* Kuala Lumpur: Rural and Industrial Development Authority, 1959.

————. *Annual Report, 1959.* Kuala Lumpur: Rural and Industrial Development Authority, 1960.

————. *Annual Report, 1960.* Kuala Lumpur: Rural and Industrial Development Authority, 1961.

Federation of Malaya, The Treasury. *Estimates of Federal Revenue and Expenditure for 1963.* Kuala Lumpur: Government Printer, 1962. 352 pp.

Feith, Herbert. *The Decline of Constitutional Democracy in Indonesia.* Ithaca: Cornell University Press, 1962. 618 pp.

Furnivall, J. S. *Netherlands India, a Study of Plural Economy.* Cambridge: Harvard University Press, 1944. 502 pp.

Geertz, Clifford, *Agricultural Involution.* Berkeley and Los Angeles: University of California Press, 1963, 176 pp.

Gerschenkron, Alexander, *Economic Backwardness in Historical Perspective.* Cambridge: Harvard University Press, 1962. 456 pp.

Grist, D. H. *Malayan Agricultural Statistics, 1939.* Kuala Lumpur: Department of Agriculture, 1940.

——. *Nationality of Ownership and Nature of Constitution of Rubber Estates in Malaya.* Kuala Lumpur: Department of Agriculture, 1933. 26 pp.

Guerney, Henry. "Government Proposal for Improvement of Social and Economic Well-being of Malays." Kuala Lumpur, 19 May 1950, mimeographed.

Gullick, J. M. *Indigenous Political Systems of Western Malaya.* London School of Economics Monographs on Social Anthropology No. 17. London: University of London, 1958. 151 pp.

Han, Su-yin. *And the Rain My Drink.* Boston: Little, Brown, Inc., 1956. 306 pp.

Hobsbawn, Eric J. *The Age of Revolution.* London: Weidenfeld and Nicolson, 1962. 356 pp.

Holland, W. L. (ed.). *Asian Nationalism and the West.* New York: Macmillan, 1953. 449 pp.

Hoselitz, Bert F., and Moore, Wilbert E. *Industrialization and Society.* Paris: UNESCO, 1963. 437 pp.

International Bank for Reconstruction and Development, *The Economic Development of Malaya.* Baltimore: Johns Hopkins University Press, 1955. 707 pp.

Jackson, R. N. *Immigrant Labour and the Development of Malaya 1786–1920.* Kuala Lumpur: Government Printer, 1961. 161 pp.

Kautsky, J. H. (ed.). *Political Change in Underdeveloped Countries.* New York: John Wiley, 1962. 347 pp.

Kuznets, Simon. *Six Lectures on Economic Growth.* Glencoe: The Free Press, 1960. 122 pp.

Levin, Jonathan V. *The Export Economies.* Cambridge: Harvard University Press, 1960. 347 pp.

Lipset, S. M. *The First New Nation.* New York: Basic Books, 1963. 366 pp.

Mahajani, Usha. *The Role of Indian Minorities in Burma and Malaya.* New York: Institute of Pacific Relations, 1960. 344 pp.

McGee, T. G. "The Malayan Elections of 1959, A Study in Political Geography." *The Journal of Tropical Geography,* October 1962, pp. 70–99.

McVey, Ruth. *The Calcutta Conference and the Southeast Asian Uprisings.* Cornell Modern Indonesia Project, Interim Report Series. Ithaca: Cornell University Press, 1958. 28 pp.

Millikan, Max F., and Blackmer, Donald L. M. *The Emerging Nations.* London: Asia Publishing House, 1961. 168 pp.

Mills, Lennox, *Malaya: A Political and Economic Appraisal.* Minneapolis: University of Minnesota Press, 1958, 234 pp.

Ness, Gayl D. "Cooperative Development and Industrial Capitalism in England and Denmark," *Berkeley Journal of Sociology,* Spring, 1961, pp. 1–15.

——. "Modernization and Indigenous Control of the Bureaucracy in Malaysia," *Asian Survey,* Vol. V, No. 9, September, 1965, pp. 467–473.

Parmer, J. N. *Colonial Labor Policy and Administration: A History of Labor in the Rubber Plantation Industry in Malaya, 1910–1941.* Monographs of the Association for Asian Studies, IX. New York: Association for Asian Studies, 1960. 294 pp.

Purcell, Victor. *The Chinese in Southeast Asia.* London: Oxford University Press, 1951. 801 pp.

Pye, Lucien. *Guerilla Communism in Malaya.* Princeton: Princeton University Press, 1956. 369 pp.

Rawlings, G. S. "First Steps in Community Development in Malaya." Kuala Lumpur, 1958, mimeographed.

Rosovsky, H. *Capital Formation in Japan.* Glencoe: Free Press, 1961. 358 pp.

Shils, Edward. "Political Development in the New States," *Comparative Studies in Society and History,* Vol. II, 1959–1960, pp. 265–292 and 379–411.

Silcock, T. H., and Aziz, Ungku. "Nationalism in Malaya," in W. L. Holland (ed.), *Asian Nationalism and the West.* New York: Macmillan, 1953. 449 pp.

Smith, T. E. *Population Growth in Malaya.* Princeton: Princeton University Press, 1952. 126 pp.

Stokes, Eric T. *The English Utilitarians in India.* Oxford: Clarendon Press, 1959. 350 pp.

Tilman, Robert O. *Bureaucratic Transition in Malaya.* Durham, N.C.: Duke University Press, 1964. 175 pp.

United Nations Food and Agricultural Organization. *Yearbook of Food and Agricultural Statistics, 1957.* Rome: UN, FAO, 1957. 2 parts.

Weber, Max. *General Economic History.* Glencoe: The Free Press, 1950. 401 pp.

Wilson, T. Bryan. *The Economics of Padi Production in North Malaya.* Department of Agriculture Bulletin, No. 103. Kuala Lumpur: Federation of Malaya, Department of Agriculture, 1958. 113 pp.

Wong, Lin Ken. *The Malayan Tin Industry to 1914.* Monographs of the Association for Asian Studies XIV. Tucson: The University of Arizona Press, 1965. 302 pp.

Index

DATE DUE

NOV 1 5 70			
NOV 3 0 '70			
MAY 2 '74			
MAY 1 6 '74			
APR 2 9 '81			
MAY 14 '81			
MAR 8 1983			•
FEB 1 8 1983			
MAY 2 1 '85			
MAY 7 '85			
GAYLORD			PRINTED IN U.S.A.